THE BOOK-HUNTER

etc

The Book-Hunter

etc

By JOHN HILL BURTON

With Additional Notes

By RICHARD GRANT WHITE

NEW YORK
SHELDON AND COMPANY 335 Broadway
1863

RIVERSIDE, CAMBRIDGE:
PRINTED BY H. O. HOUGHTON.

PREFATORY NOTE

TO THIS EDITION.

ROM the beginning books have been reckoned almost among the necessaries of life by the people of this country. Of later years they have become objects of taste and luxury, and of collection for the purpose of special study. This disposition to possess books other than standard works of reference and the miscellaneous literature of the day is increasing rapidly among us; and the desire is very generally accompanied, at least in a certain degree, by the means for its gratification. To all those who have this taste, and to many who have it not, the following desultory dissertation on books, book-collecting, and book-collectors, cannot fail to be welcome for its always interesting, often serviceable, and sometimes amusing, information. Its influence upon those whose brains are touched with bibliomania cannot fail to be good; for it deals firmly, though gently, with their cherished folly, and leads them away from that petty dilettanteism into which a love of rare and beautiful books is apt to fall, toward a manly and sensible indulgence of their inclination. The true book-lover will delight in the outside as well as the inside of his treasures ; and he is more than mortal, if he does not glory a little in their accumulation, "for to have meny is a plesaunt thynge ;" but he has passed a perilous line whose books have become to him other than the means and signs of culture, or the loved companions of his solitude. Against that danger there is in the following pages many a wholesome warning.

It must be confessed, however, that there is much in this book which, though good in itself, is very wide of its main purpose. Not to speak of previous pages, the connection of the chapters upon John Spalding and Robert Wodrow with a dissertation upon bibliomania is of the slenderest ; while the thread which served as the author's clue in passing to the curious and interesting accounts of the Early Northern Saints and the Early British Church Architecture is to my eye quite invisible. The "etc." of the title-page must be accepted in its widest meaning. "The Book-Hunter and other things" is certainly a title broad enough to shelter any and all of the topics that have been treated under it; for in fact it stops only just short of *de omnibus rebus et quibusdam aliis.* The author, conscious of this, half apologizes for making the book so large and so discursive; and if he had reason, how much more have I, who have added to its length and even to its discursiveness! But as he had concerned himself not a little with the social and literary condition of this country, and had almost always led his reader to false conclusions, it was thought that in an edition intended for the United States these should be corrected. The doing of this naturally led to the doing of a little more; the occupation beguiled hours of suffering when more serious and exacting duties could not be attended to; and the result may perhaps be deemed not entirely superfluous, except by that sort of men who would regard it as the greatest glory of the compilers of the Justinian Pandects that they reduced three millions of lines in the works of their predecessors to one hundred and fifty thousand. An excellent work, truly; and they who did it, public benefactors, and worthy of all the praise which their record of the feat silently solicited and artfully won. Yet in the interests of us all there must be some limit to the spare diet of words upon which some folk would have literature exist;

else, being reduced to its one straw, it will cease from off the earth, and the functions of author and reader will cease together with it: — a catastrophe sufficiently remote, however, to allow our solicitude to slumber. And had I possessed the needful information before the body of the book was put in type, instead of one less, I should have written one more note, to say that among the Mighty Book-Hunters of whom the author gives such lively sketches, Thomas Papaverius, the most interesting of them all, is intended for Thomas De Quincey; who, indeed, seems rather to have been a robber, a ravisher, and a destroyer of books than a collector or even a hunter of them, — a very Ishmaelite, against whom, in spite of what he was and what he wrote, all book-lovers had common cause. He on the one side and the Irish Vampire on the other furnish extreme examples of what the book-hunter should not be. None of the other sketches have yet been publicly identified by the British critics.

For the Index which adds value to this edition the reader is indebted to F. F. HEARD, Esq., of the Boston Bar. The additional notes are inclosed in brackets, and signed with the last initial of their writer.

R. G. W.

ADVERTISEMENT.

THIS book owes its existence to a concurrence of accidents. The Author had the honor of contributing to Blackwood's Magazine some sketches of the ways of book-collectors, scholars, literary investigators, desultory readers, and other persons whose pursuits revolve round books and literature. Some friendly criticisms having induced him to reflect on what he had written, he saw, as will generally happen in such cases, that were he to go over the ground again, he would find much that he would desire to alter, and many things that might be added. He therefore resolved to recast the whole and expand it to the compass of a thin volume. The thin volume, however, fattened as it approached maturity, until it reached the respectable dimensions in which it now awaits the appreciation of any reader who may think it worthy of his attention.

The Book-Hunter.

CONTENTS.

Part I.—His Nature.

Part II.—His Functions.

Part III.—His Club.

Part IV.—Book-Club Literature.

transfer them from the class of free self-regulators to that of persons "under treatment." In Owen's parallelograms there were to be no prisons: he admitted no power in one man to inflict punishment upon another for merely obeying the dictates of natural propensities which could not be resisted. But, at the same time, there were to be "hospitals" in which not only the physically diseased, but also the mentally and *morally* diseased, were to be detained until they were cured; and when we reflect that the laws of the parallelogram were very stringent and minute, and required to be absolutely enforced to the letter, otherwise the whole machinery of society would come to pieces, like a watch with a broken spring, — it is clear that these hospitals would have contained a very large proportion of the unrationalized population.

There is rather an alarming amount of this sort of communism now among us; and it is therefore with some little misgiving that one sets down any thing that may betray a brother's weakness, and lay bare the diagnosis of a human frailty. Indeed, the bad name that proverbially hangs the dog has already been given to it, for bibliomania is older in the technology of this kind of nosology than dipsomania, which is now understood to be an almost established ground for seclusion, and deprivation of the management of one's own affairs. There is one ground of consolation, however, — the people who, being all right themselves, have undertaken the duty of keeping in order the rest of the world, have far too serious a task in hand to afford time for idle reading. There is a good chance, therefore, that this little book may pass them unnoticed, and the harmless class on whose peculiar frailties the present occasion is taken for devoting a gentle and kindly exposition, may yet be permitted to go at large.

So having spoken, I now propose to make the reader acquainted with some characteristic specimens of the class.

A Vision of Mighty Book-Hunters.

AS the first case, let us summon from the shades my venerable friend, Archdeacon Meadow, as he was in the body. You see him now—tall, straight, and meagre, but with a grim dignity in his air which warms into benignity as he inspects a pretty little, clean Elzevir, or a tall, portly Stephens, concluding his inward estimate of the prize with a peculiar grunting chuckle, known by the initiated to be an important announcement. This is no doubt one of the milder and more inoffensive types, but still a thoroughly confirmed and obstinate case. Its parallel to the classes who are to be taken charge of by their wiser neighbors is only too close and awful; for have not sometimes the female members of his household been known on occasion of some domestic emergency—or, it may be, for mere sake of keeping the lost man out of mischief — to have been searching for him on from bookstall unto bookstall, just as the mothers, wives, and daughters of other lost men hunt them through their favorite taverns? Then, again, can one forget that occasion of his going to London to be examined by a committee of the House of Commons, when he suddenly disappeared with all his money in his pocket, and returned penniless, followed by a wagon containing 372 copies of rare editions of the Bible? All were fish that came to his net. At one time you might find him securing a minnow for sixpence at a stall; and presently afterwards he outbids some princely collector, and secures with frantic impetuosity, "at any price," a great fish he has been patiently watching year after year. His hunting-grounds were wide and distant, and there were mysterious rumors about the numbers of copies, all identically the same in edition and minor individualities, which he possessed of certain books. I have known him, indeed, when beaten at an auction, turn round resignedly and say, "Well, so be it — but I dare say I have ten or twelve copies at home, if I could lay hands on them."

It is a matter of extreme anxiety to his friends, and, if he have a well-constituted mind, of sad misgiving to himself, when the collector buys his first *duplicate*. It is like the first secret dram swallowed in the forenoon — the first pawning of the silver spoons — or any other terrible first step downwards you may please to liken it to. There is no hope for the patient after this. It rends at once the veil of decorum spun out of the flimsy sophisms by which he has been deceiving his friends, and partially deceiving himself, into the belief that his previous purchases were necessary, or at all events serviceable, for professional and literary purposes. He now becomes shameless and hardened; and it is observable in the career of this class of unfortunates, that the first act of duplicity is immediately followed by an access of the disorder, and a reckless abandonment to its propensities. The Archdeacon had long passed this stage ere he crossed my path, and had become thoroughly hardened. He was not remarkable for local attachment; and in moving from place to place, his spoil, packed in innumerable great boxes, sometimes followed him, to remain unreleased during the whole period of his tarrying in his new abode, so that they were removed to the next stage of his journey through life with modified inconvenience.

Cruel as it may seem, I must yet notice another and a peculiar vagary of his malady. He had resolved, at least once in his life, to part with a considerable proportion of his collection — better to suffer the anguish of such an act than endure the fretting of continued restraint. There was a wondrous sale by auction accordingly; it was something like what may have occurred at the dissolution of the monasteries at the Reformation, or when the contents of some time-honored public library were realized at the period of the French Revolution.

Before the affair was over, the Archdeacon himself made his appearance in the midst of the miscellaneous self-invited guests who were making free with his treasures. He pretended, honest man, to be a mere casual spectator, who, having seen, in passing, the announcement of a sale by auction, stepped in like the rest of the public. By degrees he got excited, gasped once or twice as if mastering some desperate impulse, and at length fairly bade. He could not brazen out the effect of this escapade, however, and disappeared from the scene. It was remarked, however, that an unusual number of lots were afterwards knocked down to a military gentleman, who seemed to have left portentously large orders with the auctioneer. Some curious suspicions began to arise, which were settled by that presiding genius bending over his rostrum, and explaining in a confidential whisper that the military hero was in reality a pillar of the church so disguised.

The Archdeacon lay under what, among a portion of the victims of his malady, was deemed a heavy scandal. He was suspected of reading his own books — that is to say, when he could get at them; for there are those who may still remember his rather shamefaced apparition of an evening, petitioning, somewhat in the tone with which an old schoolfellow down in the world requests your assistance to help him to go to York to get an appointment — petitioning for the loan of a volume of which he could not deny that he possessed numberless copies lurking in divers parts of his vast collection.

This reputation of reading the books in his collection, which should be sacred to external inspection solely, is, with a certain school of book-collectors, a scandal, such as it would be among a hunting set to hint that a man had killed a fox. In the dialogues, not always the most entertaining, of Dibdin's *Bibliomania*, there is this short passage: "'I will frankly confess,' rejoined Lysander, 'that I am an arrant *bibliomaniac*,—that I love books dearly, —that the very sight, touch, and mere perusal' —— 'Hold, my friend,' again exclaimed Philemon; 'you have renounced your profession—you talk of *reading* books—do *bibliomaniacs* ever *read* books?'"

Yes, the Archdeacon read books,—he devoured them; and he did so to full prolific purpose. His was a mind enriched with varied learning, which he gave forth with full, strong, easy flow, like an inexhaustible perennial spring coming from inner reservoirs, never dry, yet too capacious to exhibit the brawling, bubbling symptoms of repletion. It was from a majestic heedlessness of the busy world and its fame that he got the character of indolence, and was set down as one who would leave no lasting memorial of his great learning. But when he died, it was not altogether without leaving a sign; for from the casual droppings of his pen has been preserved enough to signify to many generations of students in the walk he chiefly affected how richly his mind was stored, and how much fresh matter there is in those fields of inquiry where compilers have left their dreary tracks, for ardent students to cultivate into a rich harvest. In him truly the bibliomania may be counted among the many illustrations of the truth so often moralized on, that the highest natures are not exempt from human frailty in some shape or other.

Let us now summon the shade of another departed victim — Fitzpatrick Smart, Esq. He, too, through a long life, had been a vigilant and enthusiastic collector, but after a totally different fashion. He was far from omnivorous. He had a principle of selection peculiar and separate from all other's, as was his own individuality from other men's. You could not classify his library according to any of the accepted nomenclatures peculiar to the initiated. He was not a black-letter man, or a tall-copyist, or an uncut man, or a rough-edge man, or an early-English-dramatist, or an Elzevirian, or a broadsider, or a pasquinader, or an old-brown-calf man, or a Grangerite, or a tawny-moroccoite, or a gilt-topper, a marbled-insider, or an *editio princeps* man ; neither did he come under any of the more vulgar classifications of an antiquarian, or a *belles-lettres*, or a classical collector. There was no way of defining his peculiar walk save by his own name — it was the Fitzpatrick-Smart walk. In fact, it wound itself in infinite windings through isolated spots of literary scenery, if we may so speak, in which he took a personal interest. There were historical events, bits of family history, chiefly of a tragic or a scandalous kind, — efforts of art or of literary genius on which, through some intellectual law, his mind and memory loved to dwell; and it was in reference to these that he collected. If the book were the one desired by him, no anxiety and toil, no payable price, was to be grudged for its acquisition. If the book were an inch out of his own line, it might be trampled in the mire for aught he cared, be it as rare or costly as it could be.

It was difficult, almost impossible, for others to predicate what would please this wayward sort of taste, and he was the torment of the book-caterers, who were sure of a princely price for the right article, but might have the wrong one thrown in their teeth with contumely. It was a perilous, but, if successful, a gratifying thing to present him with a book. If it happened to hit his fancy, he felt the full force of the compliment, and overwhelmed the giver with his courtly thanks. But it required great observation and tact to fit one for such an adventure, for the chances against an ordinary thoughtless gift-maker were thousands to one; and those who were acquainted with his strange nervous temperament, knew that the existence within his dwelling-place of any book not of his own special kind, would impart to him the sort of feeling of uneasy horror which a bee is said to feel when an earwig comes into its cell. Presentation copies by authors were among the chronic torments of his existence. While the complacent author was perhaps pluming himself on his liberality in making the judicious gift, the recipient was pouring out all his sarcasm, which was not feeble or slight, on the odious object, and wondering why an author could have entertained against him so steady and enduring a malice as to take the trouble of writing and printing all that rubbish with no better object than disturbing the peace of mind of an inoffensive old man. Every tribute from such *dona ferentes* cost him much uneasiness and some want of sleep — for what could he do with it? It was impossible to make merchandise of it, for he was every inch a gentleman. He could not burn it, for under an acrid exterior he had a kindly nature. It was believed, indeed, that he had established some limbo of his own, in which such unwelcome commodities were subject to a kind of burial or entombment, where they remained in existence, yet were decidedly outside the circle of his household gods.

These gods were a pantheon of a very extraordinary description, for he was a hunter after other things besides books. His acquisitions included pictures, and the various commodities which, for want of a distinctive name, auctioneers call "miscellaneous articles of vertu." He started on his accumulating career with some old family relics, and these, perhaps, gave the direction to his subsequent acquisitions, for they were all, like his books, brought together after some self-willed and peculiar law of association that pleased himself. A bad, even an inferior picture he would not have, — for his taste was exquisite, — unless, indeed, it had some strange history about it, adapting it to his wayward fancies, and then he would adopt the badness as a peculiar recommendation, and point it out with some pungent and appropriate remark to his friends. But though, with these peculiar exceptions, his works of art were faultless, no dealer could ever calculate on his buying a picture, however high a work of art or great a bargain. With his ever-accumulating collection, in which tiny sculpture and brilliant color predominated, he kept a sort of fairy world around him. But each one of the mob of curious things he preserved had some story linking it with others, or with his peculiar fancies; and each one had its precise place in a sort of *epos*, as certainly as each of the persons in the confusion of a pantomime or a farce has his own position and functions.

After all, he was himself his own greatest curiosity. He had come to manhood just after the period of gold-laced waistcoats, small-clothes, and shoe-buckles, otherwise he would have been long a living memorial of these now antique habits. It happened to be his lot to preserve down to us the earliest phase of the pantaloon dynasty. So, while the rest of the world were booted or heavy shod, his silk-stockinged feet were thrust into pumps of early Oxford cut, and the predominant garment was the surtout, blue in color, and of the original make before it came to be called a frock. Round his neck was wrapped an ante-Brummelite neckerchief (not a tie), which projected in many wreaths like a great poultice, — and so he took his walks abroad, a figure which he could himself have turned into admirable ridicule.

One of the mysteries about him was, that his clothes, though unlike any other person's, were always old. This characteristic could not even be accounted for by the supposition that he had laid in a sixty years' stock in his youth, for they always appeared to have been a good deal worn. The very umbrella was in keeping — it was of green silk, an obsolete color ten years ago — and the handle was of a peculiar crosier-like formation in cast-horn, obviously not obtainable in the market. His face was ruddy, but not with the ruddiness of youth; and, bearing on his head a Brutus wig of the light-brown hair which had long ago legitimately shaded his brow, when he stood still — except for his linen, which was snowy white — one might suppose that he had been shot and stuffed on his return home from college, and had been sprinkled with the frowzy mouldiness which time imparts to stuffed animals and other things, in which a semblance to the freshness of living nature is vainly attempted to be preserved. So if he were motionless; but let him speak, and the internal freshness was still there, an ever-blooming garden of intellectual flowers. His antiquated costume was no longer grotesque — it harmonized with an antiquated courtesy and high-bred gentleness of manner, which he had acquired from the best sources, since he had seen the first company in his day, whether for rank or genius. And conversation and manner were far from exhausting his resources. He had a wonderful pencil — it was potent for the beautiful, the terrible, and the ridiculous; but it took a wayward wilful course, like everything else about him. He had a brilliant pen, too, when he chose to wield it; but the idea that he should exercise any of these his gifts in common display before the world, for any even of the higher motives that make people desire fame and praise, would have sickened him. His faculties were his own as much as his collection, and to be used according to his caprice and pleasure. So fluttered through existence one who, had it been his fate to have his own bread to make, might have been a great man. Alas for the end! Some curious annotations are all that remain of his literary powers — some drawings and etchings in private collections all of his artistic. His collection, with its long train of legends and associations, came to what he himself must have counted as dispersal. He left it to his housekeeper, who, like a wise woman, converted it into cash while its mysterious reputation was fresh. Huddled in a great auction-room, its several catalogued items lay in humiliating contrast with the decorous order in which they were wont to be arranged. *Sic transit gloria mundi.*

Let us now call up a different and a more commonplace type of the book-hunter — it shall be Inchrule Brewer. He is guiltless of all intermeddling with the contents of books, but in their external attributes his learning is marvellous. He derived his nickname from the practice of keeping, as his inseparable pocket-companion, one of those graduated folding measures of length which may often be seen protruding from the moleskin pocket of the joiner. He used it at auctions, and on other appropriate occasions, to measure the different elements of a book — the letter-press — the unprinted margin — the external expanse of the binding; for to the perfectly scientific collector all these things are very significant.[1] They are, in fact, on record among the craft, like the pedigrees and physical characteristics recorded in stud-books and short-horn books. One so accomplished in this kind of analysis could tell at once, by this criterion, whether the treasure under the hammer was the same that had been knocked down before at the Roxburghe sale — the Askew, Gordonstown, or the Heber, perhaps — or was veritably an impostor — or was in reality a new and previously unknown prize well worth contending for. The minuteness and precision of his

[1] Of the copy of the celebrated 1635 Elzevir *Cæsar*, in the Imperial Library at Paris, Brunet triumphantly informs us that it is four inches and ten twelfths in height, and occupies the high position of being the tallest copy of that volume in the world, since other illustrious copies put in competition with it have been found not to exceed four inches and eight, or, at the utmost, nine, twelfths.

"Ces détails," he subjoins, "paroitront sans doute puérils à bien des gens : mais puisque c'est la grandeur des marges de ces sorts de livres qu'en determine la valeur, il faut bien fixer le *maximum* de cette grandeur, afin que les amateurs puissent apprécier les exemplaires qui approchent plus ou moins de la mésure donnée."

knowledge excited wonder, and, being anomalous in the male sex even among collectors, gave occasion to a rumor that its possessor must veritably be an aged maiden in disguise.

His experience, aided by a heaven-born genius tending in that direction, rendered him the most merciless detector of sophisticated books. Nothing, it might be supposed on first thought, can be a simpler or more easily recognized thing than a book genuine as printed. But in the old-book trade there are opportunities for the exercise of ingenuity inferior only to those which render the picture-dealer's and the horse-dealer's functions so mysteriously interesting. Sometimes entire fac-similes are made of eminent volumes. More commonly, however, the problem is to complete an imperfect copy. This will be most satisfactorily accomplished, of course, if another copy can be procured imperfect also, but not in the same parts. Great ingenuity is sometimes shown in completing a lightly esteemed edition with fragments from one highly esteemed. Sometimes a colophon or a decorated capital has to be imitated, and bold operators will reprint a page or two in fac-simile; these operations, of course, involve the inlaying of paper, judiciously staining it, and other mysteries. Paris is the great centre of this kind of work; but it has been pretty extensively pursued in Britain; and the manufacture of first-folio Shakspeares has been nearly as staple a trade as the getting up of genuine portraits of Mary Queen of Scots. It will establish a broad distinction to note the fact, that whereas our friend the Archdeacon would collect several imperfect copies of the same book in the hope of finding materials for one perfect one among them, Inchrule would remorselessly spurn from him the most voluptuously got-up specimen (to use a favorite phrase of Dibdin's) were it tainted by the very faintest "restoration."

Among the elements which constitute the value of a book — rarity of course being equal — one might say he counted the binding highest. He was not alone in this view, for it would be difficult to give the uninitiated a conception of the importance attached to this mechanical department of book-making by the adepts. About a third of Dibdin's *Bibliographical Decameron* is, if I recollect rightly, devoted to bindings. There are binders who have immortalized themselves — as Staggemier, Walther, Payne, Padaloup, Hering, De Rome, Faulkner, Lewis, Hayday, and Thomson. Their names may sometimes be found on their work, not with any particularities, as if they required to make themselves known, but with the simple brevity of illustrious men. Thus you take up a morocco-bound work of some eminence, on the title-page of which the author sets forth his full name and profession, with the distinctive initials of certain learned societies to which it is his pride to belong; but the simple and dignified enunciation, deeply stamped in his own golden letters, "Bound by Hayday," is all that that accomplished artist deigns to tell.

And let us, after all, acknowledge that there are few men who are entirely above the influence of binding. No one likes sheep's clothing for his literature, even if he should not aspire to russia or morocco. Adam Smith, one of the least showy of men, confessed himself to be a beau in his books. Perhaps the majority of men of letters are so to some extent, though poets are apt to be ragamuffins. It was Thomson, I believe, who used to cut the leaves with the snuffers. Perhaps an event in his early career may have soured him of the proprieties. It is said that he had an uncle, a clever active mechanic, who could do many things with his hands, and contemplated James's indolent, dreamy, "feckless" character with impatient disgust. When the first of *The Seasons* — "Winter" it was, I believe — had been completed at press, Jamie thought, by a presentation copy, to triumph over his uncle's scepticism, and to propitiate his good opinion he had the book handsomely bound. The old man never looked inside, or asked what the book was about, but, turning it round and round with his fingers in gratified admiration, exclaimed — "Come, is that really our Jamie's doin' now? — weel, I never thought the cratur wad hae had the handicraft to do the like!"

The feeling by which this worthy man was influenced was a mere sensible practical respect for good workmanship. The aspirations of the collectors, however, in this matter, go out of the boundaries of the sphere of the utilitarian into that of the æsthetic. Their priests and prophets, by the way, do not seem to be aware how far back this veneration for the coverings of books may be traced, or to know how strongly their votaries have been influenced in the direction of their taste by the traditions of the Middle Ages. The binding of a book was, of old, a shrine on which the finest workmanship in bullion and the costliest gems were lavished. The psalter or the breviary of some early saint, a portion of the Scriptures, or some other volume held sacred, would be thus enshrined. It has happened sometimes that tattered fragments of them have been preserved as effective relics within outer shells or shrines; and in some instances, long after the books themselves have disappeared, specimens of these old bindings have remained to us beautiful in their decay; — but we are getting far beyond the Inchrule.

Your affluent omnivorous collector, who has more of that kind of business on hand than he can perform for himself, naturally brings about him a train of satellites, who make it their business to minister to his importunate cravings. With them the phraseology of the initiated degenerates into a hard business sort of slang. Whatever slight remnant of respect towards literature as a vehicle of knowledge may linger in the conversation of their employers, has never belonged to theirs. They are dealers who have just two things to look to, — the price of their wares, and the peculiar propensities of the unfortunates who employ them. Not that they are destitute of all sympathy with the malady which they feed. The caterer generally gets infected in a superficial cutaneous sort of way. He has often a collection himself, which he eyes complacently of an evening as he smokes his pipe over his brandy-and-water, but to which he is not so distractedly devoted but that a pecuniary consideration will tempt him to dismember it. It generally consists, indeed, of blunders or false speculations — books which have been obtained in a mistaken reliance on their suiting the craving of some wealthy collector. Caterers unable to comprehend the subtle influences at work in the mind of the book-hunter, often make miscalculations in this way. Fitzpatrick Smart punished them so terribly that they at last abandoned him in despair to his own devices.

Several men of this class were under the authority of the Inchrule, and their communings were instructive. "Thorpe's catalogue just arrived, sir, — several highly important announcements," says a portly person with a fat volume under his arm, hustling forward with an air of assured consequence. There is now to be a deep and solemn consultation, as when two ambassadors are going over a heavy protocol from a third. It happened to me to see one of these myrmidons returning from a bootless errand of inspection to a reputed collection; he was hot and indignant. "A *collection*," he sputtered forth — "that a *collection!* — mere rubbish, sir — irredeemable trash. What do you think, sir? — a set of the common quarto edition of the Delphini classics, copies of Newton's works and Bacon's works, Gibbon's *Decline and Fall*, and so forth — nothing better, I declare to you: and to call *that* a collection!" Whereas, had it contained *The Pardoner and the Frere*, *Sir Clyomon and Clamydes*, *A Knacke to knowe a Knave*, *Banke's Bay Horse in a trance*, or the works of those eminent dramatists, Nabbes, May, Glapthorne, or Chettle, then would the collection have been worthy of distinguished notice. On another occasion, the conversation turning on a name of some repute, the remark is ventured, that he is "said to know something about books," which brings forth the fatal answer — "*He* know about books! — Nothing — nothing at all, I assure you; unless, perhaps, about their insides."

The next slide of the lantern is to represent a quite peculiar and abnormal case. It introduces a strangely fragile, unsubstantial, and puerile figure, wherein, however, resided one of the most potent and original spirits that ever frequented a tenement of clay. He shall be called, on account of associations that may or may not be found out, Thomas Papaverius. But how to make palpable to the ordinary human being one so signally divested of all the material and common characteristics of his race, yet so nobly endowed with its rarer and loftier attributes, almost paralyzes the pen at the very beginning.

In what mood and shape shall he be brought forward? Shall it be as first we met at the table of Lucullus, whereto he was seduced by the false pretence that he would there meet with one who entertained novel and anarchical opinions regarding the Golden Ass of Apuleius? No one speaks of waiting dinner for him. He will come and depart at his own sweet will, neither burdened with punctualities nor burdening others by exacting them. The festivities of the afternoon are far on when a commotion is heard in the hall as if some dog or other stray animal had forced its way in. The instinct of a friendly guest tells him of the arrival; he opens the door, and fetches in the little stranger. What can it be? a street-boy of some sort? His costume, in fact, is a boy's duffle great-coat, very threadbare, with a hole in it, and buttoned tight to the chin, where it meets the fragments of a particolored belcher handkerchief; on his feet are list-shoes, covered with snow, for it is a stormy winter night; and the trousers — some one suggests that they are inner linen garments blackened with writing-ink, but that Papaverius never would have been at the trouble so to disguise them. What can be the theory of such a costume? The simplest thing in the world — it consisted of the fragments of apparel nearest at hand. Had chance thrown to him a court single-breasted coat, with a bishop's apron, a kilt, and top-boots, in these he would have made his entry.

The first impression that a boy has appeared vanishes instantly. Though in one of the sweetest and most genial of his essays he shows how every man retains so much in him of the child he originally was — and he himself retained a great deal of that primitive simplicity — it was buried within the depths of his heart — not visible externally. On the contrary, on one occasion when he corrected an erroneous reference to an event as being a century old, by saying that he recollected its occurrence, one felt almost a surprise at the necessary limitation in his age, so old did he appear with his arched brow loaded with thought, and the countless little wrinkles which ingrained his skin, gathering thickly round the curiously expressive and subtle lips. These lips are speedily opened by some casual remark, and presently the flood of talk passes forth from them, free, clear, and continuous — never rising into declamation — never losing a certain mellow earnestness, and all consisting of sentences as exquisitely jointed together, as if they were destined to challenge the criticism of the remotest posterity. Still the hours stride over each other, and still flows on the stream of gentle rhetoric, as if it were *labitur et labetur in omne volubilis ævum.* It is now far in to the night, and slight hints and suggestions are propagated about separation and home-going. The topic starts new ideas on the progress of civilization, the effect of habit on men in all ages, and the power of the domestic affections. Descending from generals to the special, he could testify to the inconvenience of late hours; for, was it not the other night that, coming to what was, or what he believed to be, his own door, he knocked, and knocked; but the old woman within either couldn't or wouldn't hear him; so he scrambled over a wall, and having taken his repose in a furrow, was able to testify to the extreme unpleasantness of such a couch. The predial groove might indeed nourish kindly the infant seeds and shoots of the peculiar vegetable to which it was appropriated, but was not a comfortable place of repose for adult man.

Shall I try another sketch of him, when, travel-stained and foot-sore, he glided in on us one night like a shadow, the child by the fire gazing on him with round eyes of astonishment, and suggesting that he should get a penny and go home — a proposal which he subjected to some philosophical criticism very far wide of its practical tenor. How far he had wandered since he had last refreshed himself, or even whether he had eaten food that day, were matters on which there was no getting articulate utterance from him. Though his costume was muddy, however, and his communications about the material wants of life very hazy, the ideas which he had stored up during his wandering poured themselves forth as clear and sparkling, both in logic and language, as the purest fountain that springs from a Highland rock.

How that wearied, worn, little body was to be refreshed was a difficult problem: soft food disagreed with him — the hard he could not eat. Suggestions pointed at length to the solution of that vegetable unguent to which he had given a sort of lustre, and it might be supposed that there were some fifty cases of acute toothache to be treated in the house that night. How many drops? Drops! nonsense. If the wineglasses of the establishment were not beyond the ordinary normal size, there was no risk — and so the weary is at rest for a time.

At early morn a triumphant cry of *Eureka!* calls me to his place of rest. With his unfailing instinct he has got at the books, and lugged a considerable heap of them around him. That one which specially claims his attention — my best bound quarto — is spread upon a piece of bedroom furniture readily at hand, and of sufficient height to let him pore over it as he lies recumbent on the floor, with only one article of attire to separate him from the condition in which Archimedes, according to the popular story, shouted the same triumphant cry. He had discovered a very remarkable anachronism in the commonly received histories of a very important period. As he expounded it, turning up his unearthly face from the book with an almost painful expression of grave eagerness, it occurred to me that I had seen something like the scene in Dutch paintings of the Temptation of St. Anthony.

Suppose the scene changed to a pleasant country house, where the enlivening talk has made a guest forget

> "The lang Scots miles,
> The mosses, waters, slaps, and stiles,"

that lie between him and his place of rest. He

must be instructed in his course, but the instruction reveals more difficulties than it removes, and there is much doubt and discussion, which Papaverius at once clears up as effectually as he had ever dispersed a cloud of logical sophisms; and this time the feat is performed by a stroke of the thoroughly practical, which looks like inspiration, — he will accompany the forlorn traveller, and lead him through the difficulties of the way — for have not midnight wanderings and musings made him familiar with all its intricacies? Roofed by a huge wideawake, which makes his tiny figure look like the stalk of some great fungus, with a lantern of more than common dimensions in his hand, away he goes down the wooded path, up the steep bank, along the brawling stream, and across the waterfall — and ever as he goes there comes from him a continued stream of talk concerning the philosophy of Immanuel Kant, and other kindred matters. Surely if we two were seen by any human eyes, it must have been supposed that some gnome, or troll, or kelpie was luring the listener to his doom. The worst of such affairs as this was, the consciousness that, when left, the old man would continue walking on until, weariness overcoming him, he would take his rest, wherever that happened, like some poor mendicant. He used to denounce, with his most fervent eloquence, that barbarous and brutal provision of the law of England which rendered sleeping in the open air an act of vagrancy, and so punishable, if the sleeper could not give a satisfactory account of himself — a thing which Papaverius never could give under any circumstances. After all, I fear this is an attempt to describe the indescribable. It was the commonest of sayings when any of his friends were mentioning to each other "his last," and creating mutual shrugs of astonishment, that, were one to attempt to tell all about him, no man would believe it, so separate would the whole be from all the normal conditions of human nature.

The difficulty becomes more inextricable in passing from specific little incidents to an estimation of the general nature of the man. The logicians lucidly describe definition as being *per genus et differentiam*. You have the characteristics in which all of the *genus* partake as common ground, and then you individualize your object by showing in what it differs from the others of the genus. But we are denied this standard for Papaverius, so entirely did he stand apart, divested of the ordinary characteristics of social man — of those characteristics without which the human race as a body could not get on or exist. For instance, those who knew him a little might call him a loose man in money matters; those who knew him closer laughed at the idea of coupling any notion of pecuniary or other like responsibility with his nature. You might as well attack the character of the nightingale, which may have nipped up your five-pound note and torn it to shreds to serve as nest-building material. Only immediate craving necessities could ever extract from him an acknowledgment of the common vulgar agencies by which men subsist in civilized society; and only while the necessity lasted did the acknowledgment exist. Take just one example, which will render this clearer than any generalities. He arrives very late at a friend's door, and on gaining admission — a process in which he often endured impediments — he represents, with his usual silver voice and measured rhetoric, the absolute necessity of his being then and there invested with a sum of money in the current coin of the realm — the amount limited, from the nature of his necessities, which he very freely states, to seven shillings and sixpence. Discovering, or fancying he discovers, signs that his eloquence is likely to be unproductive, he is fortunately reminded that, should there be any difficulty in connection with security for the repayment of the loan, he is at that moment in possession of a document, which he is prepared to deposit with the lender — a document calculated, he cannot doubt, to remove any feeling of anxiety which the most prudent person could experience in the circumstances. After a rummage in his pockets, which develops miscellaneous and varied, but as yet by no means valuable possessions, he at last comes to the object of his search, a crumpled bit of paper, and spreads it out — a fifty-pound bank-note! The friend, who knew him well, was of opinion that, had he, on delivering over the seven shillings and sixpence, received the bank-note, he never would have heard anything more of the transaction from the other party. It was also his opinion that, before coming to a personal friend, the owner of the note had made several efforts to raise money on it among persons who might take a purely business view of such transactions; but the lateness of the hour, and something in the appearance of the thing altogether, had induced these mercenaries to forget their cunning, and decline the transaction.

He stretched till it broke the proverb, *Bis dat qui cito dat.* His giving was quick enough on the rare occasions when he had wherewithal to give, but then the act was final, and could not be repeated. If he suffered in his own person from this peculiarity, he suffered still more in his sympathies, for he was full of them to all breathing creatures, and, like poor Goldy, it was agony to him to hear the beggar's cry of distress, and to hear it without the means of assuaging it, though in a departed fifty pounds there were doubtless the elements for appeasing many a street wail. All sums of money were measured by him through the common standard of immediate use; and with more solemn pomp of diction than he applied to the bank-note, might he inform you that, with the gentleman opposite, to whom he had hitherto been entirely a stranger, but who happened to be nearest to him at the time when the exigency occurred to him, he had just succeeded in negotiating a loan of "twopence." He was and is a great authority in political economy. I have known great anatomists and physiologists as careless of their health as he was of his purse, whence I have inferred that something more than a knowledge of the abstract truth of political economy is necessary to keep some men from pecuniary imprudence, and that something more than a knowledge of the received principles of physiology is necessary to bring others into a course of perfect sobriety and general obedience to the laws of health. Further, Papaverius had an extraordinary insight into practical human life; not merely in the abstract, but in the concrete; not merely as a philosopher of human nature, but as one who saw into those who passed him in the walk of life with the kind of intuition attributed to expert detectives — a faculty that is known to have belonged to more than one dreamer, and is one of the mysteries in the nature of J. J. Rousseau; and, by the way, like Rousseau's, his handwriting was clear, angular, and unimpassioned, and not less uniform and legible than printing — as if the medium of conveying so noble a thing as thought ought to be carefully, symmetrically, and decorously constructed, let all other material things be as neglectfully and scornfully dealt with as may be.

This is a long proemium to the description of his characteristics as a book-hunter — but these can be briefly told. Not for him were the common enjoyments and excitements of the pursuit. He cared not to add volume unto volume, and heap up the relics of the printing-press. All the external niceties about pet editions, peculiarities of binding or of printing, rarity itself, were to him as if they were not. His pursuit, indeed, was like that of the savage who seeks but to appease the hunger of the moment. If he catch a prey just sufficient for his desires, it is well; yet he will not hesitate to bring down the elk or the buffalo, and, satiating himself with the choicer delicacies, abandon the bulk of the carcass to the wolves or the vultures. So of Papaverius. If his intellectual appetite were craving after some passage in the Œdipus, or in the Medeia, or in Plato's Republic, he would be quite contented with the most tattered and valueless fragment of the volume if it contained what he wanted; but, on the other hand, he would not hesitate to seize upon your tall copy in russia gilt and tooled. Nor would the exemption of an *editio princeps* from everyday sordid work restrain his sacrilegious hands. If it should contain the thing he desires to see, what is to hinder him from wrenching out the twentieth volume of your *Encyclopédie Méthodique* or *Ersch und Gruber*, leaving a vacancy like an extracted front tooth, and carrying it off to his den of Cacus? If you should mention the matter to any vulgar-mannered acquaintance given to the unhallowed practice of jeering, he would probably touch his nose with his extended palm and say, "Don't you wish you may get it?" True, the world at large has gained a brilliant essay on Euripides or Plato. — but what is that to the rightful owner of the lost sheep?

The learned world may very fairly be divided

into those who return the books borrowed by them, and those who do not. Papaverius belonged decidedly to the latter order. A friend addicted to the marvellous boasts that, under the pressure of a call by a public library to replace a mutilated book with a new copy, which would have cost £30, he recovered a volume from Papaverius, through the agency of a person specially bribed and authorized to take any necessary measures, insolence and violence excepted — but the power of extraction that must have been employed in such a process excites very painful reflections. Some legend, too, there is of a book creditor having forced his way into the Cacus den, and there seen a sort of rubble-work inner wall of volumes, with their edges outwards, while others, bound and unbound, the plebeian sheepskin and the aristocratic russian, were squeezed into certain tubs drawn from the washing establishment of a confiding landlady. In other instances the book has been recognized at large, greatly enhanced in value by a profuse edging of manuscript notes from a gifted pen — a phenomenon calculated to bring into practical use the speculations of the civilians about pictures painted on other people's panels.[1] What became of all his waifs and strays, it might be well not to inquire too curiously. If he ran short of legitimate

[1] "Si quis in aliena tabula pinxerit, quidam putant, tabulam picturæ cedere: aliis videtur picturam (qualiscunque sit) tabulæ cedere: sed nobis videtur melius esse tabulam picturæ cedere. Ridiculum est enim picturam Apellis vel Parrhasii in accessionem vilissimæ tabulæ cedere." — *Inst.* ii. 1, 34.

tabula raza to write on, do you think he would hesitate to tear out the most convenient leaves of any broad-margined book, whether belonging to himself or another? Nay, it is said he once gave in "copy" written on the edges of a tall octavo, *Somnium Scipionis;* and as he did not obliterate the original matter, the printer was rather puzzled, and made a funny jumble between the letter-press Latin and the manuscript English. All these things were the types of an intellectual vitality which despised and thrust aside all that was gross or material in that wherewith it came in contact. Surely never did the austerities of monk or anchorite so entirely cast all these away as his peculiar nature removed them from him. It may be questioned if he ever knew what it was "to eat a good dinner," or could even comprehend the nature of such a felicity. Yet in all the sensuous nerves which connect as it were the body with the ideal, he was painfully susceptible. Hence a false quantity or a wrong note in music was agony to him; and it is remembered with what ludicrous solemnity he apostrophized his unhappy fate as one over whom a cloud of the darkest despair had just been drawn — a peacock had come to live within hearing distance from him, and not only the terrific yells of the accursed biped pierced him to the soul, but the continued terror of their recurrence kept his nerves in agonizing tension during the intervals of silence.

Peace be with his gentle and kindly spirit, now

for some time separated from its grotesque and humble tenement of clay. It is both right and pleasant to say that the characteristics here spoken of were not those of his latter days. In these he was tended by affectionate hands; and I have always thought it a wonderful instance of the power of domestic care and management that, through the ministrations of a devoted offspring, this strange being was so cared for, that those who came in contact with him then, and then only, might have admired him as the patriarchal head of an agreeable and elegant household.

Let us now, for the sake of variety, summon up a spirit of another order — Magnus Lucullus, Esq. of Grand Priory. He is a man with a presence — tall, and a little portly, with a handsome pleasant countenance looking hospitality and kindliness towards friends, and a quiet but not easily solvable reserve towards the rest of the world. He has no literary pretensions, but you will not talk long with him without finding that he is a scholar, and a ripe and good one. He is complete and magnificent in all his belongings, only, as no man's qualities and characteristics are of perfectly uniform balance and parallel action, his library is the sphere in which his disposition for the complete and the magnificent has most profusely developed itself.

As you enter its Gothic door a sort of indistinct slightly musky perfume, like that said to frequent Oriental bazaars, hovers around. Everything is of perfect finish — the mahogany-railed gallery —

the tiny ladders — the broad-winged lecterns, with leathern cushions on the edges to keep the wood from grazing the rich bindings — the books themselves, each shelf uniform with its facings or rather backings, like well-dressed lines at a review. Their owner does not profess to indulge much in quaint monstrosities, though many a book of rarity is there. In the first place, he must have the best and most complete editions, whether common or rare; and, in the second place, they must be in perfect condition. All the classics are there — one complete set of Valpy's in good russia, and many separate copies of each, valuable for text or annotation. The copies of Bayle, Moreri, the Trevoux Dictionary, Stephens's Lexicon, Du Cange, Mabillon's Antiquities, the Benedictine historians, the Bolandists' Lives of the Saints, Grævius and Gronovius, and heavy books of that order, are in their old original morocco, without a scratch or abrasure, gilt-edged, vellum-jointed, with their backs blazing in tooled gold. Your own dingy well-thumbed Bayle or Moreri possibly cost you two or three pounds, his cost forty or fifty. Further, in these affluent shelves may be found those great costly works which cross the border of "three figures," and of which only one or two of the public libraries can boast, such as the *Celebri Famiglie Italiane* of Litta, Denon's Egypt, the great French work on the arts of the Middle Ages, and the like; and many is the scholar who, unable to gratify his cravings elsewhere, has owed it to Lucullus that he has seen something he was in search after in one of these great books, and has been able to put it to public use.

Throughout the establishment there is an appearance of care and order, but not of restraint. Some inordinately richly-bound volumes have special grooves or niches for themselves lined with soft cloth, as if they had delicate lungs, and must be kept from catching cold. But even these are not guarded from the hand of the guest. Lucullus says his books are at the service of his friends; and, as a hint in the same direction, he recommends to your notice a few volumes from the collection of the celebrated Grollier, the most princely and liberal of collectors, on whose classic book-plate you find the genial motto, "*Joannis Grollierii et amicorum.*" Having conferred on you the freedom of his library, he will not concern himself by observing how you use it. He would as soon watch you after dinner to note whether you eschew common sherry and show an expensive partiality for that madeira at twelve pounds a dozen, which other men would probably only place on the table when it could be well invested in company worthy of the sacrifice. Who shall penetrate the human heart, and say whether a hidden pang or gust of wrath has vibrated behind that placid countenance, if you have been seen to drop an ink-spot on the creamy margin of the Mentelin Virgil, or to tumble that heavy Aquinas from the ladder and dislocate his joints? As all the world now knows, however, men assimilate to the conditions by which they are surrounded, and we civilize our city savages by substituting cleanness and purity for the putrescence which naturally accumulates in great cities. So, in a noble library, the visitor is enchained to reverence and courtesy by the genius of the place. You cannot toss about its treasures as you would your own rough calfs and obdurate hogskins; as soon would you be tempted to pull out your meerschaum and punk-box in a cathedral. It is hard to say, but I would fain believe that even Papaverius himself might have felt some sympathetic touch from the spotless perfection around him and the noble reliance of the owner; and that he might perhaps have restrained himself from tearing out the most petted rarities, as a wolf would tear a fat lamb from the fold.

Such, then, are some "cases" discussed in a sort of clinical lecture. It will be seen that they have differing symptoms — some mild and genial, others ferocious and dangerous. Before passing to another and the last case, I propose to say a word or two on some of the minor specialties which characterize the pursuit in its less amiable or dignified form. It is, for instance, liable to be accompanied by an affection, known also to the agricultural world as affecting the wheat crop, and called "the smut." Fortunately this is less prevalent among us than the French, who have a name for the class of books affected by this school of collectors in the *Bibliothèque bleue*. There is a sad story connected with this peculiar frailty. A great and high-minded scholar of the seventeenth century had a savage trick played on him by some mad wags, who collected a quantity of the brutalities of which Latin literature affords an endless supply, and published them in his name. He is said not long to have survived this practical joke; and one does not wonder at his sinking before such a prospect, if he anticipated an age and a race of book-buyers among whom his great critical works are forgotten, and his name is known solely for the spurious volume, sacred to infamy, which may be found side by side with the works of the author of *Trimalcion's Feast* — "par nobile fratrum."

There is another failing, without a leaning to virtue's side, to which some collectors have been, by reputation at least, addicted — a propensity to obtain articles without value given for them — a tendency to be larcenish. It is the culmination, indeed, of a sort of lax morality apt to grow out of the habits and traditions of the class. Your true collector — not the man who follows the occupation as a mere expensive taste, and does not cater for himself — considers himself a finder or discoverer rather than a purchaser. He is an industrious prowler in unlikely regions, and is entitled to some reward for his diligence and his skill. Moreover, it is the essence of that very skill to find value in those things which, in the eye of the ordinary possessor, are really worthless. From estimating them at little value, and paying little for them, the steps are rather too short to estimating them at nothing, and paying nothing for them. What matters it, a few dirty black-letter leaves picked out of that volume of miscellaneous trash — leaves which the owner never knew he had, and cannot miss — which he would not know the value of, had you told him of them? What use of putting notions into the greedy barbarian's head, as if one were to find treasures for him? And the little pasquinade is *so* curious, and will fill a gap in that fine collection so nicely! The notions of the collector about such spoil are indeed the converse of those which Cassio professed to hold about his good name, for the scrap furtively removed is supposed in no way to impoverish the loser, while it makes the recipient rich indeed.[1]

Those habits of the prowler which may gradually lead a mind not strengthened by strong principle into this downward career, are hit with his usual vivacity and wonderful truth by Scott. The speaker is our delightful friend Oldenbuck of Monkbarns,

[1] [It is not Cassio but Iago who says that good name in man and woman is the immediate jewel of their souls, the loss of which enriches not others, but makes them poor indeed. The error is worth correcting; for there is no more exquisite touch of art, no finer exhibition of subtle and profound knowledge of man than the teaching by the lips of this supremest scoundrel the wide difference between the intellectual perception of a moral sentiment and its actual possession. Joseph Surface is the fruit of a bold and clumsy imitation of this single trait of Iago's character. Iago is a human creature, and is therefore a complex machine. Joseph Surface is an attribute of humanity made to wear clothes and do the work of a puppet. — W.]

the Antiquary, and it has just enough of confession in it to show a consciousness that the narrator has gone over dangerous ground, and, if we did not see that the narrative is tinged with some exaggeration, has trodden a little beyond the limits of what is gentlemanly and just.

"See this bundle of ballads, not one of them later than 1700, and some of them a hundred years older. I wheedled an old woman out of these, who loved them better than her psalm-book. Tobacco, sir, snuff, and the *Complete Syren*, were the equivalent! For that mutilated copy of the *Complaynt of Scotland* I sat out the drinking of two dozen bottles of strong ale with the late learned proprietor, who in gratitude bequeathed it to me by his last will. These little Elzevirs are the memoranda and trophies of many a walk by night and morning through the Cowgate, the Canongate, the Bow, St. Mary's Wynd — wherever, in fine, there were to be found brokers and trokers, those miscellaneous dealers in things rare and curious. How often have I stood haggling on a halfpenny, lest by a too ready acquiescence in the dealer's first price he should be led to suspect the value I set upon the article! How have I trembled lest some passing stranger should chop in between me and the prize, and regarded each poor student of divinity that stopped to turn over the books at the stall as a rival amateur or prowling bookseller in disguise! And then, Mr. Lovel — the sly satisfaction with which one pays the consideration, and pockets the article, affecting a cold indifference while the hand is trembling with pleasure! Then to dazzle the eyes of our wealthier and emulous rivals by showing them such a treasure as this (displaying a little black smoked book about the size of a primer) — to enjoy their surprise and envy; shrouding, meanwhile, under a veil of mysterious consciousness, our own superior knowledge and dexterity; — these, my young friend — these are the white moments of life, that repay the toil and pains and sedulous attention which our profession, above all others, so peculiarly demands."

There is a nice subtle meaning in the worthy man calling his weakness his "profession," but it is in complete keeping with the mellow Teniers-like tone of the whole picture. Ere we have done we shall endeavor to show that the grubber among book-stalls has, with other grubs or grubbers, his useful place in the general dispensation of the world. But his is a pursuit exposing him to moral perils, which call for peculiar efforts of self-restraint to save him from them; and the moral Scott holds forth — for a sound moral he always has — is, If you go as far as Jonathan Oldenbuck did — and I don't advise you to go so far, but hint that you should stop earlier — say to yourself, Thus far, and no farther.

So much for a sort of clinical exposition of the larcenous propensities which accompany book-hunting.[1] There is another peculiar, and, it may be

[1] [Nothing could be more correct or in better tone than the author's remarks upon these larcenous propensities, the exist-

said, vicious propensity, exhibited occasionally in conjunction with the pursuit. It is entirely antagonistic in spirit to the tenth commandment, and consists in a desperate coveting of the neighbor's goods, and a satisfaction, not so much in possessing for one's self, as in dispossessing him. This spirit is said to burn with still fiercer flame in the breasts of those whose pursuit would externally seem to be the most innocent in the world, and the least excitive of the bad passions — namely, among flower-fanciers. From some mysterious cause, it has been

ence of which he recognizes in such a candid matter-of-course way. There is, too, a genuine air about what he says which is unmistakable. But we on this side of the water, while confessing to our full share of human frailty, cannot but be unpleasantly surprised at the frequent imputations upon the personal honor, in this respect, of men of letters in Great Britain, which we see publicly made by members of the fraternity, and plainly without fear of contradiction. Dreadful stories of the purloining of rare manuscripts and books, and that not by needy thieves who steal to sell or pawn, (for books of course are little more than other goods exempt from ordinary theft,) but by men of position in literature, who abuse the trust placed in them to despoil even private collections only for the sake of satisfying their greed of what is scarce and curious. There are several men whose reputations extend beyond the limits of the British empire who are resting under these accusations. These stories are almost incredible to us. Mayhap our men of letters have not yet attained a sufficient appreciation of the value of old books to be subjected to the temptations which assail their brethren of the mother-country. But we shall, nevertheless, mourn the day when an advance in learning shows itself in such a way as to invite restraint of that perfect freedom with which the owner or keeper of a library in this country now admits to his shelves any man of letters, although a perfect stranger, who is known to him even by reputation. — W.]

known to develop itself most flagrantly among tulip-collectors, insomuch that there are legends of Dutch devotees of this pursuit who have paid their thousands of dollars for a duplicate tuber, that they might have the satisfaction of crushing it under the heel.[1] This line of practice is not entirely alien to the book-hunter. Dibdin warmed his convivial guests at a comfortable fire, fed by the woodcuts which had been printed from in the impression of the *Bibliographical Decameron.* It was a quaint fancy, and deemed to be a pretty and appropriate form of hospitality, while it effectually assured the subscribers to his costly volumes that the vulgar world who buy cheap books was definitely cut off from participating in their privileges.

Let us, however, summon a more potent spirit of this order. He is a different being altogether from those gentle shades who have flitted past us already.

[1] "The great point of view in a collector is to possess that not possessed by any other. It is said of a collector lately deceased, that he used to purchase scarce prints at enormous prices, in order to destroy them, and thereby render the remaining impressions more scarce and valuable." — GROSE's *Olio*, p. 57. I do not know to whom Grose alludes; but it strikes me, in realizing a man given to such propensities — taking them as a reality and not a joke — that it would be interesting to know how, in his moments of serious thought, he could contemplate his favorite pursuit — as, for instance, when the conscientious physician may have thought it necessary to warn him in time of the approaching end — how he could reckon up his good use of the talents bestowed on him, counting among them his opportunities for the encouragement of art, or an elevator and improver of the human race.

He was known in the body by many hard names, such as the Vampire, the Dragon, &c. He was an Irish absentee, or, more accurately, a refugee, since he had made himself so odious on his ample estate that he could not live there. How on earth he should have set about collecting books, is one of the inscrutable mysteries which ever surround the diagnosis of this peculiar malady. Setting aside his using his books by reading them as out of the question, he yet was never known to indulge in that fondling and complacent examination of their exterior and general condition, which, to Inchrule and others of his class, seemed to afford the highest gratification that, as sojourners through this vale of tears, it was their lot to enjoy. Nor did he luxuriate in the collective pride — like that of David when he numbered his people — of beholding how his volumes increased in multitude, and ranged with one another, like well-sized and properly-dressed troops, along an ample area of book-shelves. His collection — if it deserved the name — was piled in great heaps in garrets, cellars, and warerooms, like unsorted goods. They were accumulated, in fact, not so much that the owner might have them, as that other people might not. If there were a division of the order into positive, or those who desire to make collections — and negative, or those who desire to prevent them being made, his case would properly belong to the latter. Imagine the consternation created in a small circle of collectors by a sudden alighting among them of a *heluo librorum* with such propensities, armed with illimitable means, enabling him to desolate the land like some fiery dragon! What became of the chaotic mass of literature he had brought together no one knew. It was supposed to be congenial to his nature to have made a great bonfire of it before he left the world; but a little consideration showed such a feat to be impossible: for books may be burnt in detail by extraneous assistance, but it is a curious fact that, combustible as paper is supposed to be, books won't burn. If you doubt this, pitch that folio Swammerdam or Puffendorf into a good rousing fire, and mark the result.

No — it is probable that, stored away in some forgotten repositories, these miscellaneous relics still remain; and should they be brought forth, some excitement might be created; for, ignorant as the monster was, he had an instinct for knowing what other people wanted, and was thus enabled to snatch rare and curious volumes from the grasp of systematic collectors. It was his great glory to get hold of a unique book and shut it up. There were known to be just two copies of a spare quarto, called *Rout upon Rout, or the Rabblers Rabbled,* by Felix Nixon, Gent. He possessed one copy; the other, by indomitable perseverance, he also got hold of, and then his heart was glad within him; and he felt it glow with well-merited pride when an accomplished scholar, desiring to complete an epoch in literary history on which that book threw some light, besought the owner to allow him a sight of it, were it but for a few minutes, and the request was refused. "I might as well ask him," said the animal, who was rather proud of his firmness than ashamed of his churlishness, "to make me a present of his brains and reputation." [1]

It was among his pleasant ways to attend book-sales, there to watch the biddings of persons on whose judgment he relied, and cut in as the contest was becoming critical. This practice soon betrayed to those he had so provoked the chinks in the monster's armor. He was assailable and punishable at last, then, this potent monster; but the attack must be made warily and cautiously. Accordingly, impartial bystanders, ignorant of the plot, began to observe that he was degenerating by

[1] [Having the note on page 49 in mind, and with eyes quite open to the risk of a charge of pharisaic gratitude, I here remark upon another restriction upon the use of books to which our British kinsmen are subjected, and from which we are free. No one can have read much in London reprints of scarce books or new editions of old authors, without noticing evidence of the frequent inaccessibility to editorial seekers of well-known rare or unique copies, which were absolutely necessary to the satisfactory performance of their labors. The students of this department of literature have again and again seen editorial short-comings excused, in a preface, by the statement that the possessor of a certain unique copy of an old edition could not be persuaded to allow the editor to make a transcript from it, or even to consult it. Nor is this aspect of affairs (so unpleasant to us) much modified by the profuse and particular thanks of editors in the many cases in which an opposite course was pursued. These, hardly less than the apologies, are signs of an exclusiveness for mere exclusion's sake, which surely show that where they are expected the generous influence of letters is counteracted and circumscribed by some power which here is quite unknown. In

degrees in the rank of his purchases, and at last becoming, utterly reckless, buying, at the prices of the sublimest rarities, common works of ordinary literature to be found in every book-shop. Such was the result of judiciously drawing him on, by biddings for valueless books, on the part of those whom he had outbid in the objects of their desire. Auctioneers were surprised at the gradual change coming over the book-market; and a few fortunate people obtained considerable prices for articles they were told to expect nothing for. But this farce, of course, did not last long; and whether or not he found out that he had been beaten at his own weapons, the devouring monster disappeared as mysteriously as he had come.

all my intercourse with lovers of books, whether they were professionally men of letters or not, I have heard but of a single instance in which the possessor of a collection, or a copy, however rare and costly, did not give any properly introduced student the right of free warren over his shelves. I have known men who never had seen each other, or held any previous communication, write for the loan of a volume of which there was but a single copy in the country, and not half a dozen in the world; and I never knew the request refused, although the book had often to be sent more than a hundred miles by express, and sometimes to be kept for three months and more. Nor did I ever know of an instance in which there was cause given to regret this courtesy; — for which, by the way, there is not much bowing and hat-doffing in type, for very shame's sake; it being taken for granted that any man who has enough of the humanities to obtain and to prize a good book is entirely willing that all the world, and particularly the men of his fellowship, should share his good fortune. — W.]

Reminiscences.

SUCH incidents bring vividly before the eye the scenes in which they took place long long ago. If any one in his early youth has experienced some slight symptoms of the malady under discussion, which his constitution, through a tough struggle with the world, and a busy training in after life, has been enabled to throw off, he will yet look back with fond associations to the scenes of his dangerous indulgence. The auction-room is often the centre of fatal attraction towards it, just as the billiard-room and the *rouge-et-noir* table are to excesses of another kind. There is that august tribunal, over which at one time reigned Scott's genial friend Ballantyne, succeeded by the sententious Tait, himself a man of taste and a collector, and now presided over by the great Nisbet. I bow with deferential awe to the august tribunal before which so vast a mass of literature has changed hands, and where the future destinies of so many thousands — or, shall it be rather said, millions — of volumes have been decided, each carrying with it its own little train of suspense and triumph.

More congenial, however, in my recollection, is that remote and dingy hall where rough Carfrae, like Thor, flourished his thundering hammer. There it was that one first marked, with a sort of sympathetic awe, the strange and varied influence of their peculiar maladies on the book-hunters of the last generation. There it was that one first handled those pretty little pets, the Elzevir classics, a sort of literary bantams, which are still dear to memory, and awaken old associations by their dwarfish ribbed backs like those of ponderous folios, and their exquisite, but now, alas! too minute type. The eyesight that could formerly peruse them with ease has suffered decay, but *they* remain unchanged; and in this they are unlike to many other objects of early interest. Children, flowers, animals, scenery even, all have undergone mutation, but no perceptible shade of change has passed over these little reminders of old times.[1]

There it was that one first could comprehend how a tattered dirty fragment of a book once common might be worth a deal more than its weight in gold. There it was too, that, seduced by bad example, the present respected pastor of Ardsnischen purchased that beautiful Greek New Testament, by Jansen of Amsterdam, which he loved so, in the freshness of its acquisition, that he took it with him to church,

1 [This is but partly true. The inexperienced collector of books, and especially of the ancient classics, should not be tempted into paying high prices for Elzevir editions, unless in a case where there is something particularly attractive to his taste in the individual copy, and he pays for his whim — for which, alas! we are all too ready. The Elzevirs have fallen much in estimation and value of late years. Their accuracy has been found to have been too much vaunted; and the page is a bad one for the eye; not on account of its smallness, or poor press-work, but because of the shape of the letter. — W.]

and, turning up the text, handed it to a venerable woman beside him, after the fashion of an absorbed and absent student who was apt to forget whether he was reading Greek or English. The presiding genius of the place, with his strange accent, odd sayings, and angular motions, accompanied by good-natured grunts of grotesque wrath, became a sort of household figure. The dorsal breadth of pronunciation with which he would expose "Mr. Ivory's *Erskine*," used to produce a titter which he was always at a loss to understand. Though not the fashionable mart where all the thorough libraries in perfect condition went to be hammered off — though it was rather a place where miscellaneous collections were sold, and therefore bargains might be expected by those who knew what they were about — yet sometimes extraordinary and valuable collections of rare books came under his hammer, and created an access of more than ordinary excitement among the denizens of the place. On one of these occasions a succession of valuable fragments of early English poetry brought prices, so high and far beyond those of ordinary expensive books in the finest condition, that it seemed as if their imperfections were their merit; and the auctioneer, momentarily carried off with this feeling, when the high prices began to sink a little, remonstrated thus, "Going so low as thirty shillings, gentlemen, — this curious book — so low as thirty shillings — and *quite imperfect!*" [1]

[1] [Let not this occasion pass without brief tribute to that wit

Those who frequented this howf, being generally elderly men, have now nearly all departed. The

among literary auctioneers, that ever-welcomed companion among men of letters, Mr. John Keese; — alas that his bright eye is forever closed, his trenchant tongue forever silent! It cannot be but that many of the Book-Hunters who will read this most interesting history of their species have at some time or other pursued the objects of their chase with him as master of the hunt; and they, who have forgiven him even the high prices which he sometimes beguiled them into paying, will cherish the memory of the man who diffused over the dull and selfish contests of the auction-room, the charms of innocent, intellectual gayety. The joke into which the Scotch auctioneer blundered was one of a kind that he would have struck out upon the spur of the occasion. Little that he said has been preserved; and little perhaps would bear preserving. For, from the necessity of the case, the greater number of his jests, being born of the circumstances of the moment, died with them; and their short-lived prosperity lay in the ears which heard them. His knowledge of literature, too, was chiefly that which a man of quick apprehension acquires by constant intercourse with men of letters. But his ready and apt use of it made his companionship an uncloying pleasure. The quickness of his repartee was perhaps its greatest merit. A wit like him is a loaded piece, which surely gives a flash and a report, no matter how dull a finger pulls the trigger. One evening a little volume of wretched religious poetry, by Miss ——, was put up. Before a bid, "Who was Miss ——?" asked a book-stall keeper. Keese glanced at the biographical sketch: — "A poor and pious girl — who wrote poor and pious poetry." The book dropped dead; but the laugh which accompanied its fall raised the spirits of the "company" and told on the subsequent bidding. He was courageous, too, as well as ready. At a sale of unusual interest, attention was attracted by the presence and the purchases of a notorious political bully, then in office, and since rewarded with a better place. The creature was as innocent of humane letters as of humanity of any other kind, and bought for some political satrap of higher culture, in whose service he was retained. He claimed a very curious and valuable book which had been

thunderer's hammer, too, has long been silenced by the great quieter. One living memorial still exists of that scene — the genial and then youthful assistant, whose partiality for letters and literary pursuits made him often the monitor and kindly guide of the raw student, and who now, in a higher field, exercises a more important influence on the destinies of literature. I passed the spot the other day — it was not desolate and forsaken, with the moss growing on the hearth-stone; on the contrary, it flared with many lights — a thronged gin-palace. When one heard the sounds that issued from the old familiar spot, the reflection not unnaturally occurred that, after all, there are worse pursuits in the world than book-hunting.

knocked down to the bid of another person. This was explained to him in vain, and he began at once to be abusive. It was then offered to put up the book again. But he refused consent to this arrangement, and began to threaten, exclaiming that he "asked justice, and meant to have it." "Sir," instantly replied Keese, in a distinct, low voice, as he fixed his steel gray eye upon the bully, who could have torn his slight little form to pieces, "I know no man who deserves justice more than you do, and I heartily wish that you may get it." The animal's hide was not proof against that dart. He turned livid with impotent rage, and slunk silently away. Keese's memory will last his generation; and, as dead men are remembered, that is much. His was the kindest of hearts, the readiest with sympathy and with cheer, and with aid to the very extent of his ability. He helped many a young author into print, for whose unsalable books when the heavy "remainders" came under his hammer, even his humor could not extract the worth of the paper on which they were printed. If he had failings, which of us is free from them? and how many of us can reckon among ours one so kindly as this, though, perhaps, publishers may think so culpable? — W.]

Classification.

ERHAPS it would be a good practical distribution of the class of persons under examination, to divide them into private prowlers and auction-hunters. There are many other modes of classifying them, but none so general. They might be classified by the different sizes of books they affect — as folios, quartos, octavos, and duodecimos — but this would be neither an expressive nor a dignified classification. In enumerating the various orders to which Fitzpatrick Smart did *not* belong, I have mentioned many of the species, but a great many more might be added. Some collectors lay themselves out for vellum-printed volumes almost solely. There are such not only among very old books, but among very new; for of a certain class of modern books it frequently happens that a copy or two may be printed on vellum, to catch the class whose weakness takes that direction.

It may be cited as a signal instance of the freaks of book-collecting, that of all men in the world Junot, the hard-fighting soldier, had a vellum library; but so it was. It was sold in London for about £1400. "The crown octavos," says Dibdin, "especially of ancient classics, and a few favorite English authors, brought from four to six guineas. The first virtually solid article of any importance, or rather of the greatest importance, in the whole collection, was the matchless Didot *Horace*, of 1799, folio, containing the original drawings from which the exquisite copperplate vignettes were executed. This was purchased by the gallant Mr. George Hibbert for £140. Nor was it in any respect an extravagant or even dear purchase." It now worthily adorns the library of Norton Hall.

Some collectors may be styled Rubricists, being influenced by a sacred rage for books having the contents and marginal references printed in red ink. Some "go at" flowered capitals, others at broad margins. These have all a certain amount of magnificence in their tastes ; but there are others again whose priceless collections are like the stock-in-trade of a wholesale ballad-singer, consisting of chap-books, as they are termed — the articles dealt in by pedlers and semi-mendicants for the past century or two. Some affect collections relating to the drama, and lay great store by heaps of play-bills arranged in volumes, and bound, perhaps, in costly russia. Of a more dignified grade are perhaps those who have lent themselves to the collection of the theses on which aspirants after university honors held their disputations or impugnments. Sometimes out of a great mass of rubbish of this kind the youthful production of some man who has afterwards become great turns up. Of these theses and similar tracts a German, Count Dietrich, collected some hundred and forty thousand, which are now in this country.

Collectors there have been, not unimportant for number and zeal, whose mission it is to purchase books marked by peculiar mistakes or errors of the press. The celebrated Elzevir *Cæsar* of 1635 is known by this, that the number of the 149th page is misprinted 153. All that want this peculiar distinction are counterfeits. The little volume being, as Brunet says, "une des plus jolies et plus rares de la collection des Elzevier," gave a temptation to fraudulent imitators, who, as if by a providential arrangement for their detection, lapsed into accuracy at the critical figure.[1]

1 [There are not a few happy mistakes of this kind which serve for the protection of the book collector, who will find almost all of them carefully recorded in Brunet's *Manuel du Libraire,* without consulting which no inexperienced buyer should ever make an important purchase. It is, however, much less full in this respect, as well as in others, with regard to books printed in our own language than with regard to those, both ancient and modern, in the languages of the continent of Europe. It is to be regretted that Lowndes's Bibliographer's Manual is very deficient upon this point, a consideration of which did not enter into the plans of either Watts or Brydges. Apropos, the lovers of beautiful books more suited to the general taste than Elzevir classics, will be glad to know of an error which affords assistance in the selection of a copy of that much prized, and most beautiful volume, Rogers' Italy with Turner's, Prout's, and Stothard's illustrations. The proof copies of this book maintain their high price, and will probably increase rather than diminish in value. They can never be mistaken, because in the corner of each impression, after the engraver's signature, is the word "proof." But there are a few copies, not thus marked, which rank next to them, and which are, to all intents and purposes, as good as proofs, they being the first which were struck off after the proof-mark was erased. These are known by the misplacing of the two illustrations to the lines upon Arqua.

The mere printers' blunders that have been committed upon editions of the Bible are reverenced in literary history; and one edition — the Vulgate issued under the authority of Sixtus V. — achieved immense value from its multitude of errors. The well-known story of the German printer's wife who surreptitiously altered the passage importing that her husband should be her lord (Herr) so as to make him be her fool (Narr), needs confirmation. If such a misprint were found, it might quite naturally be attributed to carelessness. Valarian Flavigny, who had many controversies on his hand, brought on the most terrible of them all with Abraham Ecchellensis for a mere dropped letter. In the rebuke about the mote in thy brother's eye,

The view of the tomb should be at the beginning, and that of Petrarch's house at the end of the lines; but in these copies the positions are reversed. After a few copies were printed the error was discovered and corrected; and the consequence is that the copies in which the tomb appears on page 88, and the house on page 91, have a special value, hitherto not generally known.

The obscurity of a learned language veils the most formidable error of the press that probably ever occurred, except one in the London "Morning Chronicle" on the morning after the birth of the Princess of Wales at Buckingham Palace, the vernacular enormity of which makes it absolutely unmentionable. The former fell to the lot of Erasmus in his book *Vidua Christiana,* which he dedicated to Charles the Fifth's sister, the Queen of Hungary. In this volume, and of that illustrious princess herself, he wrote *Mente illâ usam eam semper fuisse quæ talem feminam deceret;* but the printer, as if seized upon by the spirit of Aretino, made him say, *Mentula usam eam,* &c., which stupendous announcement went through the whole of a large edition. — W.]

and the beam in thine own, the first letter in the Latin for eye was carelessly dropped out, and left a word which may be found occasionally in Martial's Epigrams, but not in books of purer Latin and purer ideas.[1]

Questions as to typographical blunders in editions of the classics are mixed up with larger critical inquiries into the purity of the ascertained text, and

[1] A traditional anecdote represents the Rev. William Thomson, a clergyman of the Church of Scotland, as having got into a scrape by a very indecorous alteration of a word in Scripture. A young divine, on his first public appearance, had to read the solemn passage in 1st Corinthians, "Behold, I show you a mystery; we shall not all sleep, but we shall all be changed, in a moment, in the twinkling of an eye, at the last trump." Thomson scratched the letter *c* out of the word changed. The effect of the passage so mutilated can easily be tested. The person who could play such tricks was ill suited for his profession; and, being relieved of its restraints, he found a more congenial sphere of life among the unsettled crew of men of letters in London, over whom Smollett had just ceased to reign. He did a deal of hard work, and the world owes him at least one good turn in his translation of Cunningham's Latin *History of Britain, from the Revolution to the Hanover Succession.* The value of this work, in the minute light thrown by it on one of the most memorable periods of British history, is too little known. The following extract may give some notion of the curious and instructive nature of this neglected book. It describes the influences which were in favor of the French alliance, and against the Whigs, during Marlborough's campaign. "And now I shall take this opportunity to speak of the French wine-drinkers as truly and briefly as I can. On the first breaking out of the Confederate war, the merchants in England were prohibited from all commerce with France, and a heavy duty was laid upon French wine. This caused a grievous complaint among the topers, who have great interest in the Parliament, as if they had been poisoned by port wines. Mr. Portman Sey-

thus run in veins through the mighty strata of philological and critical controversy which, from the days of Poggio downwards, have continued to form that voluminous mass of learning which the outer world contemplates with silent awe.

To some extent the same spirit of critical inquiry has penetrated into our own language. What we have of it clusters almost exclusively around the mighty name of Shakspeare. Shakspearian criticism is a branch of knowledge by itself. To record its triumphs — from that greatest one by which the senseless "Table of Greenfield," which interrupted the touching close of Falstaff's days, was replaced

mour, who was a jovial companion, and indulged his appetites, but otherwise a good man; General Churchill, the Duke of Marlborough's brother, a man of courage, but a lover of wine; Mr. Pereira, a Jew and smell-feast, and other hard drinkers, declared, that the want of French wine was not to be endured, and that they could hardly bear up under so great a calamity. These were joined by Dr. Aldridge, who, though nicknamed the priest of Bacchus, was otherwise an excellent man, and adorned with all kinds of learning. Dr. Ratcliffe, a physician of great reputation, who ascribed the cause of all diseases to the want of French wines, though he was very rich, and much addicted to wine, yet, being extremely covetous, bought the cheaper wines; but at the same time he imputed the badness of his wine to the war, and the difficulty of getting better. Therefore the Duke of Beaufort and the Earl of Scarsdale, two young noblemen of great interest among their acquaintance, who had it in their power to live at their ease in magnificence or luxury, merrily attributed all the doctor's complaints to his avarice. All those were also for peace rather than war. And all the bottle companions, many physicians, and great numbers of the lawyers and inferior clergy, and, in fine, the loose women too, were united together in the faction against the Duke of Marlborough." — ii. 200.

by "'a babbled of green fields" — would make a large book of itself. He who would undertake it, in a perfectly candid and impartial spirit, would give us, varied no doubt with much erudition and acuteness, a curious record of blundering ignorance and presumptuous conceit, the one so intermingling with the other that it would be often difficult to distinguish them.[1]

The quantity of typographical errors exposed in those pages where they are least to be expected, and are least excusable, opens up some curious considerations. Compositors are a placid and unimpressionable race, who do their work dutifully, with-

[1] Without venturing too near to this very turbulent arena, where hard words have lately been cast about with much reckless ferocity, I shall just offer one amended reading, because there is something in it quite peculiar, and characteristic of its literary birthplace beyond the Atlantic. The passage operated upon is the wild soliloquy, where Hamlet resolves to try the test of the play, and says, —

> "The devil hath power
> T' assume a pleasing shape; yea, and perhaps,
> Out of my weakness and my melancholy,
> As he is very potent with such spirits,
> Abuses me to damn me."

The amended reading stands —

> "As he is very potent with such spirits,
> Abuses me too — damme." *

[* I may be very dull, or very ignorant of this side of the Atlantic; but I am quite unable to see in this emendation, (which must be classed rather with the "ingenious" than the erudite,) anything peculiarly characteristic of its literary birth-place. It is humorous indeed, and humor is perhaps more of an every-day matter here than in the mother-country; but the humor is of the kind peculiarly English, and the oath which is made its vehicle has been the distinctive oath of our race since Joan d'Arc called us "English God-out yielding to the intellectual influences represented by it. A clause of an Act of Parliament, with all its whereases, and be it enacteds, and hereby repealeds, creates quite as much emotion in them as the most brilliant burst of the fashionable poet of the day. They will set you up a psalm or a blasphemous ditty with the same equanimity, not retaining in their minds any clear distinction between them. Your writing must be something very wonderful indeed, before they distinguish it from other "copy," except by the goodness or badness of the hand. A State paper which all the world is mad to know about, is quite safe in a printing-office; and they will set up what is here set down of them,

damns" four hundred years ago; and doubtless William the Norman found this hearty curse with many other hearty and better things among the English whom his race conquered, and by whom it was swallowed up. In respect of our swearing, at least, we vindicate our birthright; except at the South, indeed, where new and elaborate monstrosities of profanity have been ingeniously struck out.

But here is an emendation which should commend itself to the attention of the British critics. The passage is in "Anthony and Cleopatra," Act III. Sc. 11.

"Ah, dear! if I be so,
From my cold heart let heaven engender hail
And poison it in the source."

The critic remarks, "What absurdity! Who ever heard of poisoning hail? Cleopatra plainly desires that her heart's blood should be turned into that delicious fluid the poisoning of which would indeed be a public calamity. Its name is often incorrectly pronounced, we know, especially by Yankees, without the aspirate, and the error was therefore easy. Read, without a doubt,

"'Ah dear! if I be so,
From my cold heart let heaven engender *ale*
And poison it in the source.'"

I am not prepared to assert positively that this emendation, which must be pronounced both ingenious and elaborate, had its literary birth-place beyond the Atlantic; but it certainly smacks more peculiarly of London than the former does of New York or Boston. — W.]

without noting that it refers to themselves. It is said that this stoic indifference is a wonderful provision for the preservation of the purity of literature; and that, were compositors to think with the author under "the stick," they might make dire havoc.

Allowing for these peculiarities, it may surely be believed that, between the compositors who put the types together and the correctors of the press, the printing of the Bible has generally been executed with more than average care. Yet the editions of the sacred book have been the great mine of discovered printers' blunders. The inference from this, however, is not that blunders abound less in other literature, but that they are not worth finding there. The issuing of the true reading of the Scripture is of such momentous consequence, that a mistake is sure of exposure, like those minute incidents of evidence which come forth when a murder has been committed, but would never have left their privacy for the detection of a petty fraud.

The value to literature of a pure Shakspearian text, has inspired the zeal of the detectives who work on this ground. Some casual detections have occurred in minor literature, — as, for instance, when Akenside's description of the Pantheon, which had been printed as "serenely great," was restored to "severely great." The reason, however, why such detections are not common in common books, is the rather humiliating one that they are not worth making. The specific weight of individual words is in them of so little influence, that one does as well as another. Instances could indeed be pointed out, where an incidental blunder has much improved a sentence, giving it the point which its author failed to achieve — as a scratch or an accidental splash of the brush sometimes supplies the painter with the ray or the cloud which the cunning of his hand cannot accomplish. Poetry in this way sometimes endures the most alarming oscillations without being in any way damaged, but, on the contrary, sometimes rather improved. I might refer to a signal instance of this, where, by some mysterious accident at press, the lines of a poem written in quatrains got their order inverted, so that the second and fourth of each quatrain changed places. This transposition was pronounced to operate a decided improvement on the spirit and originality of the piece, — an opinion in which, unfortunately, the author did not concur; nor could he appreciate the compliment of a critic, who remarked that the experiment tested the soundness of the lines, which could find their feet whatever way they were thrown about.[1]

There have been, no doubt, cruel instances of printers' blunders in our own days, like the fate of the youthful poetess in the Fudge family: —

[1] One curious service of printer's blunders, of a character quite distinct from their bibliological influence, is their use in detecting plagiarisms. It may seem strange that there should be any difficulty in critically determining the question, when the plagiarism is so close as to admit of this test; but there are pieces of very hard work in science, tables of reference, and the like, where, if two people go through the same work, they will

'When I talked of the dewdrops on freshly-blown roses,
The nasty things printed it — freshly-blown noses."

A solid scholar there was, who, had he been called to his account at a certain advanced period of his career, might have challenged all the world to say that he had ever used a false quantity or committed an anomaly in syntax, or misspelt a foreign name, or blundered in a quotation from a Greek or Latin classic — to misquote an English author is a far lighter crime, but even to this he could have pleaded not guilty. He never made a mistake in a date, nor left out a word in copying the title-page of a volume; nor did he ever, in affording an intelligent analysis of its contents, mistake the number of pages devoted to one head. As to the higher literary virtues too, his sentences were all carefully balanced in a pair of logical and rhetorical scales of the most sensitive kind; and he never perpetrated the atrocity of ending a sentence with a monosyllable, or using the same word twice within the same five lines, choosing always some judicious method of circumlocution to obviate reiteration. Poor man! in the pride of his unspotted purity, he little knew what a humiliation fate had prepared for him. It happened to him to have to state how

come to the same conclusion. In such cases, the prior worker has sometimes identified his own by a blunder, as he would a stolen china vase by a crack. Peignot complains that some thirty or forty pages of his *Dictionnaire Bibliographique* were incorporated in the *Siècles Littéraires de la France,* "avec une exactitude si admirable, qu'on y a precieusement conservé toutes les fautes typographiques."

Theodore Beza, or some contemporary of his, went to sea in a Candian vessel. This statement, at the last moment, when the sheet was going through the press, caught the eye of an intelligent and judicious corrector, more conversant with shipping-lists than with the literature of the sixteenth century, who saw clearly what had been meant, and took upon himself, like a man who hated all pottering nonsense, to make the necessary correction without consulting the author. The consequence was, that people read with some surprise, under the authority of the paragon of accuracy, that Theodore Beza had gone to sea in a *Canadian* vessel. The victim of this calamity had undergone minor literary trials, which he had borne with philosophical equanimity; as, for instance, when inconsiderate people, destitute of the organ of veneration, thoughtlessly asked him about the last new popular work, as if it were something that he had read or even heard of, and actually went so far in their contumelious disrespect as to speak to him about the productions of a certain Charles Dickens. The "Canadian vessel," however, was a more serious disaster, and was treated accordingly. A charitable friend broke his calamity to the author at a judicious moment, to prevent him from discovering it himself at an unsuitable time, with results the full extent of which no one could foresee. It was an affair of much anxiety among his friends, who made frequent inquiries as to how he bore himself in his affliction, and what continued to be the condition of his health, and especially of his spirits. And although he was a confirmed book-hunter, and not unconscious of the merits of the peculiar class of books now under consideration, it may be feared that it was no consolation to him to reflect that, some century or so hence, his books and himself would be known only by the curious blunder which made one of them worth the notice of the book-fanciers.

An odd accident occurred to a well-known book lately published, called *The Men of the Time.* It sometimes happens in a printing-office that some of the types, perhaps a printed line or two, fall out of "the forme." Those in whose hands the accident occurs, generally try to put things to rights as well as they can, and may be very successful in restoring appearances with the most deplorable results to the sense. It happened thus in the instance referred to. A few lines dropping out of the Life of Robert Owen, the parallelogram Communist, were hustled, as the nearest place of refuge, into the biography of his closest alphabetical neighbor — "Oxford, Bishop of." The consequence is, that the article begins as follows: —

"OXFORD, THE RIGHT REVEREND SAMUEL WILBERFORCE, BISHOP OF, was born in 1805. A more kind-hearted and truly benevolent man does not exist. A sceptic, as regards religious revelation, he is nevertheless an out-and-out believer in spirit movements."

Whenever this blunder was discovered, the leaf

was cancelled; but a few copies of the book had got into circulation, which some day or other may be very valuable.[1]

In the several phases of the book-hunter, he whose peculiar glory it is to have his books illustrated — the Grangerite, as he is technically termed — must not be omitted. "Illustrating" a volume consists in inserting in or binding up with it portraits, landscapes, and other works of art bearing a reference to its contents. This is materially different from the other forms of the pursuit, in as far as the quarry hunted down is the raw material, the finished article being a result of domestic manufacture. The illustrator is the very Ishmaelite of collectors — his hand is against every man, and every man's hand is against him. He destroys unknown quantities of books to supply portraits or other illustrations to a single volume of his own; and as it is not always known concerning any book that

[1] [Hardly. The book, even in its last corrected and augmented form, is too full of blunders to be specially prized for any particular one. With regard to this country its mistakes are equally monstrous, manifold, and laughable. The variation of even twenty years from the truth in the date, or from one hundred to five hundred miles in the place, of a man's birth is not very uncommon. And what shall be said of the absurdity, for instance, of such a remark as that with regard to Mr. Bryant that "probably we owe 'Thanatopsis'" — that solemn philosophic poem upon death — "to the inspirations of his early love." I will notice here a strange mistake made by Lowndes in his Bibliographers' Manual which remains in the new edition, to which Mr. Bohn has made so many valuable additions. "The Federalist" is said to be "a collection of essays in which John Williams *alias* Anthony Pasquins was concerned." Shades of

he has been at work on it, many a common book-buyer has cursed him on inspecting his own last bargain, and finding that it is deficient in an interesting portrait or two. Tales there are, fitted to make the blood run cold in the veins of the most sanguine book-hunter, about the devastations committed by those who are given over to this special pursuit. It is generally understood that they received the impulse which has rendered them an important sect, from the publication of Granger's biographical history — hence their name of Grangerites. So it has happened that this industrious and respectable compiler is contemplated with mysterious awe, as a sort of literary Attila or Gengis Khan, who has spread terror and ruin around him. In truth, the illustrator, whether green-eyed or not, being a monster that doth make the meat he feeds on, is apt to become excited with his work, and to go on ever widening the circle of his purveyances,

Hamilton and Monroe, founders of the Great Republic, and revered expositors of its Constitution, your noble work, which stands almost alone, as being at once an undisputed authority in politics and a classic in letters, is a series of essays in which a pasquinading *alias* "was concerned;" and this is all! Not to know who wrote "The Federalist," and what it is, and that the men who wrote it, although of what a member of Parliament, unrebuked in presence of the British Premier, calls "the scum of the earth," were yet of a sort which does not admit the companionship of the Anthony Pasquins of London, is not culpable in a British subject; the matter may be of no interest to him; but when, pretending to speak with authority, he exhibits such density of ignorance, both his ignorance and his pretence become ridiculous. — W.]

and opening new avenues toward the raw material on which he works. To show how widely such a person may levy contributions, I propose to take, not a whole volume, not even a whole page, but still a specific and distinguished piece of English literature, and describe the way in which a devotee of this peculiar practice would naturally proceed in illustrating it. The piece of literature to be illustrated is as follows: —

> "How doth the little busy bee
> Improve each shining hour,
> And gather honey all the day
> From every opening flower."

The first thing to be done is to collect every engraved portrait of the author, Isaac Watts. The next, to get hold of any engravings of the house in which he was born, or houses in which he lived. Then will come all kinds of views of Southampton — of its Gothic gate, and its older than Gothic wall. Any scrap connected with the inauguration of the Watts statue must of course be scrupulously gathered. To go but a step beyond such commonplaces — there is a traditional story about the boyhood of Isaac which has been told as follows. He took precociously to rhyming: like Pope, he lisped in numbers, for the numbers came. It happened that this practice was very offensive to his father, a practical man, who, finding admonition useless, resolved to stop it in an effectual manner. He accordingly, after the practice of his profession —

being a schoolmaster — assailed with a leathern thong, duly prepared, the cuticle of that portion of the body which has from time immemorial been devoted to such inflictions. Under torture, the divine songster abjured his propensity in the following very hopeful shape —

"Oh, father, do some pity take,
And I will no more verses make."

It is not likely that this simple domestic scene has been engraved either for the Divine Hymns, or the Improvement of the Mind. The illustrator will therefore require to get a picture of it for his own special use, and will add immensely to the value of his treasure while he gives scope to the genius of a Cruikshank or a Doyle.

We are yet, it will be observed, only on the threshold. We have next to illustrate the substance of the poetry. All kinds of engravings of bees, Attic and other, and of bee-hives, will be appropriate, and will be followed by portraits of Huber and other great writers on bees, and views of Mount Hybla and other honey districts. Some Scripture prints illustrative of the history of Samson, who had to do with honey and bees, will be appropriate, as well as any illustrations of the fable of the bear and the bees, or of the Roman story of the *sic vos non vobis*. A still more appropriate form of illustration may, however, be drawn upon by remembering that a periodical called *The Bee* was edited by Dr. Anderson; and it is important to observe that the name was adopted in the very spirit which inspired Watts. In both instances the most respected of all winged insects was brought forward as the type of industry. Portraits, then, of Dr. Anderson, and any engravings that can be connected with himself and his pursuits, will have their place in the collection. It will occur, perhaps, to the intelligent illustrator, that Dr. Anderson was the grandfather of Sir James Outram, and he will thus have the satisfaction of opening his collection for all illustrations of the career of that distinguished officer. Having been aptly called the Bayard of the Indian service, the collector who has exhausted him and his services, will be justified by the principles of the craft in following up the chase, and picking up any wood-cuts or engravings referring to the death of the false Bourbon, or any other scene in the career of the Knight without Fear or Reproach. Here, by a fortunate and interesting coincidence, through the Bourbons the collector gets at the swarms of bees which distinguish the insignia of royalty in France. When the illustrator comes to the last line, which invites him to add to what he has already collected a representation of "every opening flower," it is easy to see that he has indeed a rich garden of delights before him.

In a classification of book-hunters, the aspirants after large-paper copies deserve special notice, were it only for the purpose of guarding against a common fallacy which confounds them with the lovers of tall copies. The difference is fundamental: large-paper copies being created by system, while tall copies are merely the creatures of accident; and Dibdin bestows due castigation in a celebrated instance in which a mere tall copy had, whether from ignorance or design, been spoken of as a large-paper copy. This high development of the desirable book is the result of an arrangement to print so many copies of a volume on paper of larger size than that of the bulk of the impression. The tall copy is the result of careful cutting by the binder, or of no cutting at all. In this primitive shape a book has separate charms for a distinct class of collectors who esteem rough edges, and are willing, for the sake of this excellence, to endure the martyrdom of consulting books in that condition.[1]

[1] "But devious oft, from ev'ry classic muse,
The keen collector meaner paths will choose:
And first the margin's breadth his soul employs,
Pure, snowy, broad, the type of nobler joys.
In vain might Homer roll the tide of song,
Or Horace smile, or Tully charm the throng;
If crost by Pallas' ire, the trenchant blade,
Or too oblique, or near the edge, invade,
The Bibliomane exclaims, with haggard eye,
'No Margin!'—turns in haste, and scorns to buy."

FERRIER'S *Bibliomania*, v. 34–43

[Few, very few book collectors, I would fain believe, are so wedded to a whim as to have books with the *top edges* rough. It would seem that only such bibliomaniacs as read no books, except catalogues, could really desire them in such a condition. "Uncut" is understood among all sane bibliomaniacs to refer to the fore-edge and the bottom edge. A book which is intended to fulfil any function, to which a block of wood, leathered and gilt and lettered in like manner is not equally fitted, should have the

The historian of the private libraries of New York makes us acquainted with a sect well known in the actually sporting world, but not heretofore familiar in the biblical.[1] Here is a description of

top edge cut and gilt or stained ; otherwise not only will the consulting, or even the showing, of it be a penance for folly, but the rough top edges will retain dust which will sift down between the leaves and thus deface the book inside as well as out. This dust can be blown from a book, the top edges of which have been polished, as if from glass. The top edge being thus cared for, the condition of the fore-edge and the bottom edge are subjects of legitimate caprice; for no man who is worthy of being the possessor of a good book will ever dream of turning the leaves in any other way than with the thumb on the page and fore finger at the top. All other modes are barbarous.

It is worth while to caution the collector against indiscriminate large paper gathering. There is always, of course, a certain distinction about a large paper copy, because it is one of a small number, specially prepared, and much costlier than those of the ordinary size. To certain books this luxury of margins is very appropriate, if the margin is well proportioned to the page ; though it should be always remembered that the addition to the margin adds to the weight of the book, makes it less convenient to handle, and in effect diminishes by so much the capacity of the library shelves. The omnivorous Mr. Heber, of whom the author subsequently speaks, looked upon large paper with abhorrence, on account of the room which it took up. Sometimes, too, it is pushed to a ridiculous and uncomely extreme. There are many books which have been printed on paper of three sizes, — ordinary, large, and largest ; and of these the largest is not always the most beautiful. Other things being equal, quality is of more importance than size of paper ; and of many books there are special copies on laid, on fine, and on India paper, which, with reason, are eagerly sought by those who, like the author of "The Wealth of Nations," are dandies in their libraries. — W.]

1 [The author errs here, whether he uses the word "biblical" with reference to books in general, or to men who are profes-

the Waltonian library of the Reverend Dr. Bethune. In the sunshine he is a practical angler, and —

"During the darker seasons of the year, when forbidden the actual use of his rod, our friend has occupied himself with excursions through sale catalogues, fishing out from their dingy pages whatever tends to honor his favorite author or favorite art, so that his spoils now number nearly five hundred volumes, of all sizes and dates. Pains have been taken to have not only copies of the works included in the list, but also the several editions; and when it is of a work mentioned by Walton, an edition which the good old man himself may have seen. Thus the collection has all the editions of Walton, Cotton, and Venables in existence, and, with few exceptions, all the works referred to by Walton, or which tend to illustrate his favorite rambles by the Lea or the Dove. Every scrap of Walton's writing, and every compliment paid to him, have been carefully gathered and garnered up, with prints and autographs and some precious manuscripts. Nor

sional expounders of The Book, or quibbles between the two. The Waltonians have been a long-recognized sept of the race of book-hunters; and the vigor and pertinacity with which they pursue their game put Piscator, Auceps, and Nimrod himself to shame, as any one must know who has entered the lists with them. As to Reverend fishermen, the author must have forgotten Dr. Paley, not to speak of Peter, and the sons of the father of Zebedee's children, the puzzle as to whose immediate paternal ancestor has so often shown that it is not only a wise child that knows his own father. Apostles and saints though these were, they could hardly have had purer minds or kinder hearts than he who is the occasion of this note. — W.]

does the department end here, but embraces most of the older and many of the modern writers on ichthyology and angling."

The Prowler and the Auction-Haunter.

THESE incidental divisions are too numerous and complex for a proper classification of book-hunters, and I am inclined to go back to the idea that their most effective and comprehensive division is into the private prowler and the auction-haunter. The difference between these is something like, in the sporting world, that between the stalker and the hunter proper. Each function has its merits, and calls for its special qualities and sacrifices. The one demands placidity, patience, caution, plausibility, and unwearied industry — such attributes as those which have been already set forth in the words of the *Antiquary*. The auction-room, on the other hand, calls forth courage, promptness, and the spirit of adventure. There is wild work sometimes there, and men find themselves carried off by enthusiasm and competition towards pecuniary sacrifices which at the threshold of the auction-room they had solemnly vowed to themselves to eschew. But such sacrifices are the tribute paid to the absorbing interest of the pursuit, and are looked upon in their own peculiar circle as tending to the immortal honor of those who make them. This field of prowess has, it is said, undergone a prejudicial change in these days, the biddings being nearly all by dealers, while gentlemen-collectors are gradually moving out of the field. In old days one might have reaped for himself, by bold and emphatic biddings at a few auctions, a niche in that temple of fame, of which the presiding deity is Dr. Frognall Dibdin — a name familiarly abbreviated into that of Foggy Dibdin. His descriptions of auction-contests are perhaps the best and most readable portions of his tremendously overdone books.[1]

1 [Dibdin's books are not only excessively written, but they are brimful of apparently inbred, and hugely developed flunkyism and snobbishness, (unpleasant words, but without more acceptable equivalents,) and their language is defiled with cant not less offensive than that of the ring, the turf, or the conventicle, or any cant, indeed, for all of it is loathsome. Some book-hunters, when they get together to "talk book," seem to think it necessary to show their command of this nauseous vocabulary, which even before it became cant was but silly babble. Let men who really love books, and read them, eschew it. Dibdin's books are valuable for their information and their illustrations; although in the former respect they frequently lead astray. I have seen a letter from the late Thomas Rodd, bookseller, of London, who in bibliography could have put Dibdin to school, in which he speaks of Sir Walter Scott as the most inaccurate of writers, except Thomas Frognall Dibdin. The charge is exaggerated in both cases; but not so much so in the former as most readers are ready to believe. Scott, standing head and shoulders above all British writers of imaginative literature, (for he cannot properly be called an English author,) and next to Shakespeare among those who have used the English tongue, has yet written hardly a page in which there cannot be detected some error of fact or of language, generally trivial, of course, but sometimes important. — W.]

Conspicuous beyond all others stands forth the sale of the Roxburghe library, perhaps the most eminent contest of that kind on record. There were of it some ten thousand separate "lots," as auctioneers call them, and almost every one of them was a book of rank and mark in the eyes of the collecting community, and had been, with special pains and care and anxious exertion, drawn into the vortex of that collection. Although it was created by a Duke, yet it has been rumored that most of the books were bargains, and that the noble collector drew largely on the spirit of patient perseverance and enlightened sagacity for which Monkbarns claims credit. The great passion and pursuit of his life having been of so peculiar a character — he was almost as zealous a hunter of deer and wild swans, by the way, as of books, but this was not considered in the least peculiar — it was necessary to find some strange influencing motive for his conduct; so it has been said that it arose from his having been crossed in love in his early youth. Such crosses, in general, arise from the beloved one dying, or proving faithless and becoming the wife of another. It was, however, the peculiarity of the Duke's misfortune, that it arose out of the illustrious marriage of the sister of his elected. She was the eldest daughter of the Duke of Mecklenburg-Strelitz. Though purchased by a sacrifice of regal rank, yet there would be many countervailing advantages in the position of an affluent British Duchess, which might reconcile a young lady even of so illustrious a descent, to the sacrifice, had it not happened that Lord Bute and the Princess of Wales selected her younger sister to be the wife of George III. and the Queen of Great Britain, long known as the good Queen Charlotte. Then there arose, it seems, the necessity, as a matter of state and political etiquette, that the elder sister should abandon the alliance with a British subject.[1]

So, at all events, goes the story of the origin of the Duke's bibliomania; and it is supposed to have been in the thoughts of Sir Walter Scott, when he said of him that "youthful misfortunes, of a kind against which neither wealth nor rank possess a talisman, cast an early shade of gloom over his prospects, and gave to one splendidly endowed with the means of enjoying society that degree of reserved melancholy which prefers retirement to the splendid scenes of gaiety." Dibdin, with more

1 [Could there be a more telling illustration of the childish triviality as well as of the oppressive tyranny of the State and political etiquette which still maintains itself in the monarchies of Europe, — which in fact spreads and strengthens, as monarchy is passing into a feeble show, a dumb and grotesque image of what was once a living power! Is it not strange that an intelligent and independent people will suffer the continued existence of such a patent absurdity, — one which costs so much, beside. Kings, if you please, so that they are kings; but these kings of "shreds and patches," which, if they were not bolstered up and bombasted out with State and political etiquette, would fall flatlong into the rag-bag, — not having the wherewith to go headlong, — fit only to be thrust into the rubbish-room or sold to curiosity hunters and old clo' dealers! The German lad named Albert Edward who was here a year or two ago seemed an intelligent, well-mannered, well-meaning youth, — high praise for one

specific precision, after rambling over the house where the great auction-sale occurred, as inquisitive people are apt to do, tells us of the solitary room occupied by the Duke, close to his library, in which he slept and died: "all his migrations," says the bibliographer, "were *confined* to these two rooms. When Mr. Nichol showed me the very bed on which this bibliomaniacal Duke had expired, I felt — as I trust I ought to have felt on the occasion." Scott attributed to an incidental occurrence at his father's table the direction given to the great pursuit of his life. "Lord Oxford and Lord Sunderland, both famous collectors of the time, dined one day with the second Duke of Roxburghe, when their conversation happened to turn upon the *editio princeps* of Boccaccio, printed in Venice in 1474, and so rare that its very existence was doubted of." It so happened that the Duke remembered this vol-

of his family, on the mother's side, — is it not, Mr. Thackeray? As a man, he won the respect of all with whom he came in contact; nay, he awoke a tender solicitude for one to whom the future might bring woes, surely would bring trials. But as a prince, his three ostrich-feathers are not a lighter vanity; as a king, his crown, with or without his or any other head in it, it makes no matter, will not be an emptier show. And to sacrifice to these things the heart's happiness, and the hard wrung sweat, the very life's blood of great peoples! A Czar is something, — nay, even an Emperor of the French, while he lasts, — but a king over English men, who have common sense, and who call themselves free, and are so, and who know most of them, and who all in a few months might be safely taught, what a costly sham such a creature is, being no more regal, in fact, than John Doe and Richard Roe, — such a fiction should have long since passed away, and would have done so but for the few who keep it up for their own aggrandizement. — W.]

ume having been offered to him for £100, and he believed he could still trace and secure it: he did so, and laid it before his admiring friends at a subsequent sitting. "His son, then Marquess of Beaumont, never forgot the little scene upon this occasion, and used to ascribe to it the strong passion which he ever afterwards felt for rare books and editions, and which rendered him one of the most assiduous and judicious collectors that ever formed a sumptuous library."[1] And this same Boccaccio was the point of attack which formed the climax in the great contest of the Roxburghe roup, as the Duke's fellow-countrymen called it.

The historian of the contest terms it "the Waterloo among book-battles," whereto "many a knight came far and wide from his retirement, and many an unfledged combatant left his father's castle to partake of the glory of such a contest." He also tells us that the honor of the first effective shot was due to a house in the trade — Messrs. Payne and Foss — by whom "the Aldine Greek Bible was killed off the first in the contest. It produced the sum of £4, 14s. 6d. Thus measuredly, and guardedly, and even fearfully, did this tremendous battle begin." The earliest brilliant affair seems to have come off when Lord Spencer bought two Caxtons for £245, a feat of which the closing scene is recorded, with a touching simplicity, in these terms:—"His Lordship put each volume under his

1 Article on Pitcairn's *Criminal Trials* in the 21st vol. of Miscellaneous Prose Works.

coat, and walked home with them in all the flush of victory and consciousness of triumph." As every one does not possess a copy of the three costly volumes of which the *Bibliographical Decameron* consists — and, further, as many a one so fortunate as to possess them has not had patience and perseverance enough to penetrate to the middle of the third volume, where the most readable part is to be found — a characteristic extract, describing the heat of the contest, may not be unwelcome: —

"For two-and-forty successive days — with the exception only of Sundays — were the voice and hammer of Mr. Evans heard with equal efficacy in the dining-room of the late Duke, which had been appropriated to the vendition of the books; and within that same space (some thirty-five feet by twenty) were such deeds of valor performed, and such feats of book-heroism achieved, as had never been previously beheld, and of which the like will probably never be seen again. The shouts of the victors and the groans of the vanquished stunned and appalled you as you entered. The striving and press, both of idle spectators and determined bidders, was unprecedented. A sprinkling of Caxtons and De Wordes marked the first day, and these were obtained at high, but, comparatively with the subsequent sums given, moderate prices. Theology, jurisprudence, philosophy, and philology chiefly marked the earlier days of this tremendous contest; and occasionally during these days there was much stirring up of courage, and many hard and heavy blows were interchanged; and the combatants may be said to have completely wallowed themselves in the conflict. At length came poetry, Latin, Italian, and French: a steady fight yet continued to be fought; victory seemed to hang in doubtful scales — sometimes on the one, sometimes on the other side of Mr. Evans, who preserved throughout (as it was his bounden duty to preserve) a uniform, impartial, and steady course; and who may be said on that occasion, if not 'to have rode the whirlwind,' at least to have 'directed the storm.'"

But the dignity and power of the historian's narrative cannot be fully appreciated until we find him in the midst of the climax of the contest — the battle, which gradually merged into a single combat, for the possession of the Venetian Boccaccio. According to the established historical practice, we have in the first place a statement of the position taken up by the respective "forces."

"At length the moment of sale arrived. Evans prefaced the putting-up of the article by an appropriate oration, in which he expatiated on its extreme rarity, and concluding by informing the company of the regret, and even anguish of heart, expressed by Mr. Van Praet that such a treasure was not to be found in the Imperial collection at Paris. Silence followed the address of Mr. Evans. On his right hand, leaning against the wall, stood Earl Spencer; a little lower down, and standing at right angles with his Lordship, appeared the Marquess of Blandford. Lord Althorp stood a little backward, to the right of his father, Earl Spencer."

The first movement of the forces gives the historian an opportunity of dropping a withering sneer at an unfortunate man, so provincial in his notions as to suppose that a hundred pounds or two would be of any avail in such a contest.

"The honor of firing the first shot was due to a gentleman of Shropshire, unused to this species of warfare, and who seemed to recoil from the reverberation of the report himself had made. 'One hundred guineas,' he exclaimed. Again a pause ensued; but anon the biddings rose rapidly to five hundred guineas. Hitherto, however, it was evident that the firing was but masked and desultory. At length all random shots ceased, and the champions before named stood gallantly up to each other, resolving not to flinch from a trial of their respective strengths. *A thousand guineas* were bid by Earl Spencer — to which the Marquess added *ten.* You might have heard a pin drop. All eyes were turned — all breathing wellnigh stopped — every sword was put home within its scabbard — and not a piece of steel was seen to move or to glitter except that which each of these champions brandished in his valorous hand."

But even this exciting sort of narrative will tire one when it goes on page after page, so that we must take a leap to the conclusion. "Two thousand two hundred and fifty pounds," said Lord Spencer. "The spectators were now absolutely electrified. The Marquess quietly adds his usual *ten*," and so there an end. "Mr. Evans, ere his hammer fell, made a short pause — and indeed, as if by something preternatural, the ebony instrument itself seemed to be charmed or suspended in the mid air. However, at last down dropped the hammer."

Such a result naturally created excitement beyond the book-collectors' circle, for here was an actual stroke of trade in which a profit of more than two thousand per cent. had been netted. It is easy to believe in Dibdin's statement of the crowds of people who imagined they were possessors of the identical Venetian Boccaccio, and the still larger number who wanted to do a stroke of business with some old volume, endowed with the same rarity and the same or greater intrinsic value. The general excitement created by the dispersal of the Roxburghe collection proved an epoch in literary history, by the establishment of the Roxburghe Club, followed by a series of others, the history of which has to be told farther on.

Of the great book-sales that have been commemorated, it is curious to observe how seldom they embrace ancestral libraries accumulated in old houses from generation to generation, and how generally they mark the shortlived duration of the accumulations of some collector freshly deposited. One remarkable exception to this was in the Gordonstoun library, sold in 1816. It was begun by Sir Robert Gordon, a Morayshire laird of the time of the great civil wars of the seventeenth century. He was the author of the History of the Earldom of Sutherland, and a man of great political as well as literary account. He laid by heaps of the pamphlets, placards, and other documents of his stormy period; and thus many a valuable morsel, which had otherwise disappeared from the world, left a representative in the Gordonstoun collection.[1] It was increased by a later Sir Robert, who had the reputation of being a wizard. He belonged to one of those terrible clubs from which Satan is entitled to take a victim annually; but when Gordon's turn came, he managed to get off with merely the loss of his shadow; and many a Morayshire peasant has testified to having seen him riding forth on a sunny day, the shadow of his horse visible, with those of his spurs and his whip, but his body offering no impediment to the rays of the sun. He enriched the library with books on necromancy, demonology, and alchemy.

The greatest book-sale probably that ever was in the world, was that of Heber's collection in 1834. There are often rash estimates made of the size of libraries, but those who have stated the number of his books in six figures, seem justified when one looks at the catalogue of the sale, bound up in five thick octavo volumes. For results so

[1] [It is perhaps worthy of remark that this library was barren of Shakespeare's works, although it was collected by a gentleman of wealth and of curious as well as literary tastes, at a time when the now almost priceless quartos might have been bought for a shilling. — W.]

magnificent, Richard Heber's library had but a small beginning, according to the memoir of him in the *Gentleman's Magazine*, where it is said, that "having one day accidentally met with a little volume, called *The Vallie of Varietie*, by Henry Peacham, he took it to the late Mr. Bindley of the Stamp-office, the celebrated collector, and asked him if this was not a curious book. Mr. Bindley, after looking at it, answered, 'Yes — not very — but rather a curious book.'" This faint morsel of encouragement was, it seems, sufficient to start him in his terrible career; and the trifle becomes important as a solemn illustration of the *obsta principiis*. His labors, and even his perils, were on a par with those of any veteran commander who has led armies and fought battles during the great part of a long life. He would set off on a journey of several hundred miles any day in search of a book not in his collection. Sucking in from all around him whatever books were afloat, he of course soon exhausted the ordinary market; and to find a book obtainable which he did not already possess, was an event to be looked to with the keenest anxiety, and a chance to be seized with promptitude, courage, and decision. At last, however, he could not supply the cravings of his appetite without recourse to duplicates, and far more than duplicates. His friend Dibdin said of him, "He has now and then an ungovernable passion to possess more copies of a book than there were ever parties to a deed or stamina to a plant; and therefore I cannot call him a duplicate or a triplicate collector." He satisfied his own conscience by adopting a creed, which he enounced thus: — "Why, you see, sir, no man can comfortably do without three copies of a book. One he must have for a show copy, and he will probably keep it at his country-house; another he will require for his own use and reference; and unless he is inclined to part with this, which is very inconvenient, or risk the injury of his best copy, he must needs have a third at the service of his friends."

This last necessity is the key-note to Heber's popularity: he was a liberal and kindly man, and though, like Wolsey, he was unsatisfied in getting, yet, like him, in bestowing he was most princely. Many scholars and authors obtained the raw material for their labors from his transcendent stores. These, indeed, might be said less to be personal to himself than to be a feature in the literary geography of Europe. "Some years ago," says the writer in the *Gentleman's Magazine*, "he built a new library at his house at Hodnet, which is said to be full. His residence at Pimlico, where he died, is filled, like Magliabechi's at Florence, with books, from the top to the bottom — every chair, every table, every passage, containing piles of erudition.[1]

[1] [This reminds me of a story which I heard the wife of a book-lover of incomparably humbler means and more modest pretensions than Heber tell, with rueful merriment. She had gone into the country to pass the summer months, leaving the man that owned her in town, to solace himself with his dearly beloved silent companions, interrupting his ruminations by occa-

He had another house in York Street, leading to Great James's Street, Westminster, laden from the ground-floor to the garret with curious books. He had a library in the High Street, Oxford, an immense library at Paris, another at Antwerp, another at Brussels, another at Ghent, and at other places in the Low Countries and in Germany."

sional flying visits to those of a noisier sort. When she went away, every shelf, not only of every case, but of every closet to which a man could lay claim, was loaded down with books, and every available trunk and box was stuffed to bursting with the same ponderous and dusty wealth. As autumn approached, she had occasion to go suddenly to town, and went without warning. Having reached home, she entered the library, expecting to find her husband. He was not there; and had he been there, he would have been obliged to stand or perch; for every table and every chair was heaped to groaning with books — new-comers. This was exciting; but it might have been expected; it was not unnatural. She went up to her own apartments. The same sight met her astonished eye. Her very dressing-bureau, which she had opportunely emptied before her departure, was filled to the last inch of the last drawer; nay, even her wash-stand itself, top and bottom, was stuffed with musty lore, the outside of which seemed much in need of the soap and water which it had displaced. And last aggravation of all, there was the gude-man himself stretched at full length upon the nuptial couch, in breezy undress, hard at work with pencil and paper, and surrounded with a barricade of books, over which she peered to see it doubly strong along the place where her lovely limbs had lain. She declared war upon the spot. But, as in the case of all wives like her, there was a cherished traitor in her own camp; and she was utterly defeated. — W.]

PART II.—HIS FUNCTIONS.

The Hobby.

AVING devoted the preceding pages to the diagnosis of the book-hunter's condition, or, in other words, to the different shapes which the phenomena peculiar to it assume, I now propose to offer some account of his place in the dispensations of Providence, which will probably show that he is not altogether a mischievous or a merely useless member of the human family, but does in reality, however unconsciously to himself, minister in his own peculiar way to the service both of himself and others. This is to be a methodical discourse, and therefore to be divided and subdivided, insomuch that, taking in the first place his services to himself, this branch shall be subdivided into the advantages which are purely material and those which are properly intellectual.

And, first, of material advantages. Holding it to be the inevitable doom of fallen man to inherit some frailty or failing, it would be difficult, had he a Pandora's box-full to pick and choose among, to find one less dangerous or offensive. As the judicious physician informs the patient, suffering under some cutaneous or other external torture, that the poison lay deep in his constitution — that it must have worked in some shape — and well it is that it has taken one so innocuous — so may even the book-hunter be congratulated on having taken the innate moral malady of all the race in a very gentle and rather a salubrious form. To pass over gambling, tippling, and other practices which cannot be easily spoken of in good society, let us look to the other shapes in which man lets himself out — for instance to horse-racing, hunting, photography, shooting, fishing, cigars, dog-fancying, dog-fighting, the ring, the cockpit, phrenology, revivalism, socialism; which of these contains so small a balance of evil? counting of course that the amount of pleasure conferred is equal — for it is only on the datum that the book-hunter has as much satisfaction from his pursuit as the fox-hunter, the photographer, and so on, has in his that a fair comparison can be struck. These pursuits, one and all, leave little or nothing that is valuable behind them, except, it may be, that some of them are conducive to health, by giving exercise to the body and a genial excitement to the mind; but every hobby gives the latter, and the former may be easily obtained in some other shape. They leave little or nothing behind: even the photographer's portfolio will bring scarcely anything under the hammer after the death of him whose solace and pursuit it had been, should the positives remain visible, which may be doubted. And as to the other enumerated pursuits, some of them, as we all know, are immensely costly, all unproductive as they are.

But the book-hunter may possibly leave a little fortune behind him. His hobby, in fact, merges into an investment. This is the light in which a celebrated Quaker collector of paintings put his conduct, when it was questioned by the brethren, in virtue of that right to admonish one another concerning the errors of their ways, which makes them so chary in employing domestic servants of their own persuasion. "What had the brother paid for that bauble (a picture by Wouvermans), for instance?" "Well, £300." "Was not that, then, an awful wasting of his substance on vanities?" "No. He had been offered £900 for it. If any of the Friends was prepared to offer him a better investment of his money than one that could be realized at a profit of 200 per cent., he was ready to alter the existing disposal of his capital."

It is true that amateur purchasers do not, in the long run, make a profit, though an occasional bargain may pass through their hands. It is not maintained that, in the general case, the libraries of collectors would be sold for more than they cost, or even for nearly so much; but they are always worth something, which is more than can be said of the residue of other hobbies and pursuits. Nay, farther; the scholarly collector of books is not like the ordinary helpless amateur; for although, doubtless, nothing will rival the dealer's instinct for knowing the money-value of an article, though he may know nothing else about it, yet there is often a subtle depth in the collector's educated knowledge which the other cannot match, and bargains may be obtained off the counters of the most acute.

A small sprinkling of these — even the chance of them — excites him, like the angler's bites and rises, and gives its zest to his pursuit. It is the reward of his patience, his exertion, and his skill, after the manner in which Monkbarns has so well spoken; and it is certain that, in many instances, a collector's library has sold for more than it cost him.

No doubt, a man may ruin himself by purchasing costly books, as by indulgence in any other costly luxury, but the chances of calamity are comparatively small in this pursuit. A thousand pounds will go a great way in book-collecting, if the collector be true to the traditions of his pursuit, such as they are to be hereafter expounded. There has been one instance, doubtless, in the records of bibliomania, of two thousand pounds having been given for one book. But how many instances far more flagrant could be found in picture-buying? Look around upon the world and see how many men are the victims of libraries, and compare them with those whom the stud, the kennel, and the preserve have brought to the *Gazette*. Find out, too, anywhere, if you can, the instances in which the money scattered in these forms comes back again, and brings with it a large profit, as the expenditure of the Duke of Roxburghe did when his library was sold.[1]

But it is necessary to arrest this train of argument, lest its tenor might be misunderstood. The mercenary spirit must not be admitted to a share in the enjoyments of the book-hunter. If, after he has taken his last survey of his treasures, and spent his last hour in that quiet library, where he has ever found his chief solace against the wear and worry of the world, the book-hunter shall be taken

1 [True, the discreet expenditure of money in books is, under ordinary circumstances, and if the books be well cared for, a safe, and sometimes a profitable, investment. But let not any man be therefore tempted into spending money thus which he cannot well afford to do without and let lie idle. A library pays no interest; and more volumes than an ordinary bookcaseful, or two, are an occasion of great trouble and of some expense. And above all, let no man gather together more books than all of us who are tolerably well-to-do have in this country, unless he has good reason to believe himself settled in a home for life. The moving and reshelving of anything like a library — that is, of more than a thousand or twelve hundred volumes — is inexpressibly troublesome and vexatious; and besides, let it be done with as much care as possible, the books are almost sure to receive some injury. A well-chosen library, even a small one, of two or three thousand volumes, is a rich possession, full of pure enjoyment to a man worthy of it; but unless he is beyond the consideration of hours and dollars, and even then, it brings with it corresponding trouble, with this sad consequence, that, for that very trouble, he will love it and cling to it the more. No: the professional man of letters, or the man of elegant leisure and literary tastes, with money to spare, may justifiably collect books, to a moderate degree; but let all others, after gathering enough books to live upon, if they must collect something, collect money, which will always command money's worth. — W.]

to his final place of rest, and it is then discovered that the circumstances of the family require his treasures to be dispersed,—should the unexpected result be that his pursuit has not been so ruinously costly after all—nay, that his expenditure has actually fructified—it is well. But if the book-hunter allow money-making—even for those he is to leave behind—to be combined with his pursuit, it loses its fresh relish, its exhilarating influence, and becomes the source of wretched cares and paltry anxieties. Where money is the object, let a man speculate or become a miser—a very enviable condition to him who has the saving grace to achieve it, if we hold with Byron that the accumulation of money is the only passion that never cloys.

Let not the collector, therefore, ever, unless in some urgent and necessary circumstances, part with any of his treasures. Let him not even have recourse to that practice called barter, which political philosophers tell us is the universal resource of mankind preparatory to the invention of money as a circulating medium and means of exchange. Let him confine all his transactions in the market to purchasing only. No good ever comes of gentlemen amateurs buying and selling. They will either be systematic losers, or they will acquire shabby, questionable habits, from which the professional dealers—on whom, perhaps, they look down—are exempt. There are two trades renowned for the quackery and the imposition with which they are habitually stained — the trade in horses and the trade in old pictures; and these have, I verily believe, earned their evil reputation chiefly from this, that they are trades in which gentlemen of independent fortune and considerable position are in the habit of embarking.

The result is not so unaccountable as it might seem. The professional dealer, however smart he may be, takes a sounder estimate of any individual transaction than the amateur. It is his object, not so much to do any single stroke of trade very successfully, as to deal acceptably with the public, and make his money in the long run. Hence he does not place an undue estimate on the special article he is to dispose of, but will let it go at a loss, if that is likely to prove the most beneficial course for his trade at large. He has no special attachment to any of the articles in which he deals, and no blindly exaggerated appreciation of their merits and value. They come and go in an equable stream, and the cargo of yesterday is sent abroad to the world with the same methodical indifference with which that of to-day is unshipped. It is otherwise with the amateur. He feels towards the article he is to part with all the prejudiced attachment, and all the consequent over-estimate, of a possessor. Hence he and the market take incompatible views as to value, and he is apt to become unscrupulous in his efforts to do justice to himself. Let the single-minded and zealous collector, then, turn the natural propensity to over-estimate one's own into its proper and legitimate channel. Let him guard his treasures as things too sacred for commerce, and say, *Procul, o procul este, profani*, to all who may attempt by bribery and corruption to drag them from their legitimate shelves. If, in any weak moment, he yield to mercenary temptation, he will be forever mourning after the departed unit of his treasure — the lost sheep of his flock. If it seems to be in the decrees of fate that all his gatherings are to be dispersed abroad after he has gone to his rest, let him, at all events, retain the reliance that on them, as on other things beloved, he may have his last look: there will be many changes after that, and this will be among them. Nor, in his final reflections on his conduct to himself and to those he is to leave, will he be disturbed by the thought that the hobby which was his enjoyment, has been in any wise the more costly to him that he has not made it a means of mercenary money-getting.[1]

[1] Atticus was under the scandal of having disposed of his books, and Cicero sometimes hints to him that he might let more of them go his way. In truth, Atticus carried this so far, however, that he seems to have been a sort of dealer, and the earliest instance of a capitalist publisher. He had slaves whom he occupied in copying, and was in fact much in the position of a rich Virginian or Carolinian, who should find that the most profitable investment for his stock of slaves is a printing and publishing establishment.

The Desultory Reader, or Bohemian of Literature.

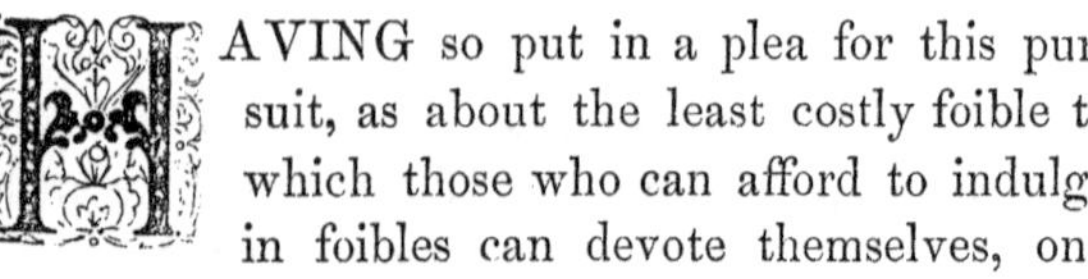

HAVING so put in a plea for this pursuit, as about the least costly foible to which those who can afford to indulge in foibles can devote themselves, one might descant on certain auxiliary advantages — as, that it is not apt to bring its votaries into low company; that it offends no one, and it is not likely to foster actions of damages for nuisance, trespass, or assault, and the like. But rather let us turn our attention to the intellectual advantages accompanying the pursuit, since the proper function of books is in the general case associated with intellectual culture and occupation. It would seem that, according to a received prejudice or opinion, there is one exception to this general connection, in the case of the possessors of libraries, who are under a vehement suspicion of not reading their books. Well, perhaps it is true in the sense in which those who utter the taunt understand the reading of a book. That one should possess no books beyond his power of perusal — that he should buy no faster than as he can read straight through what he has already bought — is a supposition alike preposterous and unreasonable. "Surely you have far more books than you can read," is sometimes the inane remark of the barbarian who gets his books, volume by volume, from some circulating library or reading club, and reads them all through, one after the other, with a dreary dutifulness, that he may be sure he has got the value of his money.

It is true that there are some books — as Homer, Virgil, Horace, Milton, Shakespeare, and Scott — which every man should read who has the opportunity — should read, mark, learn, and inwardly digest. To neglect the opportunity of becoming familiar with them is deliberately to sacrifice the position in the social scale which an ordinary education enables its possessor to reach. But is one next to read through the sixty and odd folio volumes of the Bolandist Lives of the Saints, and the new edition of the Byzantine historians, and the State Trials, and the Encyclopædia Britannica, and Moreri, and the Statutes at Large, and the Gentleman's Magazine from the beginning, each separately, and in succession? Such a course of reading would certainly do a good deal towards weakening the mind, if it did not create absolute insanity.

But in all these just named, even in the Statutes at Large, and in thousands upon thousands of other books, there is precious honey to be gathered by the literary busy bee, who passes on from flower to flower. In fact, "a course of reading," as it is sometimes called, is a course of regimen for dwarfing the mind, like the drugs which dog-breeders give to King-Charles spaniels to keep them small. Within the span of life allotted to man there is but a certain number of books that it is practicable to read through; and it is not possible to make a selection that will not, in a manner, wall in the mind from a free expansion over the republic of letters. The being chained, as it were, to one intellect in the perusal straight on of any large book, is a sort of mental slavery superinducing imbecility.[1] Even Gibbon's Decline and Fall, luminous and comprehensive as its philosophy is, and rapid and brilliant

[1] [Criticism of the style of this charming book is no part of the purpose of these notes; but I am sure that an author who writes English with so much clearness and idiomatic force, should he see this edition, will take in good part a kindly plea against the use of such a useless, overgrown pretender in our language as "superinduce." It is lamentably common, I must admit, and is becoming daily more so. But therefore all the more should we withstand it. Superinduce! why not, bring on? Is there a shade of meaning in the four syllables that there is not in the two? And yet I once heard a worthy woman who wished to be elegant, say of her husband, that he was "sufferin' very bad with bronchriches which were superinduced by excessive exposure." The truth and the English of which was that the good man had a cough brought on by getting very wet and cold. How many good and really sensible people have I heard painfully twisting simple English tongues round these slippery, many-syllabled strangers, when good home words, which they were born to speak, would have done their work much better. Nay, have we not lately seen the "Tribune" itself backsliding upon this point of sound doctrine? There we expected, and always used to find, real English; a little rough and strong sometimes, like the flavor of a wild grape, but for all that none the less welcome. But even a day or two ago was there not an article, signed, alas! "H. G.," in which it was said that the insurgent slaveholders when they determined to destroy the Republic "at once inaugurated the robbery of forts, arsenals, armories, custom-houses, and mints," and that "they had consummated at

the narrative, will become deleterious mental food if consumed straight through without variety. It will be well to relieve it occasionally with a little Boston's Fourfold State, or Hervey's Meditations, or Sturm's Reflections for Every Day in the Year, or Don Juan, or Ward's History of Stoke-upon-Trent.[1]

Isaac D'Israeli says, "Mr. Maurice, in his animated memoirs, has recently acquainted us with a

least a hundred of these gigantic thefts"! How are the mighty fallen! Why not, began the robbery, and committed the theft? Let consummate and inaugurate, except as specific terms, go with superinduce and ovation, and all their kin, into the company in which fire is called the devouring element, a drunkard, an inebriate, and a nation, a nationality. — W.]

[1] [Add to these General Butler's orders and official correspondence at New Orleans, which, for hitting the nail square upon the head, and clinching it with a twist of humor, have not been surpassed by any writing of their kind. By reading them, the man weary with the weight of the grand style or fretted with the flippancy of the familiar may obtain real mental refreshment. At the same time he cannot but admire the sagacity which contrived the measures which they announced, and the true benevolence of their purpose. Rarely has a man been placed in such trying circumstances as those in which General Butler found himself placed by the capture of New Orleans. Still more rarely has a man so placed administered affairs so wisely: — so wisely and so firmly that in that city, the most disorderly and dangerous place in the country in ordinary times, there has been such quiet and order since he settled himself well in power, (as I have been told by foreigners who came from there,) that a woman might walk at night from one end of the town to another, with a treasure in her keeping, without fear of molestation; — and this with the place in possession of a conquering army! To be sure, General Butler knew his men; and so they share his honor. — W.]

fact which may be deemed important in the life of a literary man. He tells us, 'We have been just informed that Sir William Jones *invariably* read through every year the works of Cicero.'" What a task! one would be curious to know whether he felt it less heavy in the twelve duodecimos of Elzevir, or the nine quartos of the Geneva edition. Did he take to it doggedly, as Dr. Johnson says, and read straight through according to the editor's arrangement, or did he pick out the plums and take the dismal work afterwards? For the first year or two of his task, he is not to be pitied perhaps about the Offices, or the dialogue on Friendship, or Scipio's Dream, or even the capital speeches against Verres and Catiline; but those tiresome letters, and the Tusculan Questions, and the De Natura![1] It is a pity he did not live till Angelo Mai found the De Republica. What disappointed every one else might perhaps have commanded the admiration of the great orientalist.

But here follows, on the same authority, a more wonderful performance still. "The famous Bourda-

[1] [I venture to put in a plea for the exemption of the Tusculan Questions from this censure. They are not high and mighty, or soaring, or profound, or even dramatic, like the Platonic dialogues, from the prolixity and occasional childish simplicity of which, however, they are free. But they treat of great topics with such simplicity and clearness, and in such a spirit of candid inquiry, and do this in such elegant Latin, that it seems to me that a man might read them occasionally with great pleasure. Such at least is the impression left upon my memory by a book which I have not seen since my first college year. — W.]

loue reperused every year St. Paul, St. Chrysostom, and Cicero."[1] The sacred author makes but a slight addition to the bulk, but the works of St. Chrysostom are entombed in eleven folios! Bourdaloue died at the age of seventy-two; and if he began his task at the age of twenty-two, he must have done it over fifty times. It requires nerves of more than ordinary strength to contemplate such a statement with equanimity. The tortures of the classic Hades, and the disgusting inflictions courted by the anchorites of old and the Brahmins of later times, do not approach the horrors of such an act of self-torture.

Of course any one ambitious of enlightening the world on either the political or the literary history of Rome at the commencement of the empire, must be as thoroughly acquainted with every word of Cicero as the writer of the Times leader on a critical debate is with the newly delivered speeches. The more fortunate vagabond reader, too, lounging about among the Letters, will open many little veins of curious contemporary history and biography, which he can follow up in Tacitus, Sallust, Cæsar, and the contemporary poets. Both are utterly different from the stated-task reader, who has come under a vow to work so many hours or get through so many pages in a given time. *They* are drawn by their occupation, whether work or play; *he* drives himself to his. All such work is inflic-

[1] Curiosities of Literature, iii. 339.

tion, varying from the highest point of martyrdom down to tasteless drudgery; and it is as profitless as other supererogatory inflictions, since the task-reader comes to look at his words without following out what they suggest, or even absorbing their grammatical sense, much as the stupid ascetics of old went through their penitential readings, or as their representatives of the present day, chiefly of the female sex, read "screeds of good books," which they have not "the presumption" to understand. The literary Bohemian is sometimes to be pitied when his facility of character exposes him to have a modification of this infliction forced upon him. This will occur when he happens to be living in a house frequented by "a good reader," who solemnly devotes certain hours to the perusal of passages from the English or French classics for the benefit of the company, and makes himself the mortal enemy of every guest who absents himself.[1]

As to collectors, it is quite true that they do not in general read their books successively straight through, and the practice of desultory reading, as it is sometimes termed, must be treated as part of their case, and if a failing, one cognate with their habit of collecting. They are notoriously addicted to the practice of standing arrested on some round of a ladder, where, having mounted up for some certain book, they have by wayward chance fallen

[1] [And often gains a mortal though secret enemy in every guest who comes and stays. — W.]

upon another, in which, at the first opening, has come up a passage which fascinates the finder as the eye of the Ancient Mariner fascinated the wedding-guest, and compels him to stand there poised on his uneasy perch and read. Peradventure the matter so perused suggests another passage in some other volume which it will be satisfactory and interesting to find, and so another and another search is made, while the hours pass by unnoticed, and the day seems all too short for the pursuit which is a luxury and an enjoyment, at the same time that it fills the mind with varied knowledge and wisdom.

The fact is that the book-hunter, if he be genuine, and have his heart in his pursuit, is also a reader and a scholar. Though he may be more or less peculiar, and even eccentric in his style of reading, there is a necessary intellectual thread of connection running through the objects of his search which predicates some acquaintance with the contents of the accumulating volumes. Even although he profess a devotion to mere external features — the style of binding, the cut or uncut leaves, the presence or the absence of the gilding — yet the department in literature holds more or less connection with this outward sign. He who has a passion for old editions of the classics in vellum bindings — Stephenses or Aldines — will not be put off with a copy of Robinson Crusoe or the Ready Reckoner, bound to match and range with the contents of his shelves. Those who so vehemently affect some external peculiarity are the eccentric exceptions ; yet even they have some consideration for the contents of a book as well as for its coat.

The Collector and the Scholar.

HE possession, or in some other shape the access to a far larger collection of books than can be read through in a lifetime, is in fact an absolute condition of intellectual culture and expansion. The library is the great intellectual stratification in which the literary investigator works — examining its external features, or perhaps driving a shaft through its various layers — passing over this stratum as not immediate to his purpose, examining that other with the minute attention of microscopic investigation. The geologist, the botanist, and the zoölogist, are not content to receive one specimen after another into their homes, to be thoroughly and separately examined, each in succession, as novel-readers go through the volumes of a circulating library at twopence a night — they have all the world of nature before them, and examine as their scientific instincts or their fancies suggest. For all inquirers, like pointers, have a sort of instinct, sharpened by training and practice, the power and acuteness of which astonish the unlearned. "Reading with the fingers," as Basnage said of Bayle — turning the pages rapidly over and alighting on the exact spot where the thing wanted is to be found — is far from a superficial faculty, as some deem it to be, — it is the thoroughest test of active scholarship. It was what enabled Bayle to collect so many flowers of literature, all so interesting, and yet all found in corners so distant and obscure. In fact, there are subtle dexterities, acquired by sagacious experience in searching for valuable little trinkets in great libraries, just as in other pursuits. A great deal of that appearance of dry drudgery which excites the pitying amazement of the by-stander is nimbly evaded. People acquire a sort of instinct, picking the valuables out of the useless verbiage or the passages repeated from former authors. It is soon found what a great deal of literature has been the mere "pouring out of one bottle into another," as the Anatomist of Melancholy terms it. There are those terrible folios of the scholastic divines, the civilians, and the canonists, their majestic stream of central print overflowing into rivulets of marginal notes sedgy with citations. Compared with these, all the intellectual efforts of our recent degenerate days seem the work of pigmies; and for any of us even to profess to read all that some of those indomitable giants wrote, would seem an audacious undertaking. But, in fact, they were to a great extent solemn shams, since the bulk of their work was merely that of the clerk who copies page after page from other people's writings.

Surely these laborious old writers exhibited in this matter the perfection of literary modesty. Far from secretly pilfering, like the modern plagiarist, it was their great boast that they themselves had not suggested the great thought or struck out the brilliant metaphor, but that it had been done by some one of old, and was found in its legitimate place — a book. I believe that if one of these laborious persons hatched a good idea of his own, he could experience no peace of mind until he found it legitimated by having passed through an earlier brain; and that the author who failed thus to establish a paternity for his thought would sometimes audaciously set down some great name in his crowded margin, in the hope that the imposition might pass undiscovered. Authorities, of course, enjoy priority according to their rank in literature. First come Aristotle and Plato, with the other great classical ancients; next the primitive fathers; then Abailard, Erigena, Peter Lombard, Ramus, Major, and the like. If the matter be jurisprudence, we shall have Marcianus, Papinianus, Ulpianus, Hermogenianus, and Tryphonius to begin with; and shall then pass through the straits of Bartolus and Baldus, on to Zuichemus, Sanchez, Brissonius, Ritterhusius, and Gothofridus. If all these say the same thing, each of the others copying it from the first who uttered it, so much the more valuable to the literary world is deemed the idea that has been so amply backed — it is like a vote by a great majority, or a strongly signed petition. There is only one quarter in which this practice appears to be followed at the present day — the composition, or the compilation, as it may better be termed, of English law-books. Having selected a department to be expounded, the first point is to set down all that Coke said about it two centuries and a half ago, and all that Blackstone said about it a century ago, with passages in due subordination from inferior authorities. To these are added the rubrics of some later cases, and a title-page and index, and so a new "authority" is added to the array on the shelves of the practitioner.

Whoever is well up to such repetitions has many short cuts through literature to enable him to find the scattered originalities of which he may be in search. Whether he be the enthusiastic investigator resolved on exhausting any great question, or be a mere wayward potterer, picking up curiosities by the way for his own private intellectual museum, the larger the collection at his disposal the better — it cannot be too great.[1] No one,

[1] I am quite aware that the authorities to the contrary are so high as to make these sentiments partake of heresy, if not a sort of classical profanity.

"Studiorum quoque, quæ liberalissima impensa est, tamdiu rationem habet, quamdiu modum. Quo innumerabiles libros et bibliothecas, quarum dominus vix tota vita indices perlegit? Onerat discentem turba, non instruit: multoque satius est paucis te auctoribus tradere, quam errare per multos. Quadraginta milia librorum Alexandriæ arserunt: pulcherrimum regiæ opu-

therefore, can be an ardent follower of such a pursuit without having his own library. And yet it is probably among those whose stock is the largest that we shall find the most frequent visitors to the British Museum and the State Paper Office; perhaps, for what cannot be found even there, to the Imperial Library at Paris, or the collections of some of the German universities.

lentiæ monumentum alius laudaverit, sicut et Livius, qui elegantiæ regum curæque egregium id opus ait fuisse. Non fuit elegantia illud aut cura, sed studiosa luxuria. Immo ne studiosa quidem: quoniam non in studium, sed in spectaculum comparaverant: sicut plerisque, ignaris etiam servilium literarum libri non studiorum instrumenta, sed cœnationum ornamenta sunt. Paretur itaque librorum quantum satis sit, nihil in apparatum. Honestius, inquis, hoc te impensæ, quam in Corinthia pictasque tabulas effuderint. Vitiosum est ubique, quod nimium est. Quid habes, cur ignoscas homini armaria citro atque ebore captanti, corpora conquirenti aut ignotorum auctorum aut improbatorum, et inter tot milia librorum oscitanti, cui voluminum suorum frontes maxime placent titulique? Apud desidiosissimos ergo videbis quicquid orationum historiarumque est, tecto tenus exstructa loculamenta; jam enim inter balnearia et thermas bibliotheca quoque ut necessarium domus ornamentum expolitur. Ignoscerem plane, si studiorum nimia cupidine oriretur: nunc ista conquisita, cum imaginibus suis descripta et sacrorum opera ingeniorum in speciem et cultum parietum comparantur." — *Seneca*, De Tranquillitate, c. ix.

There are some good hits here, which would tell at the present day. Seneca is reported to have had a large library; it is certain that he possessed and fully enjoyed enormous wealth; and it is amusing to find this commendation of literary moderation following on a well-known passage in praise of parsimonious living, and of the good example set by Diogenes. Modern scepticism about the practical stoicism of the ancients is surely brought to a climax by a living writer, M. Fournier, who maintains that the so-called tub of Diogenes was in reality a commo-

To every man of our Saxon race endowed with full health and strength, there is committed, as if it were the price he pays for these blessings, the custody of a restless demon, for which he is doomed to find ceaseless excitement, either in honest work, or some less profitable or more mischievous occupation.[1] Countless have been the projects devised by the wit of man to open up for this fiend fields of exertion

dious little dwelling — neat but not gorgeous. It must be supposed, then, that he spoke of his tub much as an English country gentleman does of his "box."

1 [The writer here falls into an error which all the more demands correction because it is so common. Our race is constantly spoken of, on this side of the water no less than on the other, as the Anglo-Saxon race. If there ever was a race entitled to that ambiguous name, it had disappeared before the Conquest. The people whom William conquered were Englishmen; and they were called Englishmen and their country was called England because it was the land of the English, as France was called France because it was the land of the Franks. The conduct of many of our brethren in the old home has caused most of us here to shrink from the name of English men, even those who glory that they were born and bred in New *England;* and our pride of race takes refuge in our so-called Anglo-Saxonism. The name American, so generally given to us, and so generally accepted, is most poor and unmeaning. It applies equally, and with much more propriety, to the Esquimaux and the Patagonians. It is as if the Italians or the Swedes were to be called simply Europeans. The people of this country are to all intents and purposes as surely English people as they were when in the century 1600 they were called "American Englishmen," or when in the next century our grandfathers and great-grandfathers commenced the movement which ended in our separate political existence by claiming, in specific terms, from the British Government their "rights as Englishmen." The mixture of foreign elements has been proportionally little greater here than in England. Here it has been Irish and German, there Irish

great enough for the absorption of its tireless energies; and none of them is more hopeful than the great world of books, if the demon is docile enough

and Scotch. In both cases, however, there is an immediate absorption. In the second generation, the Irishman, the Scotchman, and the German disappears, and in his place is an Englishman.

The "restless demon" of work came over the sea with the race; and that he is more active here than in his original abode (as all the world says) is because he is free here from the artificial restraints which there clog his movements and thwart his purposes. It is this hereditary disposition of every man to work, and the ability of every man to work here as he wishes to work, that has enabled us to bear and to thrive under the enormous burdens of the present war, which, though grown threefold greater than they were expected to be when the political economists of Europe, and particularly of Great Britain, predicted our reduction to beggary and consequent anarchy, have not been able to seriously impede our prosperity, or even our expenditure for foreign productions. Wise politicians and able editors abroad, when they make calculations in regard to us, must take into account our good demon, and leave out the spell from which he freed himself when he crossed the water.

— Singularly opportune, just as I am about to send this note to press, the "Saturday Review" of October 4th arrives, in the third article of which there is this characteristic sentence: — "The Americans in the noonday light of history have invented for themselves an imaginary pedigree under the blundering nickname of the great Anglo-Saxon race." This is about as near truth or courtesy as the "Saturday Review" can get when speaking of anything or any person in this country, except a slaveholding rebel against an unviolated constitutional government. But, as we have seen, the "blundering nickname" was not invented here, or specially for us, but in England, and for all English people, whether subjects of Great Britain or citizens of the United States. For the latter, however, the "Saturday Review" would prefer Mr. Roebuck's courteous and decorous designation. — W.]

to be coaxed into it. Then will its erratic restlessness be sobered by the immensity of the sphere of exertion, and the consciousness that, however vehemently and however long it may struggle, the resources set before it will not be exhausted when the life to which it is attached shall have faded away; and hence, instead of dreading the languor of inaction, it will have to summon all its resources of promptness and activity to get over any considerable portion of the ground within the short space allotted to the life of man.

That the night cometh when no man can work, haunts those who have gone so far in their investigations, and draws their entire energies into their pursuit with an exclusiveness which astonishes the rest of the world. But the energies might be more unfitly directed. Look back, for instance — no great distance back — on the great high-priest of our national school of logic and metaphysics, — he who gathered up its divers rays, and, helping them with light from all other sources of human knowledge, concentrated the whole into one powerful focus. No one could look at the massive brow, the large, full, lustrous eyes, the firm compressed lip, without seeing that the demon of energy was powerful within him, and had it not found work in the conquest of all human learning, must have sought it elsewhere. You see in him the nature that must follow up all inquiries, not by languid solicitation but hot pursuit. His conquests as he goes are rapid, but complete. Summing up the thousands upon thousands of volumes, upon all matters of human study and in many languages, which he has passed through his hands, you think he has merely dipped into them or skimmed them, or in some other shape put them to superficial use. You are wrong: he has found his way at once to the very heart of the living matter of each one; between it and him there are henceforth no secrets.[1]

Descending, however, from so high a sphere, we

[1] How a nature endowed with powerful impulses like these might be led along with them into a totally different groove, I am reminded by a traditionary anecdote of student life. A couple of college chums are under the impression that their motions are watched by an inquisitive tutor, who for the occasion may be called Dr. Fusby. They become both exceeding wroth, and the more daring of the two engages on the first opportunity to "settle the fellow." They are occupied in ardent colloquy, whether on the predicates or other matters it imports not, when a sudden pause in the conversation enables them to be aware that there is a human being breathing close on the other side of the "oak." The light is extinguished, the door opened, and a terrific blow from a strong and scientifically levelled fist hurls the listener down-stairs to the next landing-place, from which resting-place he hears thundered after him for his information, "If you come back again, you scoundrel, I'll put you into the hands of Dr. Fusby." From that source, however, no one had much to dread for some considerable period, during which the Doctor was confined to his bedroom by serious indisposition. It refreshed the recollection of this anecdote, years after I had heard it, and many years after the date attributed to it, to have seen a dignified scholar make what appeared to me an infinitesimally narrow escape from sharing the fate of Dr. Fusby, having indeed just escaped it by satisfactorily proving to a hasty philosopher that he was not the party guilty of keeping a certain copy of Occam on the sentences of Peter Lombard out of his reach.

shall find that the collector and the scholar are so closely connected with each other that it is difficult to draw the line of separation between them. As dynamic philosophers say, they act and react on each other. The possession of certain books has made men acquainted with certain pieces of knowledge which they would not otherwise have acquired. It is, in fact, one of the amiable weaknesses of the set, to take a luxurious glance at a new acquisition. It is an outcropping of what remains in the man, of the affection towards a new toy that flourished in the heart of the boy. Whether the right reverend or right honourable Thomas has ever taken his new-bought Baskerville to bed with him, as the Tommy that was has taken his humming-top, is a sort of case which has not actually come under observation in the course of my own clinical inquiries into the malady; but I am not prepared to state that it never occurred, and can attest many instances where the recent purchase has kept the owner from bed far on in the night. In this incidental manner is a general notion sometimes formed of the true object and tenor of a book, which is retained in the mind, stored for use, and capable of being refreshed and strengthened whenever it is wanted. In the skirmish for the Caxtons, which began the serious work in the great conflict of the Roxburghe sale, it was satisfactory to find, as I have already stated, on the authority of the great historian of the war, that Earl Spencer, the victor, "put each volume under his coat, and walked home with them in all the flush of victory and consciousness of triumph." [1] Ere next morning he would know a good deal more about the contents of the volumes than he did before.

The Gleaner and his Harvest.

HERE are sometimes agreeable and sometimes disappointing surprises in encountering the interiors of books. The title-page is not always a distinct intimation of what is to follow. Whoever dips into the Novellæ of Leo, or the Extravagantes, as edited by Gothofridus, will not find either of them to contain matter of a light, airy, and amusing kind. Dire have been the disappointments incurred by the Diversions of Purley — one of the toughest books in existence. It has even cast a shade over one of our best story-books, The Diversions of Hollycot, by the late Mrs. Johnston. The great scholar, Leo Allatius, who broke his heart when he lost the special pen with which he wrote during forty years, published a work called Apes Urbanæ — Urban Bees. It is a biographical work, devoted

[1] In the article in Blackwood, the author, from a vitiated reminiscence, made the unpardonable blunder of attributing this touching trait of nature to the noble purchaser of the Valderfaer Boccaccio. For this, as not only a mistake, but in some measure an imputation on the tailor who could have made for his lordship pockets of dimensions so abnormal, I received due castigation from an eminent practical man in the book-hunter's field.

to the great men who flourished during the Pontificate of Urban VIII., whose family carried bees on their coat-armorial. The History of New York, by Diedrich Knickerbocker, has sorely perplexed certain strong-minded women, who read nothing but genuine history. The book which, in the English translation, goes by the name of Marmontel's Moral Tales, has been found to give disappointment to parents in search of the absolutely correct and improving; and Edgeworth's Essay on Irish Bulls has been counted money absolutely thrown away by eminent breeders. There is a sober-looking volume, generally bound in sheep, called MacEwen on the Types — a theological book, in fact, treating of the types of Christianity in the old law. Concerning it, a friend once told me that, at an auction, he had seen it vehemently competed for by an acute-looking citizen artisan and a burly farmer from the hills. The latter, the successful party, tossed the lot to the other, who might have it and be d——d to it, he "thought it was a buik upo' the tups," a word which, it may be necessary to inform the unlearned reader, means rams: but the other competitor also declined the lot; he was a compositor or journeyman printer, and expected to find the book honestly devoted to those tools of his trade of which it professed to treat. Mr. Ruskin, having formed the pleasant little original design of abolishing the difference between Popery and Protestantism, through the persuasive influence of his own special eloquence, set forth his views upon the matter in a book which he termed a treatise "on the construction of sheepfolds." I have been informed that this work had a considerable run among the muirland farmers, whose reception of it was not flattering.

Logic has not succeeded as yet in discovering the means of framing a title-page which shall be exhaustive, as it is termed, and constitute an infallible finger-post to the nature of a book. From the beginning of all literature, it may be said that man has been continually struggling after this achievement, and struggling in vain; and it is a humiliating fact, that the greatest adepts, abandoning the effort in despair, have taken refuge in some fortuitous word, which has served their purpose better than the best results of their logical analysis. The book which has been the supreme ruler of the intellect in this kind of work stands forth as an illustrious example of failure. To those writings of Aristotle which dealt with mind, his editing pupils could give no name, — therefore they called them the things after the physics — the *metaphysics;* and that fortuitous title the great arena of thought to which they refer still bears, despite of efforts to supply an apter designation in such words as Psychology, Pneumatology, and Transcendentalism.

Writhing under this nightmare kind of difficulty, men in later times tried to achieve completeness by lengthening the title-page; but they found that the longer they made it, the more it wriggled itself into devious tracks, and the farther did they depart from a comprehensive name. Some title-pages in old folios make about half an hour's reading.[1] One advantage, however, was found in these lengthy titles — they afforded to controversialists a means of condensing the pith of their malignity towards each other, and throwing it, as it were, right in the face of the adversary. It will thus often happen that the controversialist states his case first in the title-page; he then gives it at greater length in the introduction; again, perhaps, in a preface; a third time in an analytical form, through means of a table of contents; after all this skirmishing, he brings up his heavy columns in the body of the book; and if he be very skilful, he may let fly a few Parthian arrows from the index.

It is a remarkable thing that a man should have been imprisoned, and had his ears cut off, and become one of the chief causes of our great civil wars, all along of an unfortunate word or two in the last

[1] A good modern specimen of a lengthy title-page may be found in one of the books appropriate to the matter in hand, by the diligent French bibliographer Peignot: —

"DICTIONNAIRE RAISONNÉ DE BIBLIOLOGIE: contenant — 1mo, L'explication des principaux termes relatifs à la bibliographie, à l'art typographique, à la diplomatique, aux langues, aux archives, aux manuscrits, aux médailles, aux antiquités, &c.; 2do, Des notices historiques détaillées sur les principales bibliothèques anciennes et modernes; sur les différentes sectes philosophiques; sur les plus célèbres imprimeurs, avec un indication des meilleures éditions sorties de leurs presses; et sur les bibliographes, avec la liste de leurs ouvrages; 3tio, enfin, L'exposition des différentes systèmes biliographiques, &c., — ouvrage utile aux bibliothécaires, archivistes, imprimeurs, &c." Paris, 1802.

page of a book containing more than a thousand. It was as far down in his very index as W that the great offence in Prynne's Histrio Mastyx was found, under the head "Women actors." The words which follow are rather unquotable in this nineteenth century; but it was a very odd compliment to Queen Henrietta Maria to presume that these words must refer to her — something like Hugo's sarcasm that, when the Parisian police overhear any one use the terms "ruffian" and "scoundrel," they say, "You must be speaking of the Emperor." The Histrio Mastyx was, in fact, so big and so complex a thicket of confusion, that it had been licensed without examination by the licenser, who perhaps trusted that the world would have as little inclination to peruse it as he had. The calamitous discovery of the sting in the tail must surely have been made by a Hebrew or an Oriental student, who mechanically looked for the commencement of the Histrio Mastyx where he would have looked for that of a Hebrew Bible. Successive licensers had given the work a sort of go-by, but, reversing the order of the sibylline books, it became always larger and larger, until it found a licenser who, with the notion that he "must put a stop to this," passed it without examination. It got a good deal of reading immediately afterwards, especially from Attorney-General Noy, who asked the Star-Chamber what it had to do with the immorality of stage-plays to exclaim that church-music is not the noise of men, but rather "a bleating of brute beasts — choristers bellow the tenor as it were oxen, bark a counterpoint as a kennel of dogs, roar out a treble like a set of bulls, grunt out a bass as it were a number of hogs." But Mr. Attorney took surely a more nice distinction when he made a charge against the author in these terms: "All stage-players he terms them rogues: in this he doth falsify the very Act of Parliament; for *unless they go abroad*, they are not rogues."

In the very difficulties in the way of framing a conclusive and exhaustive title, there is a principle of compensation. It clears literature of walls and hedgerows, and makes it a sort of free forest. To the desultory reader, not following up any special inquiry, there are delights in store in a devious rummage through miscellaneous volumes, as there are to the lovers of adventure and the picturesque in any district of country not desecrated by the tourist's guide-books. Many readers will remember the pleasant little narrative appended to Croker's edition of Boswell, of Johnson's talk at Cambridge with that extensive book-hunter, Dr. Richard Farmer, who boasted of the possession of "plenty of all such reading as was never read," and scandalized his visitor by quoting from Markham's Book of Armorie a passage applying the technicalities of heraldry and genealogy to the most sacred mystery of Christianity. One who has not tried it, may form an estimate of this kind of pursuit from Charles Lamb's Specimens from the Writings of Fuller. No doubt, as thus transplanted, these have not the same fresh relish which they have for the wanderer who finds them in their own native wilderness; but, like the specimens in a conservatory or a museum, they are examples of what may be found in the place they have come from. I am here tempted to relieve this desultory prattle by offering to the reader a passage or two from some old author, not exactly in the regular beat of our "English classics;" and I shall take Sir Thomas Browne. Whether the reader is already acquainted with them or not, I am sure that he will enjoy the beauty of the thoughts and the mellowed sweetness of the style. In the first, the author relieves his mind about his fellow-Christians of the Romish persuasion.

The Æsthetics of Toleration.

"We have reformed from them, not against them; for, omitting those improprieties and terms of scurrility betwixt us, which only difference our affections and not our cause, there is between us one common name and appellation, one faith and necessary body of principles common to us both; and therefore I am not scrupulous to converse and live with them, to enter their churches in defect of ours, and either pray with them or for them. I could never perceive any rational consequence from those many texts which prohibit the children of Israel to pollute themselves with the temples of the heathens; we being all Christians, and not divided by such detested impieties as might profane our prayers, or the place wherein we make them; or that a resolved conscience may not adore her Creator anywhere, especially in places devoted to his service; where, if their devotions offend him, mine may please him, if theirs profane it, mine may hallow it. Holy water and crucifix (dangerous to the common people) deceive not my judgment, nor abuse my devotion at all. I am, I confess, naturally inclined to that which misguided zeal terms superstition: my common conversation I do acknowledge austere, my behaviour full of rigour, sometimes not without morosity; yet at my devotion I love to use the civility of my knee, my hat, and hand, with all those outward and sensible motions which may express or promote my invisible devotion. I should violate my own arm rather than a church, nor willingly deface the name of saint or martyr. At the sight of a cross or crucifix I can dispense with my hat, but scarce with the thought or memory of my Saviour. I cannot laugh at, but rather pity the fruitless journeys of pilgrims, or contemn the miserable condition of friars; for though misplaced in circumstances, there is something in it of devotion. I could never hear the Ave Maria bell without an elevation; or think it a sufficient warrant, because they erred in one circumstance, for me to err in all — that is, in silence and dumb contempt. Whilst, therefore, they directed their devotions to her, I offered mine to God, and rectified the errors of their prayers by rightly ordering mine own. At a solemn procession I have wept abundantly, while my consorts, blind with opposition and prejudice, have fallen into an excess of scorn and laughter. There are, questionless, both in Greek, Roman, and African churches, solemnities and ceremonies whereof the wiser zealots do make a Christian use; and stand condemned by us, not as evil in themselves, but as allurements and baits of superstition to those vulgar heads that look asquint on the face of truth, and those unstable judgments that cannot consist in the narrow point and center of virtue, without a reel or stagger to the circumference."

Disputation.

"I could never divide myself from any man upon the difference of an opinion, or be angry with his judgment for not agreeing with me in that from which, perhaps, within a few days I should dissent myself. I have no genius to disputes in religion, and have often thought it wisdom to decline them, especially upon a disadvantage, or when the cause of truth might suffer in the weakness of my patronage. Where we desire to be informed, 'tis good to contest with men above ourselves; but to confirm and establish our opinions, 'tis best to argue with judgments below our own, that the frequent spoils and victories over their reasons may settle in ourselves an esteem and confirmed opinion of our own. Every man is not a proper champion for truth, — not fit to take up the gauntlet in the cause of verity. Many, from the ignorance of these maxims, and an inconsiderate zeal unto truth, have too rashly charged the troops of error, and remain as trophies unto the enemies of truth. A man may be in as just possession of truth as of a city, and yet be forced to surrender; 'tis therefore far better to enjoy her with peace than to hazard her on a battle. If, therefore, there arise any doubts in my way, I do forget them, or at least defer them, till my better-settled judgment and more manly reason be able to resolve them; for I perceive every man's own reason is his best Œdipus, and will, upon a reasonable truce, find a way to loose those bonds wherewith the subtilties of error have enchained our more flexible and tender judgments."

The Harmony of Nature.

"'Natura nihil agit frustra,' is the only indisputable axiom in philosophy. There are no grotesk in nature, nor anything framed to fill up empty cantons and unnecessary spaces. In the most imperfect creatures, and such as were not preserved in the ark — but, having their seeds and principles in the womb of nature, are everywhere where the power of the sun is — in these is the wisdom of his hand discovered; out of this rank Solomon chose the object of his admiration. Indeed what reason may not go to school to the wisdom of bees, ants, and spiders? What wise hand teacheth them to do what reason cannot teach us? Ruder heads stand amazed at those prodigious pieces of nature, whales, elephants, dromedaries and camels, — these, I confess, are the colossus and majestick pieces of her hand; but in these narrow engines there are more curious mathematicks, and the civility of these little citizens more neatly sets forth the wisdom of their maker. Who admires Regiomontanus his fly beyond his eagle, or wonders not more at the operation of two souls in those little bodies, than but one in the trunk of a cedar? I could never content my contemplation with those general pieces of wonder, the flux and reflux of the sea, the increase of the Nile, the conversion of the needle to the north; and have studied to match and parallel those in the more obvious and neglected pieces of nature, which without further travel I can do in the cosmography of myself. We carry with us the wonders we seek without us: there is all Africa and her prodigies in us. We are that bold and adventurous piece of nature which he that studies wisely learns in a compendium, and which others labour at in a divided piece and endless volume.

"Thus there are two books from whence I collect my divinity; besides that written one of God, another of his servant nature, that universal and publick manuscript, that lies expended unto the eyes of all. Those that never saw him in the one, have discovered him in the other. This was the scripture and theology of the heathens. The natural motion of the sun made them more admire him than its supernatural station did the children of Israel; the ordinary effect of nature wrought more admiration in them than in the other all his miracles.

Surely the heathens knew better how to join and read these mystical letters than we Christians, who cast a more careless eye on these common hieroglyphicks, and disdain to suck divinity from the flowers of nature."

The Justification of Martyrdom.

"Now as all that die in war are not termed soldiers, so neither can I properly term all those that suffer in matters of religion martyrs. The Council of Constance condemns John Huss for an heretick, the stories of his own party stile him a martyr: he must needs offend the divinity of both, who says he was neither the one nor the other. There are many, questionless, canonised on earth, who shall never be saints in heaven; and have their names in histories and martyrologies, who, in the eyes of God are not so perfect martyrs as was that wise heathen, Socrates, who suffered on a fundamental point of religion, the unity of God. I have often pitied the miserable bishop who suffered in the cause of antipodes, yet cannot chuse but accuse him of as much madness, for exposing his life on such a trifle, as those of ignorance and folly who condemned him. I think my conscience would not give me the lie, if I say there are not many extant who, in a noble way, fear the face of death less than myself; yet, from the moral duty I owe to the commandment of God, and the natural respects that I tender unto the conservation of my essence and being, I would not perish upon a ceremony, politick points, or indifferency; nor is my belief of that untractable temper as not to bow at their obstacles, or connive at matters wherein there are not manifest impieties. The leaven, therefore, and ferment of all, not only civil but religious actions, is wisdom; without which, to commit ourselves to the flames is homicide, and (I fear) but to pass through one fire into another."[1]

Ashes of the Unknown Dead.

"Time, which antiquates antiquities, and hath an art to make dust of all things, hath yet spared these minor monuments. In vain we hope to be known by open and visible conservatories, when to be unknown was the means of their continuation, and obscurity their protection. If they died by violent hands, and were thrust into their urns, these bones become considerable; and some old philosophers would honour them, whose souls they conceived most pure which were thus snatched from their bodies, and to retain a stronger propension unto them; whereas they weariedly left a languishing corpse, and with faint desires of reunion, if they fell by long and aged decay. Yet, wrapt up in the bundle of time, they fall into indistinction, and make but one blot with infants. . . . . What song the Syrens sang, or what name Achilles assumed when he hid himself among women, though puzzling questions, are not beyond all conjecture. What time the persons of these assuaries entered

[1] From the Religio Medici.

the famous nations of the dead, and slept with princes and counsellors, might admit a wide solution. But who were the proprietors of these bones, or what bodies these ashes made up, were a question above antiquarism — not to be resolved by men, nor easily, perhaps, by spirits, except we consult the provincial guardians or tutelary observators. Had they made as good provision for their names as they have done for their reliques, they had not so grossly erred in the art of perpetuation. But to subsist in bones, and be but pyramidally extant, is a fallacy in duration. Vain ashes! which, in the oblivion of names, persons, times, and sexes, have found unto themselves a fruitless continuation, and only arise unto late posterity as emblems of mortal vanities, antidotes against pride, vainglory, and madding vices."[1]

But there are passages worth finding in books less promising than the works of Browne or Fuller. Those who potter in libraries, especially if they have courage to meddle with big volumes, sometimes find curious things — for all gems are not collected in caskets. In searching through the solid pages of Hatsell's Precedents in Parliament for something one doesn't find, it is some consolation to alight on such a precedent as the following, set forth as likely to throw light on the mysterious process called "naming a member." "A story used to be told of Mr. Onslow, which those who

[1] From the Hydriotaphia.

ridiculed his strict observance of forms were fond of repeating, that as he often, upon a member's not attending to him, but persisting in any disorder, threatened to name him — 'Sir, sir, I must name you' — on being asked what would be the consequence of putting that threat in execution and naming a member, he answered, 'The Lord in heaven knows.'"

In the perusal of a very solid book on the progress of the ecclesiastical differences of Ireland, written by a native of that country, after a good deal of tedious and vexatious matter, the reader's complacency is restored by an artless statement how an eminent person "abandoned the errors of the Church of Rome, and adopted those of the Church of England."

So also a note I have preserved of a brief passage descriptive of the happy conclusion of a duel runs thus: —

"The one party received a slight wound in the breast; the other fired in the air — and so the matter terminated."[1]

[1] This passage has been quoted and read by many people quite unconscious of the arrant bull it contains. There could be no better testimony to its being endowed with the subtle spirit of the genuine article. Irish bulls, as Burke said of constitutions, "are not made — they grow," and that only in their own native soil. Those manufactured for the stage and the anecdote-books betray their artificial origin in their breadth and obviousness. The real bull carries one with it at first by an imperceptible confusion and misplacement of ideas in the mind where it has arisen, and it is not until you reason back that you see it. Horace Walpole used to say that the best of all bulls,

Professional law-books and reports are not generally esteemed as light reading, yet something may be made even of them at a pinch. Menage wrote a book upon the amenities of the civil law, which does anything but fulfil its promise. There are many much better to be got in the most unlikely corners; as, where a great authority on copyright begins a narrative of a case in point by saying, "One Moore had written a book which he called Irish Melodies;" and again, in an action of trespass on the case, "The plaintiff stated in his declaration that he was the true and only proprietor of the copyright of a book of poems entitled The Seasons, by James Thomson." I cannot lay hands at this moment on the index which refers to Mr. Justice Best — he was the man, as far as memory serves, but never mind.

from its thorough and grotesque confusion of identity, was that of the man who complained of having been "changed at nurse;" and perhaps he is right. An Irishman, and he only, can handle this confusion of ideas so as to make it a more powerful instrument of repartee than the logic of another man: take, for instance, the beggar who, when imploring a dignified clergyman for charity, was charged not to take the sacred name in vain, and answered, "Is it in vain, then? and whose fault is that?" I have doubts whether the saying attributed to Sir Boyle Roche about being in two places at once "like a bird," is the genuine article. I happened to discover that it is of earlier date than Sir Boyle's day, having found, when rummaging in an old house among some Jacobite manuscripts, one from Robertson of Strowan, the warrior poet, in which he says about two contradictory military instructions, "It seems a difficult point for me to put both orders in execution, unless, as the man said, I can be in two places at once, like a bird." A few copies of these letters were printed for the use of the Abbotsford Club. This letter of Strowan's occurs in p. 92.

A searcher after something or other, running his eye down the index through letter B, arrived at the reference "Best — Mr. Justice — his great mind." Desiring to be better acquainted with the particulars of this assertion, he turned up the page referred to, and there found, to his entire satisfaction, "Mr. Justice Best said he had a great mind to commit the witness for prevarication."

The following case is curiously suggestive of the state of the country round London in the days when much business was done on the road: — A bill in the Exchequer was brought by Everett against a certain Williams, setting forth that the complainant was skilled in dealing in certain commodities, "such as plate, rings, watches, &c.," and that the defendant desired to enter into partnership with him. They entered into partnership accordingly, and it was agreed that they should provide the necessary plant for the business of the firm — such as horses, saddles, bridles, &c. (pistols not mentioned) — and should participate in the expenses of the road. The declaration then proceeds, "And your orator and the said Joseph Williams proceeded jointly with good success in the said business on Hounslow Heath, where they dealt with a gentleman for a gold watch; and afterwards the said Joseph Williams told your orator that Finchley, in the county of Middlesex, was a good and convenient place to deal in, and that commodities were very plenty at Finchley aforesaid, and it would be almost all clear gain to them; that they went accordingly, and dealt with several gentlemen for divers watches, rings, swords, canes, hats, cloaks, horses, bridles, saddles, and other things; that about a month afterwards the said Joseph Williams informed your orator that there was a gentleman at Blackheath who had a good horse, saddle, bridle, watch, sword, cane, and other things to dispose of, which, he believed, might be had for little or no money; that they accordingly went, and met with the said gentleman, and, after some small discourse, they dealt for the said horse, &c. That your orator and the said Joseph Williams continued their joint dealings together in several places — viz., at Bagshot, in Surrey; Salisbury, in Wiltshire; Hampstead, in Middlesex; and elsewhere, to the amount of £2000 and upwards."[1]

Here follows a brief extract from a law paper, for the full understanding of which it has to be kept in view that the pleader, being an officer of the law, who has been prevented from executing his warrant by threats, requires, as a matter of form, to swear that he was really afraid that the threats would be carried into execution.

"Farther depones, that the said A. B. said that if deponent did not immediately take himself off he would pitch him (the deponent) down stairs — which the deponent verily believes he would have done.

"Farther depones, that, time and place aforesaid,

[1] This case has been often referred to in law-books, but I have never met with so full a statement of the contents of the declaration as in the Retrospective Review (vol. v. p. 81).

the said A. B. said to deponent, 'If you come another step nearer I'll kick you to hell'—which the deponent verily believes he would have done." [1]

I know not whether "lay gents," as the English bar used to term that portion of mankind who had not been called to itself,[2] can feel any pleasure in wandering over the case-books, and picking up the funny technicalities scattered over them; but I can attest from experience that, to a person trained in one set of technicalities, the pottering about among those of a different parish is exceedingly exhilarating. When one has been at work among interlocutors, suspensions, tacks, wadsets, multiplepoindings, adjudications in implement, assignations, infeftments, homologations, charges of horning, quadriennium utiles, vicious intromissions, decrees of putting to silence, conjoint actions of declarator and reduction-improbation — the brain, being satu-

[1] It is curious to observe how bitter a prejudice Themis has against her own humbler ministers. Most of the bitterest legal jokes are at the expense of the class who have to carry the law into effect. Take, for instance, the case of the bailiff who had been compelled to swallow a writ, and, rushing into Lord Norbury's court to proclaim the indignity done to justice in his person, was met by the expression of a hope that the writ was "*not returnable* in this court."

[2] [*Do* members of the English bar call any people "gents"? Do those solemn benchers, those punctilious Q. C.'s, those fearfully and wonderfully wigged judges, say "gents"? We who have not had the advantage of personal observation, supposed "gent" to be fitly given up to the use of those execrable animals who are the triumphs of John Leech's pencil, and the butts of his gentlemen,—in short, the Tittlebat Titmice of the English part of the British nation. — W.]

rated with these and their kindred, becomes refreshed by crossing the border of legal nomenclature, and getting among common recoveries, demurrers, quare impedits, tails-male, tails-female, docked tails, latitats, avowrys, nihil dicits, cestui que trusts, estoppels, essoigns, darrein presentments, emparlances, mandamuses, qui tams, capias ad faciendums or ad withernam, and so forth. After vexatious interlocutors in which the Lord Ordinary has refused interim interdict, but passed the bill to try the question, reserving expenses; or has repelled the dilatory defences, and ordered the case to the roll for debate on the peremptory defences; or has taken to avizandum; or has ordered re-revised condescendence and answers on the conjoint probation; or has sisted diligence till caution be found judicio sisti; or has done nearly all these things together in one breath, — it is like the consolation derived from meeting a companion in adversity, to find that at Westminster Hall, "In fermedon the tenant having demanded a view after a general imparlance, the demandant issued a writ of petit cape — held irregular."

Also, "If, after nulla bona returned, a testatum be entered upon the roll, quod devastavit, a writ of inquiry shall be directed to the sheriff, and if by inquisition the devastavit be found and returned, there shall be a scire facias quare executio non de propriis bonis, and if upon that the sheriff returns scire feci, the executor or administrator may appear and traverse the inquisition."

Again, "If the record of Nisi prius be a die Sancti Trinitatis in tres Septimanas nisi a 27 June, prius venerit, which is the day after the day in Bank, which was mistaken for a die Sancti Michaelis, it shall not be amended."

It is interesting to observe, that at one end of the island a panel means twelve perplexed agriculturists, who, after having taken an oath to act according to their consciences, are starved till they are of one mind on some complicated question; while, at the other end, the same term applies to the criminal on whose conduct they are going to give their verdict. It would be difficult to decide which is the more happy application; but it must be admitted that we are a great way behind the South in our power of selecting a nomenclature immeasurably distant in meaning from the thing signified. We speak of a bond instead of a mortgage, and we adjudge where we ought to foreclose. We have no such thing as chattels, either personal or real.[1] If you want to

[1] A late venerable practitioner in a humble department of the law, who wanted to write a book, and was recommended to try his hand at a translation of Latin law-maxims as a thing much wanted, was considerably puzzled with the maxim, "Catella realis non potest legari;" nor was he quite relieved when he turned up his Ainsworth and found that catella means "a little puppy." There was nothing for it, however, but obedience, so that he had to give currency to the remarkable principle of law, that "a genuine little whelp cannot be left in legacy." He also translated "messis sequitur sementem," with a fine simplicity, into "the harvest follows the seed-time;" and "actor sequitur forum rei," he made "the agent must be in court when the case is going on." Copies of the book containing these gems are ex-

know the English law of book-debts, you will have to look for it under the head of Assumpsit in a treatise on Nisi Prius; while a lawyer of Scotland would unblushingly use the word itself, and put it in his index. So, too, our bailments are merely spoken of as bills, notes, or whatever a merchant might call them. Our garnishee is merely a common debtor. Baron and feme we call husband and wife, and coverture we term marriage.[1]

Still, for the honor of our country, it is possible to find a few technicalities which would do no discredit to our neighbors. Where one of them would bring a habeas corpus — a name felicitously expressive, according to the English method of civil liberty — an inhabitant of the North, in the same unfortunate position, would take to running his letters. We have no turbary, or any other easement; but, to compensate us, we have thirlage, outsucken multures, insucken multures, and dry multures; as also we have a sowmen and rowmen, as any one who has been so fortunate as to hear Mr. Outram's pa-

ceedingly rare, some malicious person having put the author up to their absurdity.

[1] [This and the amusing account which follows of the many and great variations between the Scotch and English forms of law, which are signs of a difference at least equal in spirit, are interesting evidence of the radical unlikeness, as well in institutions as in race, of the two peoples which form the most important elements of the British nation. No shadow of such unlikeness exists or ever has existed in this country, except in one State, — Louisiana. — W.]

thetic lyric on that interesting servitude, will remember in conjunction with pleasing associations. To do the duty of a Duces Tecun we have a diligence against havers. We have no capias ad faciendum (abbreviated cap ad fac), nor have we the fieri facias, familiarly termed fi fa, but we have perhaps as good in the in meditatione fugæ warrant, familiarly abbreviated into fugie, as poor Peter Peebles termed it, when he burst in upon the party assembled at Justice Foxley's, exclaiming, "Is't here they sell the fugie warrants?"[1]

I am not sure but, in the very mighty heart of all legal formality and technicality — the Statutes at Large — some funny things might be found. The best that now occurs to the memory is not to be brought to book, and must be given as a tradition of the time when George III. was king. Its tenor is, that a bill which proposed, as the punishment of an offence, to levy a certain pecuniary penalty, one half thereof to go to his Majesty and the other half

[1] There are two old methods of paying rent in Scotland — Kane and Carriages; the one being rent in kind from the farm-yard, the other being an obligation to furnish the landlord with a certain amount of carriage, or rather cartage. In one of the vexed cases of domicile, which had found its way into the House of Lords, a Scotch lawyer argued that a landed gentleman had shown his determination to abandon his residence in Scotland by having given up his "kane and carriages." It is said that the argument went further than he expected — the English lawyers admitting that it was indeed very strong evidence of an intended change of domicile when the laird not only ceased to keep a carriage, but actually divested himself of his walking-cane.

to the informer, was altered in committee, in so far that, when it appeared in the form of an act, *the punishment* was changed to whipping and imprisonment, *the destination* being left unaltered.

It is wonderful that such mistakes are not of frequent occurrence when one remembers the hot hasty work often done by committees, and the complex entanglements of sentences on which they have to work. Bentham was at the trouble of counting the words in one sentence of an Act of Parliament, and found that, beginning with "Whereas" and ending with the word "repealed," it was precisely the length of an ordinary three-volume novel. To offer the reader that sentence on the present occasion would be rather a heavy jest, and as little reasonable as the revenge offered to a village schoolmaster who, having complained that the whole of his little treatise on the Differential Calculus was printed bodily in one of the earlier editions of the Encyclopædia Britannica (not so profitable as the later), was told that he was welcome, in his turn, to incorporate the Encyclopædia Britannica in the next edition of his little treatise.

In the supposition, however, that there are few readers who, like Lord King, can boast of having read the Statutes at Large through, I venture to give a title of an Act — a title only, remember, of one of the bundle of acts passed in one session — as an instance of the comprehensiveness of English statute law, and the lively way in which it skips from one subject to another. It is called —

"An Act to continue several laws for the better regulating of pilots, for the conducting of ships and vessels from Dover, Deal, and the Isle of Thanet, up the River Thames and Medway; and for the permitting rum or spirits of the British sugar plantations to be landed before the duties of excise are paid thereon; and to continue and amend an Act for preventing fraud in the admeasurement of coals within the city and liberties of Westminster, and several parishes near thereunto; and to continue several laws for preventing exactions of occupiers of locks and wears upon the River Thames westward; and for ascertaining the rates of water-carriage upon the said river; and for the better regulation and government of seamen in the merchant service; and also to amend so much of an Act made during the reign of King George I. as relates to the better preservation of salmon in the River Ribble; and to regulate fees in trials and assizes at nisi prius," &c.

But this gets tiresome, and we are only half way through the title after all. If the reader wants the rest of it, as also the substantial Act itself, whereof it is the title, let him turn to the 23d of Geo. II., chap. 26.

No wonder, if he anticipated this sort of thing, that Bacon should have commended "the excellent brevity of the old Scots acts." Here, for instance, is a specimen, an actual statute at large, such as they were in those pigmy days:—

"Item, it is statute that gif onie of the King's lieges passes in England, and resides and remains there against the King's will, he shall be halden as Traiter to the King."

Here is another, very comprehensive, and worth a little library of modern statute-books, if it was duly enforced: —

"Item, it is statute and ordained, that all our Sovereign lord's lieges being under his obeisance, and especially the Isles, be ruled by our Sovereign lord's own laws, and the common laws of the realm, and none other laws."

The Irish statute-book opens characteristically with "An Act that the King's officers may travel *by sea* from one place to another within *the land* of Ireland."[1] And further on we have a whole series

[1] [I am as much at loss to discover what is characteristic in this opening sentence of the Irish statute book, as I was with regard to the emendation of the passage in Hamlet, on page 67. The author plainly intimates that the passage contains a bull; but it does not, or the semblance of one. Dublin and Cork, I take it, are both "within the land of Ireland," and yet it is common enough to "travel by sea" from one to the other. The author shows elsewhere a very nice appreciation of what is essential to a bull. I do not know that a bull has ever been exactly defined; but it seems to me that its essential element is a statement of the impossible and preposterous with a ludicrous semblance to the possible and natural. Thus the account on page 136 of the duel is an absolutely perfect bull. So is the advertisement on page 158 describing a man whose age is not known, but who looks older than he is. Perhaps there is no more complete and exquisite bull than the reply of the Irishman who had been some time in this country, to the question of his newly arrived countryman, as to the political condition of the people here. "Is it thrue, Pat, that wan man's as good as another in this counthry?" "Yis, be jabers, an' betther too." The exquisite touch in this cannot be appreciated by any one who does

of acts, with a conjunction of epithets in their titles which, at the present day, sounds rather startling, "for the better suppressing Tories, Robbers, and Rapparees, and for preventing robberies, burglaries, and other heinous crimes." The classes so associated having an unreasonable dislike of being killed, difficulties are thus put in the way of those beneficially employed in killing them, insomuch that they, "upon the killing of any one of their number,

not know the presumption and self-importance of the Irishmen who come here (I except, of course, the educated and intelligent few); — a presumption in which they are confirmed by the fact, that, owing to the well-known indifference of the very large cultivated class of the North to political affairs, and their absolute non-appearance in them under ordinary circumstances, (for which indifference there are amply sufficient reasons,) the Irish formerly and now the Irish and the German citizens, though comparatively so few, hold the balance of political power, and therefore are courted not only by demagogues, but even by such honest men as have engaged in politics. But to return to the bulls. The author doubts (page 137) whether Sir Boyle Roche's often quoted saying about being in two places at once, like a bird, is a genuine bull. There can be no doubt about it at all. It is simply a stupid blunder. There is not the least semblance of truth in it. An intelligent child would not be bewildered by it for a moment. He would see instantly, if not intuitively, that quickness of passage and identity of place are a contradiction in terms. The saying is suggestive of one which *is* characteristic of its birthplace on this side of the Atlantic, where humor often consciously takes a form much like the unconscious absurdity of Irish bulls. There is a little river at the West which is said to be "so crooked that when birds fly across it they light upon the same side they started from." The story put into the negro's mouth who was sent to count the pigs, and reported that he had counted them all except one little one who ran about so fast that he couldn't count him, is also a pure bull of this country's breeding. — W.]

are thereby so alarmed and put upon their keeping, that it hath been found impracticable for such person or persons to discover and apprehend, or kill any more of them, whereby they are discouraged from discovering and apprehending or killing," and so forth. There is a strange and melancholy historical interest in these motley enactments, since they almost verbatim repeat the legislation about the Highland clans passed a century earlier by the Lowland Parliament of Scotland.

To one shelf of the law library, however, an interest attaches which few are ready to deny — that devoted to the literature of Criminal Trials. It will go hard indeed, if, besides the reports of mere technicalities, there be not here some glimpses of the sad romances which lie at their heart; and, at all events, when the page passes a very slight degree beyond the strictly professional, the technicalities will be found mingled with abundant narrative. The State Trials, for instance — surely a lawyer's book — contains the materials of a thousand romances; nor are these all attached to political offences; as, fortunately, the book is better than its name, and makes a virtuous effort to embrace all the remarkable trials coming within the long period covered by the collection. Some assistance may be got, at the same time, from minor luminaries, such as the Newgate Calendar — not to be commended, certainly, for its literary merits, but full of matters strange and horrible, which, like the gloomy forest of the Castle of

Indolence, "send forth a sleepy horror through the blood."

There are many other books where records of remarkable crimes are mixed up with much rubbish, as, The Terrific Register, God's Revenge against Murder, a little French book called Histoire Générale des Larrons (1623), and if the inquirer's taste turn towards maritime crimes, the History of the Bucaniers, by Esquemeling. A little work in four volumes, called The Criminal Recorder, by a student in the Inner Temple, can be commended as a sort of encyclopædia of this kind of literature. It professes — and is not far from accomplishing the profession — to give biographical sketches of notorious public characters, including "murderers, traitors, pirates, mutineers, incendiaries, defrauders, rioters, sharpers, highwaymen, footpads, pickpockets, swindlers, housebreakers, coiners, receivers, extortioners, and other noted persons who have suffered the sentence of the law for criminal offences." By far the most luxurious book of this kind, however, in the English language, is Captain Johnston's Lives of Highwaymen and Pirates. It is rare to find it now complete. The old folio editions have been often mutilated by over use: the many later editions in octavo are mutilated by design of their editors; and for conveying any idea of the rough truthful descriptiveness of a book compiled in the palmy days of highway robbery, they are worthless.

All our literature of that nature must, however, yield to the French Causes Célèbres, a term rendered so significant by the value and interest of the book it names, as to have been borrowed by writers in this country to render their works attractive. It must be noted as a reason for the success of this work, and also of the German collection by Feuerbach, that the despotic Continental method of procedure by secret inquiry affords much better material for narrative than ours by open trial. We make, no doubt, a great drama of a criminal trial. Everything is brought on the stage at once, and cleared off before an audience excited so as no player ever could excite; but it loses in reading; while the Continental inquiry, with its slow secret development of the plot, makes the better novel for the fireside.

There is a method by which, among ourselves, the trial can be imbedded in a narrative which may carry down to later generations a condensed reflection of that protracted expectation and excitement which disturb society during the investigations and trials occasioned by any great crime. This is by "illustrating" the trial, through a process resembling that which has been already supposed to have been applied to one of Watts's hymns. In this instance there will be all the newspaper scraps — all the hawker's broadsides — the portraits of the criminal, of the chief witnesses, the judges, the counsel, and various other persons, — everything in literature or art that bears on the great question.

He who inherits or has been able to procure a

collection of such illustrated trials, a century or so old, is deemed fortunate among collectors, for he can at any time raise up for himself the spectre as it were of the great mystery and exposure that for weeks was the absorbing topic of attraction to millions. The curtains are down — the fire burns bright — the cat purrs on the rug; Atticus, soused in his easy-chair, cannot be at the trouble of going to see Macbeth or Othello — he will sup full of horrors from his own stores. Accordingly he takes down an unseemly volume, characterized by a flabby obesity by reason of the unequal size of the papers contained in it, all being bound to the back, while the largest only reach the margin. The first thing at opening is the dingy pea-green-looking paragraph from the provincial newspaper, describing how the reapers, going to their work at dawn, saw the clay beaten with the marks of struggle, and, following the dictates of curiosity, saw a bloody rag sticking on a tree, the leaves also streaked with red, and, lastly, the instrument of violence hidden in the moss ; next comes from another source the lamentations for a young woman who had left her home — then the excitement of putting that and that together — the search, and the discovery of the body. The next paragraph turns suspense into exulting wrath : the perpetrator has been found with his bloody shirt on — a scowling murderous villain as ever was seen — an eminent poacher, and fit for anything. But the next paragraph turns the tables. The ruffian had his own secrets of what he had been about that night, and at last makes a clean breast. It would have been a bad business for him at any other time, but now he is a revealing angel, for he noted this and that in the course of his own little game, and gives justice the thread which leads to a wonderful romance, and brings home desperate crime to that quarter where, from rank, education, and profession, it was least likely to be found. Then comes the trial and the execution; and so, at a sitting, has been swallowed all that excitement which, at some time long ago, chained up the public in protracted suspense for weeks.

The reader will see, from what I have just been saying, that I am not prepared to back Charles Lamb's Index Expurgatorius.[1] It is difficult, almost

[1] "In this catalogue of *books which are no books — biblia a biblia* — I reckon court calendars, directories, pocket-books, draught-boards bound and lettered on the back, scientific treatises, alma nacs, statutes at large; the works of Hume, Gibbon, Robertson, Beattie, Soame Jenyns, and generally all those volumes which 'no gentleman's library should be without;' the histories of Flavius Josephus (that learned Jew) and Paley's Moral Philosophy. With these exceptions, I can read almost anything. I bless my stars for a taste so catholic, so unexcluding. I confess that it moves my spleen to see these *things in books' clothing* perched upon shelves, like false saints, usurpers of true shrines, intruders into the sanctuary, thrusting out the legitimate occupants. To reach down a well-bound semblance of a volume, and hope it some kind-hearted play-book, then, opening what 'seem its leaves,' to come bolt upon a withering population essay. To expect a Steele, or a Farquhar, and find — Adam Smith. To view a well-arranged assortment of block-headed encyclopædias (Anglicanas or Metropolitanas) set out in an array

impossible, to find the book from which something either valuable or amusing may not be found, if the proper alembic be applied. I know books that are curious, and really amusing, from their excessive badness. If you want to find precisely how a thing ought not to be said, you take one of them down, and make it perform the service of the intoxicated Spartan slave. There are some volumes in which, at a chance opening, you are certain to find a mere platitude delivered in the most superb and amazing climax of big words, and others in which you have a like happy facility in finding every proposition stated with its stern forward, as sailors say, or in some other grotesque mismanagement of composition. There are no better farces on or off the stage than when two or three congenial spirits ransack books of this kind, and compete with each other in taking fun out of them.

There is a solid volume, written in an inquiring spirit, but in a manner which reminds one of deep calling unto deep, about the dark superstitions of a country which was once a separate European kingdom. I feel a peculiar interest in it, from the author having informed me, by way of communicating an important fact in literary history, and also as an example to be followed by literary as-

of russia or morocco, when a tithe of that good leather would comfortably reclothe my shivering folios, would renovate Paracelsus himself, and enable old Raymund Lully to look like himself again in the world. I never see these impostors but I long to strip them, to warm my ragged veterans in their spoils." — Essays of Elia.

pirants, that, before committing the book to the press, he had written it over sixteen times. It would have been valuable to have his first manuscript, were it only that one might form some idea of the steps by which he had brought it into the condition in which it was printed. But its perusal in that condition was not entirely thrown away, since I was able to recommend it to a teacher of composition, as containing, within a moderate compass — after the manner, in fact, of a handbook — good practical specimens of every description of depravity of style of which the English language is susceptible.

In the present day, when few scholars have opportunities of enriching the world with their prison hours, perhaps the best conditions for testing how far any volume or portion of printed matter, however hopeless-looking, may yet yield edifying or amusing matter to a sufficient pressure, will occur when a bookish person finds himself imprisoned in a country inn, say for twenty-four hours. Such things are not impossible in this age of rapid movement. It is not long since a train, freighted with musical artistes, sent express to perform at a provincial concert and be back immediately in town for other engagements, were caught by a great snowstorm, which obliterated the railway, and had to live for a week or two in a wayside alehouse, in one of the dreariest districts of Scotland. The possessor and user of a large library undergoing such a calamity in a modified shape will be able to form a conception of the resources at his disposal, and to calculate how long it will take him to exhaust the intellectual treasures at his command, just as a millionnaire, haunted as such people sometimes are by the dread of coming on the parish, might test how long a life his invested capital would support by spending a winter in a Shetland cottage, and living on what he could procure. Having exhausted all other sources of excitement and interest, the belated traveller is supposed to call for the literature of the establishment. Perhaps the Directory of the county town is the only available volume. Who shall say what the belated traveller may make of this? He may do a turn in local statistics, or, if his ambition rises higher, he may pursue some valuable ethnological inquiries, trying whether Celtic or Saxon names prevail, and testing the justice of Mr. Thierry's theory by counting the Norman patronymics, and observing whether any of them are owned by persons following plebeian and sordid occupations. If in after-life the sojourner should come in contact with people interested in the politics or business of that county town, he will surprise them by exhibiting his minute acquaintance with its affairs.

If, besides the Directory, an Almanac, old or new, is to be had, the analysis may be conducted on a greatly widened basis. The rotations of the changes of the seasons may at the same time suggest many appropriate reflections on the progress of man from the cradle to the grave, and all that he meets with between the alpha and omega; and if the prisoner is a man of genius, the announcements of eclipses and other solar phenomena will suggest trains of thought which he can carry up to any height of sublimity. A person in the circumstances supposed, after he has exhausted the Directory and the Almanac, may perhaps be led to read (if he can get) Zimmerman On Solitude, Harvey's Meditations, Watts On the Improvement of the Mind, or Hannah More's Sacred Dramas. Who knows what he may be reduced to? I remember the great Irish liberator telling how, when once detained in an inn in Switzerland, he could find no book to beguile the time with but the Lettres Provinciales of Pascal. I have no doubt that the coerced perusal of them to which he had to submit did him a deal of good.

Let us imagine that nothing better is to be found than the advertising sheet of an old newspaper — never mind. Let the unfortunate man fall to and read the advertisements courageously, and make the best of them. An advertisement is itself a fact, though it may sometimes be the vehicle of a falsehood; and, as some one has remarked, he who has a fact in hand is like a turner with a piece of wood in his lathe, which he can manipulate to his liking, tooling it in any way, as a plain cylinder or a richly ornamented toy. There have been fortunate instances of people driven to read them finding good jokes and other enjoyable things in advertisements — such things as make one almost regret that so little attention has been paid to this department of literature.[1] Advertisements, in fact, bring us into the very heart of life and business, and there is a world of interest in them. Suppose that the dirty broadside you pick up in the dingy inn's soiled room contains the annual announcement of the reassembling of the school in which you spent your own years of school-boy life — what a mingled and many-figured romance does it recall of all that has befallen to yourself and others since the day when the same advertisement made you sigh, because the hour was close at hand when you were to leave home and all its homely ways to dwell among strangers! Going onward, you remember how each one after another ceased to be a stranger, and twined himself about your heart; and then comes the reflection, Where are they all now? You remember how

> "He, the young and strong, who cherished
> Noble longings for the strife,
> By the roadside fell and perished,
> Weary with the march of life."

You recall to your memory also those two insepara-

[1] Take, for instance, the announcement of the wants of an affluent and pious elderly lady, desirous of having the services of a domestic like-minded with herself, who appeals to the public for a "groom to take charge of two carriage-horses of a serious turn of mind." So also the simple-hearted innkeeper, who founds on his limited "charges and civility;" or the description given by a distracted family of a runaway member, who consider that they are affording valuable means for his identification by saying, "age not precisely known — but looks older than he is.'

bles — linked together, it would seem, because they were so unlike. The one, gentle, dreamy, and romantic, was to be the genius of the set; but alas, he "took to bad habits," and oozed into the slime of life, imperceptibly almost, hurting no creature but himself — unless it may be that to some parent or other near of kin his gentle facility may have caused keener pangs than others give by cruelty and tyranny. The other, bright-eyed, healthy, strong, and keen-tempered — the best fighter and runner and leaper in the school — the dare-devil who was the leader in every row — took to Greek much about the time when his companion took to drinking, got a presentation, wrote some wonderful things about the functions of the chorus, and is now on the fair road to a bishopric.

Next arises the vision of "the big boy," the lout — the butt of every one, even of the masters, who, when any little imp did a thing well, always made the appropriate laudation tell to the detriment of the big boy, as if he were bound to be as superfluous in intellect as in flesh. He has sufficiently dinned into him to make him thoroughly modest, poor fellow, how all great men were little. Napoleon was little, so was Frederic the Great, William III., the illustrious Condé, Pope, Horace, Anacreon, Campbell, Tom Moore, and Jeffrey. His relations have so thoroughly given in to the prejudice against him, that they get him a cadetship because he is fit for nothing at home; and now, years afterwards, the newspapers resound with his fame — how, when at the quietest of all stations when the mutiny suddenly broke out in its most murderous shape, and even experienced veterans lost heart, he remained firm and collected, quietly developing, one after another, resources of which he was not himself aware, and in the end putting things right, partly by stern vigor, but more by a quiet tact and genial appreciation of the native character. But what has become of the Dux — him who, in the predictions of all, teachers and taught, was to render the institution some day illustrious by occupying the Woolsack, or the chief place at the Speaker's right hand? A curious destiny is his: at a certain point the curve of his ascent was as it were truncated, and he took to the commonest level of ordinary life. He may now be seen, staid and sedate in his walk, which brings him, with a regularity that has rendered him useful to neighbours owning erratic watches, day by day to a lofty three-legged stool, mounted on which, all his proceedings confirm the high character retained by him through several years for the neatness of his handwriting, and especially for his precision in dotting his i's and stroking his t's.

This is all along of the use which the reflective man may make of an old advertisement. If it be old, the older the better — the more likely is it to contain matter of curious interest or instruction about the ways of men. To show this, I reprint two advertisements from British newspapers.

From the Public Advertiser of 28th March, 1769.

"TO be SOLD, A BLACK GIRL, the property of J. B ——, eleven years of age, who is extremely handy, works at her needle tolerably, and speaks English perfectly well: is of an excellent temper, and willing disposition.

"Inquire of Mr Owen, at the Angel Inn, behind St. Clement's Church in the Strand."

From the Edinburgh Evening Courant, 18th April, 1768.

"A BLACK BOY TO SELL.

"TO be SOLD, A BLACK BOY, with long hair, stout made, and well-limbed—is good-tempered, can dress hair, and take care of a horse indifferently. He has been in Britain near three years.

"Any person that inclines to purchase him may have him for £40. He belongs to Captain ABERCROMBIE at Broughton.

"This advertisement not to be repeated."

There was at that time probably more of this description of property in Britain than in Virginia. It had become fashionable, as one may see in Hogarth. Such advertisements—they were abundant—might furnish an apt text on which a philosophical historian could speculate on the probable results to this country, had not Mansfield gone to the root of the matter by denying all property in slaves.[1]

[1] It was on this occasion, and in answer to the plea of the vast property, amounting to millions, at issue on the question, that Mansfield uttered that memorable maxim which nobody can

So much for the chances which still remain to the heluo librorum or devourer of books, if, after having consumed all the solid volumes within his reach, he should be reduced to shreds and patches of literature, like a ship's crew having resort to shoe-leather and the sweepings of the locker.

Pretenders.

BUT now to return to the point whence we started — the disposition, and almost the necessity, which the true enthusiast in the pursuit feels to look into the soul, as it were, of his book, after he has got possession of the body. When he is not of the omnivorous kind, but one who desires to possess a particular book, and, having got it, dips into the contents before committing it to permanent obscurity on his loaded shelves, there is, as we have already seen, a certain thread of intelligent association linking the items of his library to each other. The collector knows what he wants, and why he wants it, and that *why* does not entirely depend on exteriors, though he may have his whim as to that also.

trace back to any other authority, "Fiat justitia — ruat cœlum." Sir Thomas Browne has, in his Religio Medici, "Ruat cœlum — fiat voluntas tua." Perhaps he may have found this in one of the Fathers.

He is a totally different being from the animal who goes to all sales, and buys every book that is cheap. That is a painfully low and grovelling type of the malady; and, fortunately for the honor of literature, the bargain-hunter who suffers under it is not in general a special votary of books, but buys all bargains that come in his way — clocks, tables, forks, spoons, old uniforms, gas-meters, magic lanterns, galvanic batteries, violins (warranted real Cremonas from their being smashed to pieces), classical busts (with the same testimony to their genuineness), patent coffee-pots, crucibles, amputating knives, wheel-barrows, retorts, cork-screws, boot-jacks, smoke-jacks, melon frames, bath-chairs, and hurdy-gurdies. It has been said that once, a coffin, made too short for its tenant, being to be had an undoubted bargain, was bought by him, in the hope that, some day or other, it might prove of service in his family. His library, if such it may be termed, is very rich in old trade-directories, justices of peace and registers of voters, road-books, and other useful manuals; but there are very learned books in it too. That clean folio Herodotus was certainly extremely cheap at half-a-crown; and you need not inform him that the ninth book is wanting, for he will never find that out. The day when he has discovered that any book has been bought by another person, a better bargain than his own copy, is a black one in his calendar; but he has a peculiar device of his own for getting over the calamity by bringing down the average cost of his own copy through fresh investments. Having had the misfortune to buy a copy of Goldsmith's History of England for five shillings, while a neighbor flaunts daily in his face a copy obtained for three, he has been busily occupied in a search for copies still cheaper. He has now brought down the average price of his own numerous copies to three shillings and twopence, and hopes in another year to get below the three shillings.

Neither is the rich man who purchases fine and dear books by deputy to be admitted within the category of the genuine book-hunter. He must hunt himself — must actually undergo the anxiety, the fatigue, and, so far as purse is concerned, the risks of the chase. Your rich man, known to the trade as a great orderer of books, is like the owner of the great game-preserve, where the sport is heavy butchery; there is none of the real zest of the hunter of the wilderness to be had within his gates. The old Duke of Roxburghe wisely sank his rank and his wealth, and wandered industriously and zealously from shop to stall over the world, just as he wandered over the moor stalking the deer. One element in the excitement of the poorer book-hunter he must have lacked — the feeling of committing something of extravagance — the consciousness of parting with that which will be missed. This is the sacrifice which assures the world, and satisfies the man's own heart, that he is zealous and earnest in the work he has set about. And it is decidedly this class who most read and use the books they possess.[1] How genial a picture does Scott give of himself at the time of the Roxburghe sale — the

[1] [I shall not resist the temptation of quoting here a charming passage from Henry Ward Beecher's "Star Papers," although thousands, and, I believe, tens of thousands of that book have been sold. What our author states as general truth is to Mr. Beecher the inspiration of a picture full of life and humor; based, however, I am sure, on a study from nature. The latter seems almost an expansion of the former, or the former a generalization of the latter; and yet the "Star Papers" were published seven years ago, and Mr. Burton, doubtless, never saw them.

"As a hungry man eats first, and pays afterward, so the book-buyer purchases, and then works at the debt afterward. This paying is rather medicinal. It cures for a time. But a relapse takes place. The same longing, the same promises of self-denial. He promises himself to put spurs on both heels of his industry; and then, besides all this, he will *somehow* get along when the time for payment comes! Ah! this SOMEHOW! That word is as big as a whole world, and is stuffed with all the vagaries and fantasies that Fancy ever bred upon Hope. And yet, is there not some comfort in buying books, *to be* paid for? We have heard of a sot, who wished his neck as long as the worm of a still, that he might so much the longer enjoy the flavor of the draught! Thus, it is a prolonged excitement of purchase, if you feel for six months in a slight doubt whether the book is honestly your own or not. Had you paid down, that would have been the end of it. There would have been no affectionate and beseeching look of your books at you, every time you saw them, saying, as plain as a book's eyes can say, 'Do not let me be taken from you.'

"Moreover, buying books before you can pay for them promotes caution. You do not feel quite at liberty to take them home. You are married. Your wife keeps an account-book. She knows to a penny what you can and what you cannot afford. She has no 'speculation' in *her* eyes. Plain figures make desperate work with airy '*somehows*.' It is a matter of no small skill and experience to get your books home, and into

creation of Abbotsford pulling him one way, on the other his desire to accumulate a library round him in his Tusculum. Writing to his familiar Terry he says, "The worst of all is, that while my trees grow and my fountain fills, my purse, in an inverse ratio, sinks to zero. This last circumstance will, I fear, make me a very poor guest at the literary entertainment your researches hold out for me. I should, however, like much to have the treatise on Dreams

their proper places, undiscovered. Perhaps the blundering Express brings them to the door just at evening. 'What is it, my dear?' she says to you. 'Oh! nothing — a few books that I cannot do without.' That smile! A true housewife that loves her husband can smile a whole arithmetic at him in one look! Of course she insists, in the kindest way, in sympathizing with you in your literary acquisition. She cuts the strings of the bundle, (and of your heart,) and out comes the whole story. You have bought a complete set of costly English books, full bound in calf, extra gilt! You are caught, and feel very much as if bound in calf yourself, and admirably lettered.

"Now, this must not happen frequently. The books must be smuggled home. Let them be sent to some near place. Then, when your wife has a headache, or is out making a call, or has lain down, run the books across the frontier and threshold, hastily undo them, stop only for one loving glance as you put them away in the closet, or behind other books on the shelf, or on the topmost shelf. Clear away the twine and wrapping-paper, and every suspicious circumstance. Be very careful not to be too kind. That often brings on detection. Only the other day we heard it said, somewhere, 'Why, how good you have been, lately. I am really afraid that you have been carrying on mischief secretly.' Our heart smote us. It was a fact. That very day we had bought a few books which 'we could not do without.' After a while, you can bring out one volume, accidentally, and leave it on the table. 'Why, my dear, *what* a beautiful book! Where *did* you borrow it?' You glance over the newspaper,

by the author of the New Jerusalem, which, as John Cuthbertson, the smith, said of the minister's sermon, 'must be neat wark.' The loyal poems by N. T. are probably by poor Nahum Tate, who was associated with Brady in versifying the Psalms, and more honorably with Dryden in the second part of Absalom and Achitophel. I never saw them, however, but would give a guinea or thirty shillings for the collection."

with the quietest tone you can command: '*That!* oh! that is *mine.* Have you not seen it before? It has been in the house these two months;' and you rush on with anecdote and incident, and point out the binding, and that peculiar trick of gilding, and everything else you can think of; but it all will not do; you cannot rub out that roguish, arithmetical smile. People may talk about the equality of the sexes! They are not equal. The silent smile of a sensible, loving woman, will vanquish ten men. Of course you repent, and in time form a habit of repenting.

"Another method which will be found peculiarly effective, is, to make a *present* of some fine work, to your wife. Of course, whether she or you have the name of buying it, it will go into your collection and be yours to all intents and purposes. But, it stops remark in the presentation. A wife could not reprove you for so kindly thinking of her. No matter what she suspects, she will say nothing. And then if there are three or four more works, which have come home with the gift-book — they will pass through the favor of the other.

"These are pleasures denied to wealth and old bachelors. Indeed, one cannot imagine the peculiar pleasure of buying books, if one is rich and stupid. There must be some pleasure, or so many would not do it. But the full flavor, the whole relish of delight only comes to those who are so poor that they must engineer for every book. They set down before them, and besiege them. They are captured. Each book has a secret history of ways and means. It reminds you of subtle devices by which you insured and made it yours, in spite of poverty!" — W.]

One of the reasons why Dibdin's expatiations among rare and valuable volumes are, after all, so devoid of interest, is, that he occupied himself in a great measure in catering for men with measureless purses. Hence there is throughout too exact an estimate of everything by what it is worth in sterling cash, with a contempt for small things, which has an unpleasant odor of plush and shoulder-knot about it. Compared with dear old Monkbarns and his prowlings among the stalls, the narratives of the Boccaccio of the book-trade are like the account of a journey that might be written from the rumble of the travelling chariot, when compared with the adventurous narrative of the pedestrian or of the wanderer in the far east. Everything is too comfortable, luxurious, and easy — russia, morocco, embossing, marbling, gilding — all crowding on one another, till one feels suffocated with riches. There is a feeling, at the same time, of the utter useless pomp of the whole thing. Books, in the condition in which he generally describes them, are no more fitted for use and consultation than white kids and silk stockings are for hard work. Books should be used decently and respectfully — reverently, if you will, but let there be no toleration for the doctrine that there are volumes too splendid for use, too fine almost to be looked at, as Brummel said of some of his Dresden china. That there should be little interest in the record of rich men buying costly books which they know nothing about and never become acquainted with, is an illustration of a wholesome truth, pervading all human endeavors after happiness. It is this, that the active, racy enjoyments of life — those enjoyments in which there is also exertion and achievement, and which depend on these for their proper relish — are not to be bought for hard cash. To have been to him the true elements of enjoyment, the book-hunter's treasures must not be his mere property, they must be his achievements — each one of them recalling the excitement of the chase and the happiness of success. Like Monkbarns with his Elzevirs and his bundle of pedler's ballads, he must have, in common with all hunters, a touch of the competitive in his nature, and be able to take the measure of a rival, — as Monkbarns magnanimously takes that of Davie Wilson, "commonly called Snuffy Davie, from his inveterate addiction to black rappee, who was the very prince of scouts for searching blind alleys, cellars, and stalls, for rare volumes. He had the scent of a slow-hound, sir, and the snap of a bull-dog. He would detect you an old black-letter ballad among the leaves of a law-paper, and find an editio princeps under the mask of a school Corderius."

In pursuing the chase in this spirit, the sportsman is by no means precluded from indulgence in the adventitious specialties that delight the commonest bibliomaniac. There is a good deal more in many of them than the first thought discloses. An "editio princeps" is not a mere toy — it has something in it that may purchase the attention even of a thinking man. In the first place, it is a very old commodity — about four hundred years of age. If you look around you in the world you will see very few movables coeval with it. No doubt there are wonderfully ancient things shown to travellers, — as in Glammis Castle you may see the identical four-posted bedstead — a very creditable piece of cabinetmakery — in which King Malcolm was murdered a thousand years ago. But genuine articles of furniture so old as the editio princeps are very rare. If we should highly esteem a poker, a stool, a drinking-can, of that age, is there not something worthy of observance, as indicating the social condition of the age, in those venerable pages, made to look as like the handwriting of their day as possible, with their decorated capitals, all squeezed between two solid planks of oak, covered with richly embossed hogskin, which can be clinched together by means of massive decorated clasps? And shall we not admit it to a higher place in our reverence than some mere item of household convenience, when we reflect that it is the very form in which some great ruling intellect, resuscitated from long interment, burst upon the dazzled eyes of Europe and displayed the fulness of its face?

His Achievements in the Creation of Libraries.

O much, then, for the benefit which the class to whom these pages are devoted derive to themselves from their peculiar pursuit. Let us now turn to the far more remarkable phenomena, in which these separate and perhaps selfish pursuers of their own instincts and objects are found to concur in bringing out a great influence upon the intellectual destinies of mankind. It is said of Brindley, the great canal engineer, that, — when a member of a committee, where he was under examination, a little provoked or amused by his entire devotion to canals, asked him if he thought there was any use of rivers, — he promptly answered, "Yes, to feed navigable canals." So, if there be no other respectable function in life fulfilled by the book-hunter, I would stand up for the proposition that he is the feeder, provided by nature, for the preservation of literature from age to age, by the accumulation and preservation of libraries, public or private. It will require perhaps a little circumlocutory exposition to show this, but here it is.

A great library cannot be constructed — it is the growth of ages. You may buy books at any time with money, but you cannot make a library like one that has been a century or two a-growing, though you had the whole national debt to do it with. I remember once how an extensive publisher, speaking of the rapid strides which literature had made of late years, and referring to a certain old public library, celebrated for its affluence in the fathers, the civilians, and the medieval chroniclers, stated how he had himself freighted for exportation, within the past month, as many books as that whole library consisted of. This was likely enough to be true, but the two collections were very different from each other. The cargoes of books were probably thousands of copies of some few popular selling works. They might be a powerful illustration of the diffusion of knowledge, but what they were compared with was its concentration. Had all the paper of which these cargoes consisted been bank-notes, they would not have enabled their owner to create a duplicate of the old library, rich in the fathers, the civilians, and the medieval chroniclers.

This impossibility of improvising libraries is really an important and curious thing; and since it is apt to be overlooked, owing to the facility of buying books, in quantities generally far beyond the available means of any ordinary buyer, it seems worthy of some special consideration. A man who sets to form a library will go on swimmingly for a short way. He will easily get Tennyson's Poems — Macaulay's and Alison's Histories — the Encyclopædia Britannica — Buckle on Civilization — all the books "in print," as it is termed. Nay, he will find no difficulty in procuring copies of others which may not happen to be on the shelves of the publisher or of the retailer of new books. Of Voltaire's works — a little library in itself — he will get a copy at his call in London, if he has not set his mind on some special edition. So of Scott's edition of Swift or Dryden, Crocker's edition of Boswell's Johnson, and the like. One can scarcely suppose a juncture in which any of these cannot be found through the electric chain of communication established by the book trade. Of Gibbon's and Hume's Histories — Jeremy Taylor's works — Bossuet's Universal History, and the like, copies abound everywhere. Go back a little, and ask for Kennet's Collection of the Historians — Echard's History, Bayle, Moreri, or Father Daniel's History of France, you cannot be so certain of immediately obtaining your object, but you will get the book in the end — no doubt about that.[1]

Everything has its caprices, and there are some books which might be expected to be equally shy, but in reality, by some inexplicable fatality, are as plentiful as blackberries; such, for instance, are

[1] [The assertion is true with regard to much scarcer books than those named by the author; although not, of course, with regard to those which may justly be called rare. I heard a very thoroughly informed and observant bookseller say, (he has too much sense, should he see these lines, to wish that he had been called a bibliopole; and, by the way, he is capable of instructing most of his customers,) that every book except those of which all the copies were known to be in certain great collections, turned up for sale once in five years. My own observation and experience lead me to think that this is very near the truth. And so,

Famianus Strada's History of the Dutch War of Independence — one of the most brilliant works ever written, and in the very best Latin after Buchanan's. There is Buchanan's own history, very common even in the shape of the early Scotch edition of 1582, which is a highly favorable specimen of Arbuthnot's printing. Then there are Barclay's Argenis, and Raynal's Philosophical History of the East and West Indies, without which no book-stall is to be considered complete, and which seem to be possessed of a supernatural power of resistance to the elements, since, month after month, in fair weather or foul, they are to be seen at their posts dry or dripping.

So the collector goes on, till he perhaps collects some five thousand volumes or so of select works. If he is miscellaneous in his taste, he may get on pretty comfortably to ten or fifteen thousand, and then his troubles will arise. He has easily got Baker's and Froissart's and Monstrelet's Chronicles, because there are modern reprints of them in the market.[1] But if he want Cooper's Chronicle, he

afflicted book-hunter, when you see the idol of your longings snatched away by another of your species, more reckless or more pecunious than you, grieve not as those that are without hope. You will have another chance in five years. Though candor compels me to confess that when that wearily expected moment arrives there will appear at least four of those who like you were disappointed; and in the lapse of five years they will have added to themselves at least five other like marplots, worse than themselves. Such are the trials of your calling. Bear them with what strength and grace you may. — W.]

[1] [A lady who sometimes does me the honor to look over my

may have to wait for it, since its latest form is still the black-letter. True, I did pick up a copy lately, at Braidwood's, for half-a-guinea, but that was a catch — it might have caused the search of a lifetime. Still more hopeless it is when the collector's ambition extends to The Ladder of Perfection of Winkin de Worde, or to his King Rycharde Cure de Lion, whereof it is reported in the Repertorium Bibliographicum, that "an imperfect copy, wanting one leaf, was sold by auction at Mr. Evans's, in June 1817, to Mr. Watson Taylor for £40 19*s*." "Woe betide," says Dibdin, "the young bibliomaniac who sets his heart upon Breton's Flourish upon Fancie and Pleasant Toyes of an Idle Head, 1557, 4to; or Workes of a Young Wyt trussed up with a Fardell of Pretty Fancies!! Threescore guineas shall hardly fetch these black-letter rarities from the pigeon-holes of Mr. Thorpe. I lack courage to add the prices for which these copies sold." But he has some comfort reserved for the hungry collector, in the intimation that The Ravisht Soul and the Blessed Weaper, by the same author, may be had

shoulder, here laughed with scorn. "Call a man a collector, or a book-hunter, who will buy a reprint when the antiquated original is to be had! Why, a reprint isn't dirty; it doesn't smell badly; it isn't tattered and torn; it doesn't need mending and rebinding to keep it from tumbling to pieces; it has little chance of harboring unnamable creeping things, which Noah might as well have kept out of the ark. Why, a reprint can be read comfortably, and by anybody! Reprints! The author must be mad!" Upon what observation any woman could have founded such extraordinary remarks, the reader is quite as well able to judge as the writer. — W.]

for £15.[1] It creates a thrilling interest to know, through the same distinguished authority, that the Heber sale must have again let loose upon the world "A merry gest and a true, howe John Flynter made his Testament," concerning which we are told with appropriate solemnity and pathos, that "Julian Notary is the printer of this inestimably precious volume, and Mr. Heber is the thrice-blessed owner of the copy described in the Typographical Antiquities."

Such works as the Knightly Tale of Galogras, The Temple of Glas, Lodge's Nettle for Nice Noses, or the Book of Fayts of Armes, by Christene of Pisa, or Caxton's Pylgremage of the Sowle, or his Myrrour of the Worlde, will be long inquired after before they come to the market, thoroughly contradicting that fundamental principle of political economy, that the supply is always equal to the demand.

He, indeed, who sets his mind on the possession of any one of these rarities, may go to his grave a disappointed man. It will be in general the consolation of the collector, however, that he is by no means the "homo unius libri." There is always something or other turning up for him, so long as he keeps within moderate bounds. If he be rich and ravenous, however, there is nothing for it but duplicating—the most virulent form of book mania. We have seen that Heber, whose collection, made during his own lifetime, was on the scale of those

[1] Library Companion, p. 699.

public libraries which take generations to grow, had, with all his wealth, his liberality, and his persevering energy, to invest himself with duplicates, triplicates — often many copies of the same book.

It is rare that the private collector runs himself absolutely into this quagmire, and has so far exhausted the market that no already unpossessed volume turns up in any part of the world to court his eager embraces. The limitation constitutes, however, a serious difficulty in the way of rapidly creating great public libraries. We would obtain the best testimony to this difficulty in America, were our brethren there in a condition to speak or think of so peaceful a pursuit as library-making.[1]

1 [In this kindly allusion to his brethren in this country, the author makes a mistake, natural enough in one who has not lived here a long while. That so peaceful a pursuit as library-making can be thought of here, is shown by the fact that at this very time the annual Book Trade Sale is going on in New York from a catalogue of 430 pages, and with very large attendance and lively bidding. The very reprinting of this book about library-making, of which, in spite of the specialty of its subject, there will be three times as many sold here as in Great Britain, is in itself evidence to the same purpose. It would probably be impossible to make the author or any of his countrymen believe that at the present time, and for a year and a half past, New York, Boston, Philadelphia, Baltimore, Cincinnati, and, recently, even New Orleans, are and have been as busy and thriving, as orderly, and as free from violence as London, Liverpool, or Edinburgh; and, as the police-records and the newspapers of both countries show, far freer than the former city from robbery and theft. If it be answered that all the robbers and thieves have gone into the army, I deny it; some of them have gone into business as contractors, which is their way in all countries. In the next

In the normal condition of society there — something like that of Holland in the seventeenth century — there are powerful elements for the promotion of art and letters, when wealth gives the means and civilization the desire to promote them. The very absence of feudal institutions — the inability to found a baronial house — turns the thoughts of the rich and liberal to other foundations calculated to transmit their name and influence to posterity. And so we have such bequests as John Jacob Astor's, who left four hundred thousand dollars for a library,[1] and the hundred and eighty thousand which were the nucleus of the Smithsonian Institution. Yes! Their efforts in this direction have fully earned for them their own peculiar form of laudation as "actually equal to cash." Hence, as the book trade and book buyers know very well, "the almighty dollar" has been hard at work, trying to rear up by its sheer force duplicates of the old European

sentence the likening of the condition of society here to that of Holland in the seventeenth century will raise a smile on the lips of those who know anything of the two societies which are compared. But I must not be tempted into writing in these notes a book on "America and the Americans." — W.]

1 [Neither the author, nor Mr. Edwards in his book on libraries, seems to have known that to Mr. John Jacob Astor's noble bequest, his son, Mr. William B. Astor, added some years ago the gift, which needs no epithet, of other four hundred thousand dollars. If the money which is given by men of wealth in this country (that is, in the Free States) in addition to the ample provision by the State, for the education and culture of the whole people, were summed and stated, the account would be looked upon out of the country with amazement and incredulity. — W.]

libraries, containing not only all the ordinary stock books in the market, but also the rarities, and those individualities — solitary remaining copies of impressions — which the initiated call uniques. It is clear, however, that when there is but one copy, it can only be in one place; and if it have been rooted for centuries in the Bodleian, or the University of Tubingen, it is not to be had for Harvard or the Astorian. Dr. Cogswell, the first librarian of the Astorian, spent some time in Europe with his princely endowment in his pocket, and showed himself a judicious, active, and formidable sportsman in the book-hunting world. Whenever, from private collections, or the breaking-up of public institutions, rarities got abroad into the open market, the collectors of the old country found that they had a resolute competitor to deal with — almost, it might be said, a desperate one — since he was in a manner the representative of a nation using powerful efforts to get possession of a share of the literary treasures of the Old World.

In the case of a book, for instance, of which half a dozen copies might be known to exist, the combatants before the auctioneer would be, on the one side, many an ambitious collector desiring to belong to the fortunate circle already in possession of such a treasure; but on the other side was one on whose exertions depended the question, whether the book should henceforth be part of the intellectual wealth of a great empire, and should be accessible for consultation by American scholars and authors without their requiring to cross the Atlantic. Let us see how far, by a brief comparison, money has enabled them to triumph over the difficulties of their position.

It is difficult to know exactly the numerical contents of a library, as some people count by volumes, and others by the separate works, small or great; and even if all should consent to count by volumes, the estimate would not be precise, for in some libraries bundles of tracts and other small works are massed in plethoric volumes for economy, while in affluent institutions every collection of leaves put under the command of a separate title-page is separately bound in cloth, calf, or morocco, according to its rank. The Imperial Library at Paris is computed to contain above eight hundred thousand volumes; the Astorian boasts of approaching a hundred thousand:[1] the next libraries in size in America are the Harvard, with from eighty thousand to ninety thousand; the Library of Congress, which has from sixty thousand to seventy thousand; and the Boston Athenæum, which has about sixty thousand.

There are many of smaller size. In fact, there is probably no country so well stocked as the States with libraries of from ten thousand to twenty thousand volumes; the evidence that they have bought what was to be bought, and have done all that a new people can to participate in the long-hoarded

[1] [The Astor Library contains more than one hundred and twenty-five thousand volumes. — W.]

treasures of literature which it is the privilege of the Old World to possess. I know that, especially in the instance of the Astorian Library, the selections of books have been made with great judgment, and that, after the boundaries of the common crowded market were passed, and individual rarities had to be stalked in distant hunting-grounds, innate literary value was still held an object more important than mere abstract rarity, and, as the more worthy quality of the two, that on which the buying power available to the emissary was brought to bear.

The zeal and wealth which the citizens of the States have thrown into the limited field from which a library can be rapidly reaped, are manifested in the size and value of their private collections. A volume, called The Private Libraries of New York, by James Wynne, M. D., affords interesting evidence of this phenomenon. It is printed on large, thick paper, after the most luxurious fashion of our book clubs, apparently for private distribution.[1] The author states, however, that "the greater part of the sketches of private libraries to be found in this volume, were prepared for and published in the Evening Post about two years since. Their origin is due to a request on the part of Mr. Bigelow, one of the editors of the Post, to the writer, to examine and sketch the more prominent private collections of books in New York."

[1] [This is the first of many erroneous conclusions with regard to the book in question. It was published, though subscriptions for a certain number of copies were first obtained. — W.]

Such an undertaking reveals, to us of the old country, a very singular social condition. With us, the class who may be thus offered up to the martyrdom of publicity is limited. The owners of great houses and great collections are doomed to share them with the public, and if they would frequent their own establishments, must be content to do so in the capacity of librarians or showmen, for the benefit of their numerous and uninvited visitors. They generally, with wise resignation, bow to the sacrifice, and, abandoning all connection with their treasures, dedicate them to the people — nor, as their affluence is generally sufficient to surround them with an abundance of other enjoyments, are they an object of much pity.

But that the privacy of our ordinary wealthy and middle classes should be invaded in a similar shape, is an idea that could not get abroad without creating sensations of the most lively horror. They manage these things differently across the Atlantic, and so here we have "over" fifty gentlemen's private collections ransacked and anatomized. If *they* like it, we have no reason to complain, but rather have occasion to rejoice in the valuable and interesting result.[1]

[1] [The "very singular social condition" revealed by the publication of "The Private Libraries of New York" is merely one in which there is a general disposition to be obliging, and communicative of information which may be useful or agreeable, and also to do anything to contribute to the honor of the community of which one is a member. Personal privacy is, I suppose, one of the very first needs to the comfort of a gentleman; — at least of

It is quite natural that their ways of esteeming a collection should not be as our ways. There is a

our race; for with the Latin and the Oriental races it appears to be not so much sought for. Certainly it could nowhere be more jealously guarded than in this country, where intrusion into the penetralia of a man's home, be it high or humble, is an offence which, among people of any decent sort, not to say among the well-bred or the cultivated, is regarded as the most unpardonable, as it surely is the rarest, of social misdemeanors. Indeed, the partial publicity of the daily life of people of rank in Europe is looked upon here as part of a dear price paid for their privileges. But what invasion of privacy is there in having a few hundred people told in a nicely printed book (what many of them doubtless knew before) that in a certain room, their more knowledge of which depends absolutely on their personal relations with you, you have a fine Caxton or Aldus or Pannartz, or five hundred or five thousand other good books which it will gratify them to know are in their country and in their town, and which you will gladly let any properly introduced person, who has occasion to do so, examine to his heart's content? It does not draw a bolt, or lift a latch, or raise a curtain in your house; or even relax for a moment those stronger, though invisible, barriers which guard the approaches to your hearth-stone. As our author says, and as we all know, in Great Britain "the owners of great houses and great collections are doomed to share them with the public." But great is a comparative term. Great collections are great because most others around them are smaller than they are. Now if the collections described in "The Private Libraries of New York" are the largest and most considerable in that city, of which the mere fact that they were selected for description is evidence, it is somewhat puzzling to discover the difference of social etiquette and individual feeling between New York and London which the publication of that book indicates. True, none of the possessors of those collections were dukes, marquises, earls, viscounts, barons, or even baronets. Those varieties of our race are not produced in this country. If it be proper to describe the collections of such people only, we are in this respect in the condition of the cherub who was asked to sit down —

story of a Cockney auctioneer, who had a location in the back settlements to dispose of, advertising that it was "almost entirely covered with fine old timber." To many there would appear to be an equal degree of verdant simplicity in mentioning among the specialties and distinguishing features of a collection — the Biographia and Encyclopædia Britannica, Lowndes's Manual, The Quarterly and

we have not the wherewith. And as to mere publicity of name, it so happens that their positions in the church, in law, in science, letters, or society, had made nearly all of Dr. Wynne's subjects almost as used to being talked about, and having their "names spelled wrong in the newspapers," as the Old World possessors of the great houses and the great collections aforesaid. The few who were not in that category consented for good-fellowship, and to be obliging. And perhaps from vanity? No. For the truth is that in most instances there was a great reluctance, sometimes long persisted in, to consent to the publication; but a feeling that it would seem churlish or over-modest to refuse, when others whose collections were of no more importance had consented, finally overcame this obstacle. But a certain pride did enter into the motives which produced "The Private Libraries." It was municipal pride, however, not personal. The libraries of New York probably would never have been described had not an account of those of Boston been previously given to the public. This was unwise on the part of the men of Athens. It opened a seam in their armor. Because, although no man in his senses would dream of denying the claim of the three-hilled city to be either the Modern Athens or the Hub of the Universe, or both, yet it was seen that in this minor matter of private libraries New York was far ahead. Thereupon men began to say to each other, like Sir Toby Belch, when Sir Andrew Aguecheek discovers his excellence in capers and back-tricks, "Wherefore are these things hid?" And so they were revealed. The revelation probably, however, abated none of the Bostonian pretension; as to the loftiness of which a Boston man once met with this illustration. Passing a negro

Edinburgh Reviews, Boyle, Ducange, Moreri, Dodsley's Annual Register, Watt's Bibliotheca, and Diodorus Siculus.

The statement that there is in Dr. Francis's collection "a complete set of the Recueil des Causes Célèbres, collected by Maurice Mejan, in eighteen volumes — a scarce and valuable work" — would throw any of our black-letter knight-errants into

Methodist church one Sunday morning, and hearing the tremendous shouting which always issues from those places, he entered to make observation, and took his stand just within the inner door. The black Boanerges certainly obeyed the injunction to cry aloud and spare not: his voice was stentorian, his denunciation tremendous. After listening awhile, the white critic became aware of the presence of a black brother, who had taken a place by his side unnoticed. He was evidently a "colored pusson" of the very highest respectability — his manner sedate and soft, his hat of a dignified breadth of brim, his coat a long frock; and he wore those two articles which always give such an irresistibly ludicrous appearance to the negro face — a white cravat and silver spectacles. The gentleman turned to him, and decorously praised the preacher. "Fair, Sar, ve-ry fair," was the reply, with a look of patronizing approval which was almost contemptuous. A decided rebuff. Presently the preacher became more uproarious than ever; his voice ran away with him, and his arms flew like those of a windmill. "Now, my friend, what do you think of that? Perhaps I can't judge; but it really seems to me as if he was laying down that matter pretty strongly. See how he stirs up the congregation, too." — "Ve-ry good, Sar; ve-ry good. Man of talent, Sar. Nothing ve-ry remarkable;" — and then glancing over the rims of his barnacles, and with an exquisite touch of serene condescension in the placid circumflexion of his voice, "New York man, Sar; New York man." I am half inclined to think that when "The Private Libraries" appeared, Boston said, in her heart at least, and with some truth, "Nothing ve-ry remarkable. New York collections." — W.]

convulsions of laughter.[1] There are also some instances of perhaps not unnatural confusion between one merely local British celebrity and another, as where it is set forth that in Mr. Noyes's collection "there is a fine copy of Sir Robert Walpole's works, in five large quarto volumes, embellished

[1] [Very likely; and the laughter, or at least the surprise, at seeing a book which stands here for weeks and months on the shelves of the old-book sellers, asking a buyer at a few dollars, styled "scarce and valuable," would not be all on one side of the water. The author has been led to a very false conclusion as to our "ways of esteeming a collection" and our "inexperience in the ways of the craft" as it is practised in Europe. A collection of books in New York or Boston is judged by the very same canons which would be brought to the measurement of its value in London or Paris. The standard books are valued for their standard value and their fitness to supply the general wants of reading people; the illustrated books, for their beauty; and the rare books, for their special significance in the history of literature or printing, and for their rarity. Dr. Wynne has, with such modest candor, disavowed, in his preface, any "pretensions to nice bibliographical knowledge," that he may well claim exemption from criticism, especially at the hands of such a bibliophile as the author of this book. But it is quite fair to say that in some of the articles in his "Private Libraries" there are passages upon bibliography and history which do not represent the acquaintance with those subjects which is general among the persons for whom his very agreeable work was prepared. It was received here as a fair and welcome exhibit of the principal private collections of New York; but I am not aware that it met with special attention on bibliographic grounds in any quarter; except that envious Boston intensified one gracious "Ve-ry good for New York" by pointing out, blandly and briefly, evidences of the lack of that bibliographic knowledge the possession of which the author, with such creditable frankness, disavowed. Indeed, "The Private Libraries" received more attention in this book published at Edinburgh, than it did from the whole periodical press of the United States. — W.]

with plates." But under all this inexperience of the ways of the craft as it is cultivated among us, and unconsciousness of such small parochial distinctions as may hold between Sir Robert Walpole, our Prime Minister, and Horace Walpole, the man of letters and trinkets, the book contains a quantity of valuable and substantial matter, both as a record of rich stores of learning heaped up for the use of the scholar, and marvellous varieties to dazzle the eyes of the mere Dibdinite. The prevailing feature throughout is the lavish costliness and luxury of these collections, several of which exceed ten thousand volumes. Where collections have grown so large that, on the principles already explained, their increase is impeded, the owner's zeal and wealth seem to have developed themselves in the lavish enshrining and decorating of such things as were attainable.[1]

[1] Take as a practical commentary on what has been said (p. 76) on "illustrating" books, the following passage describing some of the specialties of a collection, the general features of which are described farther on: —

"But the crowning glory is a folio copy of Shakespeare, illustrated by the collector himself, with a prodigality of labor and expense, that places it far above any similar work ever attempted. The letterpress of this great work is a choice specimen of Nicol's types, and each play occupies a separate portfolio. These are accompanied by costly engravings of landscapes, rare portraits, maps, elegantly colored plates of costumes, and water-color drawings, executed by some of the best artists of the day. Some of the plays have over 200 folio illustrations, each of which is beautifully inlaid or mounted, and many of the engravings are very valuable. Some of the landscapes, selected from the oldest cosmographies known, illustrating the various places mentioned in the pages of Shakespeare, are exceedingly curious as well as valuable.

The descriptions of a remorseless investigator like this have a fresh individuality not to be found here, where our habitual reserve prevents us from offering or enjoying a full, true, and particular account of the goods of our neighbors, unless they are brought to the hammer, — and then they have lost half the charm which they possessed as the household gods of some one conspicuous by position or character, and are little more estimable than other common merchandise. It would be difficult to

"In the historical plays, when possible, every character is portrayed from authoritative sources, as old tapestries, monumental brasses, or illuminated works of the age, in well-executed drawings or recognized engravings. There are in this work a vast number of illustrations, in addition to a very numerous collection of water-color drawings. In addition to the thirty-seven plays, are two volumes devoted to Shakespeare's life and times, one volume of portraits, one volume devoted to distinguished Shakespearians, one to poems, and two to disputed plays, the whole embracing a series of forty-two folio volumes, and forming, perhaps, the most remarkable and costly monument, in this shape, ever attempted by a devout worshipper of the Bard of Avon. The volume devoted to Shakespeare's portraits was purchased by Mr. Burton, at the sale of a gentleman's library, who had spent many years in making the collection, and includes various 'effigies' unknown to many laborious collectors. It contains upwards of one hundred plates, for the most part proofs. The value of this collection may be estimated by the fact, that a celebrated English collector recently offered its possessor £60 for this single volume.

"In the reading-room directly beneath the main library, are a number of portfolios of prints illustrative of the plays of Shakespeare, of a size too large to be included in the illustrated collection just noticed. There is likewise another copy of Shakespeare, based upon Knight's pictorial royal octavo, copiously illustrated by the owner; but although the prints are numerous,

find, among the countless books about books produced by us in the old country, any in which the bent of individual tastes and propensities is so distinctly represented in tangible symbols ; and the reality of the elucidation is increased by the sort of innocent surprise with which the historian approaches each "lot," evidently as a first acquaintance, about whom he inquires and obtains all available particulars, good-humoredly communicating them in bold detail to his reader. Here follows

they are neither as costly nor as rare as those contained in the large folio copy.

"Among the curiosities of the Shakespeare collection are a number of copies of the disputed plays, printed during his lifetime, with the name of Shakespeare as their author. It is remarkable, if these plays were not at least revised by Shakespeare, that no record of a contradiction of their authorship should be found. It is not improbable that many plays written by others were given to Shakespeare to perform in his capacity as a theatrical manager, requiring certain alterations in order to adapt them to the use of the stage, which were arranged by his cunning and skilful hand, and these plays afterward found their way into print, with just sufficient of his emendations to allow his authorship of them, in the carelessness in which he held his literary fame, to pass uncontradicted by him.

"There is a copy of an old play of the period, with manuscript annotations, and the name of Shakespeare written on the title-page. It is either the veritable signature of the poet, or an admirably imitated forgery. Mr. Burton inclined to the opinion that the work once belonged to Shakespeare, and that the signature is genuine. If so, it is probably the only scrap of his handwriting on this continent. This work is not included in the list given of Ireland's library, the contents of which were brought into disrepute by the remarkable literary forgeries of the son, but stands forth peculiar and unique, and furnishes much room for curious speculation." — (148–51.)

a sketch — and surely a tempting one — of a New York interior: —

"Mr. Burton's library contains nearly sixteen thousand volumes. Its proprietor had constructed for its accommodation and preservation a three-story fire-proof building, about thirty feet square, which is isolated from all other buildings, and is connected with his residence in Hudson Street by a conservatory gallery. The chief library-room occupies the upper floor of this building, and is about twenty-five feet in height. Its ceiling presents a series of groined rafters, after the old English style, in the centre of which rises a dome-skylight of stained glass. The sides of the library are fitted up with thirty-six oak book-cases of a Gothic pattern, which entirely surround it, and are nine feet in height. The space between the ceiling and the book-cases is filled with paintings, for the most part of large size, and said to be of value. Specimens of armor and busts of distinguished authors decorate appropriate compartments, and in a prominent niche, at the head of the apartment, stands a full-length statue of Shakespeare, executed by Thom, in the same style as the Tam o' Shanter and Old Mortality groups of this Scotch sculptor.

"The great specialty of the library is its Shakespeare collection; but, although very extensive and valuable, it by no means engrosses the entire library, which contains a large number of valuable works in several departments of literature.

"The number of lexicons and dictionaries is large, and among the latter may be found all the rare old English works so valuable for reference. Three book-cases are devoted to serials, which contain many of the standard reviews and magazines. One case is appropriated to voyages and travels, in which are found many valuable ones. In another are upwards of one hundred volumes of table-talk, and numerous works on the fine arts and bibliography. One book-case is devoted to choice works on America, among which is Sebastian Munster's Cosmographia Totius Orbis Regionum, published in folio at Basle in 1537, which contains full notes of Columbus, Vespucci, and other early voyagers. Another department contains a curious catalogue of authorities relating to Crime and Punishment; a liberal space is devoted to Facetiæ, another to American Poetry, and also one to Natural and Moral Philosophy. The standard works of Fiction, Biography, Theology, and the Drama, are all represented.

"There is a fair collection of classical authors, many of which are of Aldine and Elzevir editions. Among the rarities in this department is a folio copy of Plautus, printed at Venice in 1518, and illustrated with woodcuts."

The author thus coming upon a Roman writer of plays, named Plautus, favors us with an account of him, which it is unnecessary to pursue, since it by no means possesses the interest attached to his still-life sketches. Let us pass on and take a peep at the collection of Chancellor Kent, known in this country as the author of Kent's Commentaries[1]: —

"To a lawyer, the Chancellor's written remarks on his books are, perhaps, their most interesting feature. He studied pen in hand, and all of his books contain his annotations, and some are literary curiosities. His edition of Blackstone's Commentaries is the first American edition, printed in

[1] [Again the author errs. The library in question was that of the late Judge Kent, the son of Chancellor Kent. The library of the son naturally included that of the father. It is, perhaps, too much to expect that even so intelligent and well-informed a subject of Her Majesty as the writer of this book should know that Chancellor Kent died in 1847, at the advanced age of eighty-four years; but still the Chancellor was known so long ago throughout Great Britain as the author of Kent's Commentaries, that it would seem as if a moment's reflection would have decided the question rightly; although the article itself settled the point upon the best authority — that of Judge Kent himself. For there can be no impropriety in saying here, what has long been generally known in literary circles, that in the preparation of several of the articles in "The Private Libraries," the author had the advantage of assistance from the pens of the owners of the collections, and that in two or three instances the whole, or nearly the whole, article was thus written, subject, of course, to his after supervision. The description of Judge Kent's library bears unmistakable marks of his own hand. The passage, quoted by our author, in which it is remarked as to the prison and scaffold literature, (and, by the way, why should there not be a club — the Selwyn, of course — for the reprinting of this?) that "the Chancellor is not responsible for this part of the library, which owes its completeness to the morbid taste of his successor," is one which Dr. Wynne is too courteous and too good-natured to have written; but the sly humor of writing it about himself is perfectly in Judge Kent's manner. This library, though marshalled among those of New York, was at Judge Kent's house at Fishkill Landing, seventy-five miles away. — W.]

Philadelphia in 1771. It is creditable to the press of that time, and is overlaid with annotations, showing how diligently the future American commentator studied the elegant work of his English predecessor. The general reader will find still more interest in the earlier judicial reports of the State of New York, printed while he was on the bench. He will find not merely legal notes, but biographical memoranda of many of the distinguished judges and lawyers who lived at the commencement of the century, and built up the present system of laws.

"In proceeding from the legal to the miscellaneous part of the library, the visitor's attention will, perhaps, be attracted by an extensive and curious collection of the records of criminal law. Not merely the English state trials and the French *causes célèbres* are there, but the criminal trials of Scotland and of America, and detached publications of remarkable cases, Newgate Calendars, Malefactors' Register, Chronicles of Crime, with ghastly prints of Newgate and Old Bailey, with their executions. The Chancellor is not responsible for this part of the library, which owes its completeness to the morbid taste of his successor, who defends the collection as best illustrating the popular morals and manners of every period, and contends that fiction yields in interest to the gloomy dramas of real life."

The practice attributed to the Chancellor of annotating his books is looked on by collectors as in the general case a crime which should be denied benefit of clergy. What is often said, however, of other crimes may be said of this, that if the perpetrator be sufficiently illustrious, it becomes a virtue. If Milton, for instance, had thought fit to leave his autograph annotations on the first folio Shakespeare, the offence would not only have been pardoned but applauded, greatly to the pecuniary benefit of any one so fortunate as to discover the treasure. But it would be highly dangerous for ordinary people to found on such an immunity. I remember being once shown by an indignant collector a set of utterly and hopelessly destroyed copies of rare tracts connected with the religious disputes of Queen Elizabeth's day, each inlaid and separately bound in a thin volume in the finest morocco, with the title lengthways along the back. These had been lent to a gentleman who deemed himself a distinguished poet, and he thought proper to write on the margin the sensations caused within him by the perusal of some of the more striking passages, certifying the genuineness of his autograph by his signature at full length in a bold distinct hand. He, worthy man, deemed that he was adding greatly to the value of the rarities; but had he beheld the owner's face on occasion of the discovery, he would have been undeceived.

There are in Dr. Wynne's book descriptions, not only of libraries according to their kind, but according to their stage of growth, from those which, as the work of a generation or two, have reached from ten to fifteen thousand, to the collections still in their youth, such as Mr. Lorimer Graham's of five thousand volumes, rich in early editions of British poetry, and doubtless, by this time, still richer, since its owner was lately here collecting early works on the literature of Scotland, and other memorials of the land of his fathers. Certainly, however, the most interesting of the whole is the library of the Rev. Dr. Magoon, "an eminent and popular divine of the Baptist Church." He entered on active life as an operative bricklayer. There are, it appears, wall-plates extant, and not a few, built by his hands, and it was only by saving the earnings these brought to him that he could obtain an education. When an English mechanic finds out that he has a call to the ministry, we can easily figure the grim ignorant fanatical ranter that comes forth as the result. If haply he is able to read, his library will be a few lean sheepskin-clad volumes, such as Boston's Crook in the Lot, Fisher's Marrow of Modern Divinity, Booth's Apples of Gold, Bolton's Saint's Enriching Examination, and Halyburton's Great Concern. The bricklayer, however, was endowed with the heavenly gift of the high æsthetic, which no birth or breeding can secure, and threw himself into that common ground where art and religion meet — the literature of Christian mediæval art. Things must, however, have greatly changed among our brethren since the days of Cotton Mather, or even of Jonathan Edwards, when a person in Dr. Magoon's position could embellish his private sanctuary in this fashion.

"The chief characteristic of the collection is its numerous works on the history, literature, and theory of art in general, and of Christian architecture in particular. There is scarcely a church, abbey, monastery, college, or cathedral; or picture, statue, or illumination, prominent in Christian art, extant in Italy, Germany, France, or the British Islands, that is not represented either by original drawings or in some other graphic form.

"In addition to these works, having especial reference to Christian art, are many full sets of folios depicting the leading galleries of ancient, mediæval, and modern art in general. Some of these, as the six elephant folios on the Louvre, are in superb bindings; while many others, among which are the Dresden Gallery and Retzsch's Outlines, derive an additional value from once having formed a part of the elegant collection of William Reginald Courtenay.

"But what renders this collection particularly valuable, is its large number of original drawings by eminent masters which accompany the written and engraved works. Amongst these are two large sepia drawings, by Amici, of the Pantheon and St. Peter's at Rome. These drawings were engraved and published with several others by Ackermann. Both the originals, and the engravings executed from them, are in the collection. The original view near the Basilica of St. Marco, by Samuel Prout, the engraving of which is in Finden's Byron, and the interior of St. Marco, by Luke Price, the engraving of which is in Price's Venice Illustrated, grace the collection. There is likewise a superb general view of Venice, by Wyld; a fine exterior view of Rheims Cathedral, by Buckley; an exterior view of St. Peter's at Caën, by Charles Vacher; and the interior of St. Germain des Prés at Paris, by Duval."

The early history of the American settlements is naturally the object around which many of these collections cluster; but the scraps of this kind of literature which have been secured have a sadly impoverished aspect in comparison with the luxurious stores which American money has attracted from the Old World.[1] Here one is forcibly reminded

[1] "This collection [Mr. Menzies'] contains four thousand volumes, and is for the most part in the English language. Its chief specialty consists in works on American history and early American printed books. Among the latter may be mentioned a series of the earliest works issued from the press in New York. Of these, is A Letter of Advice to a Young Gentleman, by R. L., printed and sold by William Bradford, in New York, 1696. Richard Lyon, the author, came early to this country, and officiated as a private tutor to a young English student at Cambridge, to whom the letter of advice was written. It is undoubtedly the earliest work which issued from the press in New York, and is so extremely rare, that it is questionable whether another copy is to be found in the State. There is a collection of tracts, comprised in seven volumes, written by the Rev. George Keith, and published by Bradford, at New York, 1702–4. Keith was born in Scotland, and settled in East Jersey, in the capacity of surveyor-general, in 1682. The several tracts in the collection are on religious subjects, and are controversial in their char-

of those elements in the old-established libraries of Europe which no wealth or zeal can achieve elsewhere, because the commodity is not in the market.

America had just one small old library, and the lamentation over the loss of this ewe-lamb is touching evidence of her poverty in such possessions. The Harvard Library dates from the year 1638. In 1764 the college buildings were burned, and though books are not easily consumed, yet the small collection of five thousand volumes was easily overwhelmed in the general ruin. So were destroyed many books from the early presses of the mother country, and many of the firstlings of the transatlantic printers; and though its bulk was but that of an ordinary country squire's collection, the loss has been always considered national and irreparable.

It is, after all, a rather serious consideration — which it never seems as yet to have occurred to any

acter. As early specimens of printing, and as models of the manner in which the religious controversies of the day were conducted, they are both instructive and curious. In addition to these is a work entitled The Rebuker Rebuked, by Daniel Leeds, 1703; A Sermon preached at Kingston, in Jamaica, by William Corbin, 1703; The Great Mystery of Foxcraft, by Daniel Leeds, 1705; A Sermon preached at Trinity Church, in New York, by John Sharp, 1706; An Alarm Sounded to the Inhabitants of the World, by Bath Bowers, 1709; and Lex Parliamentaria, 1716. All the above works were printed by Bradford, the earliest New York publisher, aud one of the earliest printers in America. They constitute, perhaps, the most complete collection in existence of the publications of this early typographer. The whole are in an excellent state of preservation, and are nearly, if not quite, unique."

one to revolve — how entirely the new States of the West and the South seem to be cut off from the literary resources which the Old World possesses in her old libraries. Whatever light lies hidden beneath the bushel in these venerable institutions, seems forever denied to the students and inquirers of the new empire rising in the antipodes, and consequently to the minds of the people at large who receive impressions from students and inquirers. Books can be reprinted, it is true; but where is the likelihood that seven hundred thousand old volumes will be reprinted to put the Astorian Library on a par with the Imperial? Well, perhaps some quick and cheap way will be found of righting it all when we have got a tunnel to Australia, and are shot through it by something only a shade less instantaneous than the electric telegraph.[1]

In the mean time, what a lesson do these matters impress on us of the importance of preserving

[1] [These apprehensions of a narrow literary future for us of the New World are entertained in a truly philosophic and kindly spirit. But they are based, I think, on an exaggerated estimate of our privations. Not that the author overrates the value of the real treasures which have been heaped up by Time on the other continent; but that he, perhaps, rates much as treasure which is really rubbish, and regards it as more inaccessible to us than it actually is. And although his figures are correct, they leave a very false impression. Choosing, very properly, for his illustration the greatest library of the world, the Imperial Library at Paris, (poor great library! once Royal, then National, then Imperial, then Royal again, again National, and again Imperial; and all this within the memory of one man!) he asks, What is the likelihood that 700,000 old volumes will be reprinted to put the Astor Library on a par with it? There is none. But

old books! Government and legislation have done little, if anything, in Britain, towards this object,

let us see. The British Ambassador at Paris ascertained in 1850 that the number of "printed books" in the great French library was 700,000. But were all these rare, not to say unique, or scarce, or "old volumes," or even out of print? No man who knows anything of the history of books could seriously entertain the question. These 700,000 volumes, one half of which were acquired in the present century, (see Edwards's "Memoirs of Libraries," Vol. II., p. 281,) represent the literature of the whole world, from the invention of printing to the year 1850. There are not only duplicates and triplicates and quadruplicates, but whole editions of most of them scattered over the face of the earth; and our full share, at least, is in this country. But then there *are* uniques and extremely rare volumes, which can be found only there and in two or three other places? Certainly; and many of them are intrinsically of what may be called priceless value. But I venture the conjecture, that, casting aside those multitudinous books which, in the words of a British critic, "are rare now because they were always worthless," there are not one thousand printed volumes in the Imperial Library, the Library of the British Museum, and the Bodleian together, which have not yet been reprinted, and which are so rare that we may not reasonably expect to have a copy or copies of them in this country within the next fifty years. And as to the reprinting of a thousand volumes, if it were found very desirable for the interests of literature here, a few gentlemen would meet together and settle that matter very quickly; always supposing that our friends of the Museum, the Bodleian, and the Imperial, did not refuse permission to a sharing, even without a diminution, of their treasures. The great and ever unapproachable superiority of the Imperial Library, that of the Vatican, the British Museum, and a few others of their class, is in their ancient manuscripts, gathered from monasteries and other like depositories throughout Europe, in Syria, the Levant, and Egypt. These will never be printed; and although it is possible that in the advancement of art, and the more doubtful increase and spread of international comity and fellowship in letters, a few of them may be photographed, still it seems quite certain that this mountain cannot

beyond the separate help that may have been extended to individual public libraries, and the Copy-

come to Mahomet. But it is not so clear that Mahomet cannot go to the mountain. It would seem as if Sanscrit were one of the chief among the fields of literature from which we of the New World are shut out by our position. And yet I have been told on European authority that the one man to whom no other oriental scholar can teach more Sanscrit is native here, and is now living in New England. One of my own friends, on a casual meeting, the first in two or three years, spoke quite slightingly of studies in English literature of the Elizabethan period, which he heard I was pursuing. He thought that they had had their day, and that Shakespeare was obsolete. "And what have you been about this long time?" I asked; for I knew that he was bookish. "Oh, I've been giving myself up heart and soul to Coptic. I've been studying in Paris. I shall go to Egypt very soon." He could afford it; and he went before the month was out. But was it not left for Prescott of Massachusetts to spread out manuscripts before closed to the world, and first exhibit in their true aspect the ambiguous glories of the reign of Ferdinand and Isabella, and the darker, sterner record of the deeds of Cortez? Did not Motley of New York in like manner throw a flood of new light upon the struggles for liberty in the Netherlands? Has not the first truly philosophical history of the development of our language just been written by George P. Marsh of Vermont, now United States Minister at Turin? and is not the principal text-book for the study of English now used in Great Britain a mere reprint, with an Introduction and notes by the British editor, of the same thorough and thoughtful scholar's course of lectures, first delivered and printed in New York? We do not boast of these things, or of others of their kind, or even silently over-estimate their importance, which we take at European rating. Yet we may venture to ask, Have British scholars, with all their advantages and superiority, accomplished within the same time and in similar fields, anything so very much better? It yet remains, however, that even if these fruits of research were far more numerous and important than they are, they are not those results of the explorations of special scholarship into the wilderness of codices and palimpsests, which

right Act deposits. Of general measures, it is possible to point out some which have been injurious, by leading to the dispersal or destruction of books. The house and window duties have done this to a large extent. As this statement may not be quite self-evident, a word in explanation may be appropriate. The practice of the department having charge of the Assessed Taxes has been, when any furniture was left in an unoccupied house, to levy the duty — to exempt only houses entirely empty. It was a consequence of this that when, by minority, family decay, or otherwise, a mansion-house had to be shut up, there was an inducement entirely to gut it of its contents, including the library. The same cause, by the way, has been more destructive still to furniture, and may be said to have lost to our posterity the fashions of a generation or two. Tables, chairs, and cabinets first grow unfashionable, and then old; in neither stage have they any friends who will comfort or support them — they are still worse off than books. But then comes an after-stage, in which they revive as antiquities, and become exceeding precious. As Pompeiis, however, are rare in the world, the chief repositories of antique furniture have been man-

perhaps were, after all, what the author had specially in mind. And of that work we shall not do too much. If any one of us is bent upon it, be sure that it will go hard but he shall find a way of doing it. Those who are impelled to such tasks, because they are born to no other, will be put in the way of their desire. And these will be enough. It is not well to have too many young men think Shakespeare obsolete, and go down into Egypt

sions shut up for a generation or two, which, after more fashions than generations have passed away, are reopened to the light of day, either in consequence of the revival of the fortunes of their old possessors, or of their total extinction and the entry of new owners. How the house and window duties disturbed this silent process by which antiques were created is easily perceived.

One service our Legislature has done for the preservation of books, in the copies which require to be deposited under the Copyright Act at Stationers' Hall for the privileged libraries. True, this has been effected somewhat in the shape of a burden upon authors, for the benefit of that posterity which has done no more for them specially than it has for other people of the present generation. But in its present modified shape the burden should not be grudged, in consideration of the magnitude of the benefit to the people of the future — a benefit, the full significance of which it probably requires a little consideration to estimate. The right of receiving a copy of every book from Stationers' Hall has generally been looked on as a benefit to the library receiving it. The benefit, however, was but lightly esteemed by some of these

to devote themselves heart and soul to Coptic. The great mass of us, including the intelligent and the cultivated, can be better occupied within our own borders in so living and laboring as simple citizens of the Republic, that our example may hasten the time when peace, truth, justice, and good-will shall reign, and only they shall reign, — as when they do reign they must reign, — throughout all the world. — W.]

institutions, the directors of which represented that they were thus pretty well supplied with the unsalable rubbish, while the valuable publications slipped past them ; and, on the whole, they would sell their privilege for a very small annual sum, to enable them to go into the market and buy such books, old and new, as they might prefer. The view adopted by the law, however, was, that the depositing of these books created an obligation if it conferred a privilege, the institution receiving them having no right to part with them, but being bound to preserve them as a record of the literature of the age.[1]

[1] I am not aware that in the blue-books, or any other source of public information, there is any authenticated statement of the quantity of literature which the privileged libraries receive through the Copyright Act. The information would afford a measure of the fertility of the British press. It is rather curious, that for a morsel of this kind of ordinary modern statistics, one must have recourse to so scholarly a work as the quarto volume of the *Præfationes et Epistolæ Editionibus Principibus Auctorum Veterum præpositæ, curante Beriah Botfield, A.M.* The editor of that noble quarto obtained a return from Mr. Winter Jones, of the number of deposits in the British Museum from 1814 to 1860. Counting the "pieces," as they are called—that is, every volume, pamphlet, page of music, and other publication — the total number received in 1814 was 378. It increased by steady gradation until 1851, when it reached 9871. It then got an impulse, from a determination more strictly to enforce the Act, and next year the number rose to 13,934, and in 1859 it reached 28,807. In this great mass, the number of books coming forth complete in one volume or more is roundly estimated at 5000, but a quantity of the separate numbers and parts which go to make up the total, are elementary portions of books, giving forth a certain number of completed volumes annually. From the same authority, it appears that the total number of publica-

If the rule come ever to be thoroughly enforced, it will then come to pass that of every book that is printed in Britain, good or bad, five copies shall be preserved in the shelves of so many public libraries, slumbering there in peace, or tossed about by impatient readers, as the case may be. For the latter there need not perhaps be much anxiety; it is for the sake of those addicted to slumbering in peaceful obscurity that this refuge is valuable. There is thus at least a remnant saved from the relentless trunk-maker. If the day of resuscitation from the long slumber should arrive, we know where to find the

tions which issued from the French press in 1858 was estimated at 13,000; but this includes "sermons, pamphlets, plays, pieces of music, and engravings." In the same year the issues from the German press, Austria not included, are estimated at 10,000, all apparently actual volumes, or considerable pamphlets. Austria in 1855 published 4673 volumes and parts. What a contrast to all this it must be to live in sleepy Norway, where the annual literary prowess produces 146 volumes! In Holland the annual publications approach 2000. "During the year 1854, 861 works in the Russian language, and 451 in foreign languages, were printed in Russia; besides 2940 scientific and literary treatises in the different periodicals." The number of works anywhere published is, however, no indication of the number of books put in circulation, since some will have to be multiplied by tens, others by hundreds, and others by thousands. We know that there is an immense currency of literature in the American States, yet, of the quantity of literature issued there, the Publishers' Circular for February, 1859, gives the following meagre estimate:—"There were 912 works published in America during 1858. Of these 177 were reprints from England, 35 were new editions, and 10 were translations from the French or German. The new American works thus number only 690, and among them are included sermons, pamphlets, and letters, whereas the reprints are in most cases *bonâ fide* books."

book — in a privileged library. The recollection just now occurs to me of a man of unquestionable character and scholarship, who wrote a suitable and intelligent book on an important subject, and at his own expense had it brought into the world by a distinguished publisher, prudently intimating on the title-page that he reserved the right of translation. Giving the work all due time to find its way, he called at the Row, exactly a year after the day of publication, to ascertain the result. He was presented with a perfectly succinct account of charge and discharge, in which he was credited with three copies sold. Now, he knew that his family had bought two copies, but he never could find out who it was that had bought the third. The one mind into which his thoughts had thus passed, remained ever mysteriously undiscoverable. Whether or not he consoled himself with the reflection that what might have been diffused over many was concentrated in one, it is consolatory to others to reflect that such a book stands on record in the privileged libraries, to come forth to the world if it be wanted.

Nor is the resuscitation of a book unsuited to its own age, but suited to another, entirely unexampled. That beautiful poem called Albania was reprinted by Leyden, from a copy preserved somewhere: so utterly friendless had it been in its obscurity, that the author's history, and even his name, were unknown; and though it at once excited the high admiration of Scott, no scrap of intelligence concerning it could be discovered in any quarter contemporary with its first publication. The Discourse on Trade by Roger North, the author of the amusing Lives of Lord-Keeper Guildford and his other two brothers, was lately reprinted from a copy in the British Museum, supposed to be the only one existing. Though neglected in its own day, it has been considered worthy of attention in this, as promulgating some of the principles of our existing philosophy of trade. On the same principle, some rare tracts on political economy and trade were lately reprinted by a munificent nobleman, who thought the doctrines contained in them worthy of preservation and promulgation. The Spirit of Despotism, by Vicesimus Knox, was reprinted, at a time when its doctrines were popular, from a single remaining copy: the book, though instructive, is violent and declamatory, and it is supposed that its author discouraged or endeavored to suppress its sale after it was printed.[1]

In the public duty of creating great libraries, and generally of preserving the literature of the world from being lost to it, the collector's or book-hunter's services are great and varied. In the first place, many of the great public libraries have been absolute donations of the treasures to which some en-

[1] I once heard an odd anecdote about this book. A traveller who had it in his luggage, passing the Austrian frontier, was, much to his astonishment, allowed to retain it. To his equal astonishment, the book beside it, being Combe on the Constitution of Man, was prohibited — the word "constitution" was sufficient to condemn this profound volume.

thusiastic literary sportsman has devoted his life and fortune. Its gradual accumulation has been the great solace and enjoyment of his active days; he has beheld it, in his old age, a splendid monument of enlightened exertion, and he resolves that, when he can no longer call it his own, it shall preserve the relics of past literature for ages yet to come, and form a centre whence scholarship and intellectual refinement shall diffuse themselves around. We can see this influence in its most specific and material shape, perhaps, by looking round the reading-room of the British Museum — that great manufactory of intellectual produce, where so many heads are at work. The beginning of this great institution, as everybody knows, was in the fifty thousand volumes collected by Sir Hans Sloane — a wonderful achievement for a private gentleman at the beginning of the last century. When George III. gave it the libraries of the kings of England, it gained, as it were, a better start still by absorbing collections which had begun before Sloane was born — those of Cranmer, Prince Henry, and Casaubon. The Ambrosian Library at Milan was the private collection of Cardinal Borromeo, bequeathed by him to the world. It reached forty thousand volumes ere he died, and these formed a library which had arisen in free, natural, and symmetrical growth, insomuch as, having fed it during his whole life, it began with the young and economic efforts of youth and poverty, and went on accumulating in bulk and in the costliness of its contents as succeeding years brought wealth and honors to the great prelate. What those merchant princes, the Medici, did for the Laurentian Library at Florence is part of history. Old Cosmo, who had his mercantile and political correspondents in all lands, made them also his literary agents, who thus sent him goods too precious to be resold even at a profit. "He corresponded," says Gibbon, "at once with Cairo and London, and a cargo of Indian spices and Greek books were often imported by the same vessel." The Bodleian started with a collection which had cost Sir Thomas Bodley, £10,000, and it was augmented from time to time by the absorption of tributary influxes of the same kind.[1]

In many instances the collectors, whose stores have thus gone to the public, have merely followed their book-hunting propensities, without having the merit of framing the ultimate destiny of their collections, but in others the intention of doing benefit to the world has added zest and energy to the chase. Of this class there is one memorable and beautiful instance in Richard of Bury, Bishop of Durham, who lived and labored so early as the days of Edward III., and has left an autobiographical sketch infinitely valuable, as at once informing us of the social habits, and letting us into the very inner life, of the highly endowed student and the affluent col-

[1] The most complete mass of information which we probably possess in the English language about the history of libraries, both home and foreign, is in the two octavos called Memoirs of Libraries, including a Handbook of Library Concerns, by Edward Edwards.

lector of the fourteenth century. His little book, called Philobiblion, was first printed at Cologne in the fifteenth century. An English translation of it was published in 1832. It is throughout adorned with the gentle and elevated nature of the scholar, and derives a still nobler lustre from the beneficent purpose to which the author destined the literary relics which it was the enjoyment of his life to collect and study. Being endowed with power and wealth, and putting to himself the question, "What can I render to the Lord for all that he hath conferred on me?" he found an answer in the determination of smoothing the path of the poor and ardent student, by supplying him with the means of study. "Behold," he says, "a herd of outcasts rather than of elect scholars meets the view of our contemplations, in which God the artificer, and nature his handmaid, have planted the roots of the best morals and most celebrated sciences. But the penury of their private affairs so oppresses them, being opposed by adverse fortune, that the fruitful seeds of virtue, so productive in the unexhausted field of youth, unmoistened by their wonted dews, are compelled to wither. Whence it happens, as Boetius says, that bright virtue lies hid in obscurity, and the burning lamp is not put under a bushel, but is utterly extinguished for want of oil. Thus the flowery field in spring is ploughed up before harvest; thus wheat gives way to tares, the vine degenerates to woodbine, and the olive grows wild and unproductive." Keenly alive to this want, he resolved to devote himself, not merely to supply to the hungry the necessary food, but to impart to the poor and ardent scholar the mental sustenance which might possibly enable him to burst the bonds of circumstance, and, triumphing over his sordid lot, freely communicate to mankind the blessings which it is the function of cultivated genius to distribute.

The Bishop was a great and powerful man, for he went over Europe commissioned as the spiritual adviser of the great conqueror, Edward III. Wherever he went on public business — to Rome, France, or the other states of Europe — "on tedious embassies and in perilous times," he carried about with him "that fondness for books which many waters could not extinguish," and gathered up all that his power, his wealth, and his vigilance brought within his reach. In Paris he becomes quite ecstatic: "Oh blessed God of Gods in Zion! what a rush of the glow of pleasure rejoiced our heart as often as we visited Paris — the Paradise of the world! There we longed to remain, where, on account of the greatness of our love, the days ever appeared to us to be few. There are delightful libraries in cells redolent of aromatics — there flourishing greenhouses of all sorts of volumes: there academic meads trembling with the earthquake of Athenian peripatetics pacing up and down: there the promontories of Parnassus and the porticos of the stoics."

The most powerful instrument in his policy was

encouraging and bringing round him as dependents and followers, the members of the mendicant orders — the laborers called to the vineyard in the eleventh hour, as he calls them. These he set to cater for him, and he triumphantly asks, "Among so many of the keenest hunters, what leveret could lie hid? What fry could evade the hook, the net, or the trawl of these men? From the body of divine law down to the latest controversial tract of the day, nothing could escape the notice of these scrutinizers." In further revelations of his method he says, "When, indeed, we happened to turn aside to the towns and places where the aforesaid paupers had convents, we were not slack in visiting their chests and other repositories of books; for there, amidst the deepest poverty, we found the most exalted riches treasured up; there, in their satchels and caskets, we discovered not only the crumbs that fell from the master's table for the little dogs, but, indeed, the shew-bread without leaven — the bread of angels containing all that is delectable." He specially marks the zeal of the Dominicans as preachers; and in exulting over his success in the field, he affords curious glimpses into the ways of the various humble assistants who were glad to lend themselves to the hobby of one of the most powerful prelates of his day.[1]

[1] "Indeed, although we had obtained abundance both of old and new works, through an extensive communication with all the religious orders, yet we must in justice extol the Preachers with a special commendation in this respect; for we found them,

The manner in which Robert of Bury dedicated his stores to the intellectual nurture of the poor

above all other religious devotees, ungrudging of their most acceptable communications, and overflowing with a certain divine liberality; we experienced them not to be selfish hoarders, but meet professors of enlightened knowledge. Besides all the opportunities already touched upon, we easily acquired the notice of the stationers and librarians, not only within the provinces of our native soil, but of those dispersed over the kingdoms of France, Germany, and Italy, by the prevailing power of money; no distance whatever impeded, no fury of the sea deterred them; nor was cash wanting for their expenses, when they sent or brought us the wished-for books; for they knew to a certainty that their hopes reposed in our bosoms could not be disappointed, but ample redemption, with interest, was secure with us. Lastly, our common captivatrix of the love of all men (money), did not neglect the rectors of country schools, nor the pedagogues of clownish boys, but rather, when we had leisure to enter their little gardens and paddocks, we culled redolent flowers upon the surface, and dug up neglected roots (not, however, useless to the studious), and such coarse digests of barbarism, as with the gift of eloquence might be made sanative to the pectoral arteries. Amongst productions of this kind, we found many most worthy of renovation, which, when the foul rust was skilfully polished off, and the mask of old age removed, deserved to be once more remodelled into comely countenances, and which we, having applied a sufficiency of the needful means, resuscitated for an exemplar of future resurrection, having in some measure restored them to renewed soundness. Moreover, there was always about us in our halls no small assemblage of antiquaries, scribes, bookbinders, correctors, illuminators, and, generally, of all such persons as were qualified to labor advantageously in the service of books.

"To conclude. All of either sex, of every degree, estate, or dignity, whose pursuits were in any way connected with books, could, with a knock, most easily open the door of our heart, and find a convenient reposing place in our bosom. We so admitted all who brought books, that neither the multitude of first-comers

scholar, was by converting them into a library for Durham College, which merged into Trinity of Oxford. It would have been a pleasant thing to look upon the actual collection of manuscripts which awakened so much recorded zeal and tenderness in the great ecclesiastic of five hundred years ago; but in later troubles they became dispersed, and all that seems to be known of their whereabouts is, that some of them are in the library of Baliol.[1] Another eminent English prelate made a worthy, but equally ineffectual, attempt to found a great university library. This was the Rev. John Fisher, Bishop of Rochester, who gave what was called "the noblest library in England" to the newly-founded college of St. John's. It was not a bequest. To make his gift secure, it was made over directly to the college, but as he could not part with his favorites while he lived, he borrowed the whole back for life. This is probably the most extensive book loan ever negotiated; but the Reformation, and his tragic destiny, were coming on apace, and the books were lost both to himself and his favorite college.[2]

could produce a fastidiousness of the last, nor the benefit conferred yesterday be prejudicial to that of to-day. Wherefore, as we were continually resorted to by all the aforesaid persons, as to a sort of adamant attractive of books, the desired accession of the vessels of science, and a multifarious flight of the best volumes were made to us. And this is what we undertook to relate at large in the present chapter."

[1] Edwards on Libraries, vol. i. p. 586.

[2] Ibid. p. 609.

The Preservation of Literature.

HE benefactors whose private collections have, by a generous act of endowment, been thus rendered at the same time permanent and public, could be counted by hundreds. It is now, however, my function to describe a more subtle, but no less powerful influence, which the book-hunter exercises in the preservation and promulgation of literature, through the mere exercise of that instinct or passion which makes him what he is here called. What has been said above must have suggested— if it was not seen before—how great a pull it gives to any public library, that it has had an early start; and how hard it is, with any amount of wealth and energy, to make up for lost time, and raise a later institution to the level of its senior. The Imperial Library of Paris, which has so marvellously lived through all the storms that have swept round its walls, was founded in the fourteenth century. It began, of course, with manuscripts; possessing, before the beginning of the fifteenth century, the then enormous number of a thousand volumes. The reason, however, of its present greatness, so far beyond the rivalry of later establishments, is, that it was in active operation at the birth of printing, and received the first-born of the press. There they have been sheltered and preserved, while their un-

protected brethren, tossed about in the world outside, have long disappeared, and passed out of existence forever.

It is a common notion, which has been floated off from time to time, inflated with every variety of rhetorical gas, that, since the age of printing, no book once put to press has ever died. The notion is quite inconsistent with fact. When we count by hundreds of thousands the books that are in the Paris Library, and not to be had for the British Museum, we see the number of books which a chance refuge has caught up from the general destruction, and can readily see, in shadowy bulk, though we cannot estimate in numbers, the great mass which, having found no refuge, have disappeared out of separate existence, and been mingled up with the other elements of the earth's crust.

We have many accounts of the marvellous preservation of books, after they have become rare — the snatching of them as brands from the burning; their hairbreadth-'scapes i' the imminent deadly breach. It would be interesting, also, to have some account of the progress of destruction among books. A work dedicated apparently to this object, which I have been unable to find in the body, is mentioned under a very tantalizing title. It is by a certain John Charles Conrad Oelrichs, author of several scraps of literary history, and is called a Dissertation concerning the Fates of Libraries and Books, and, in the first place, concerning the books that have been eaten — such I take to be the meaning of Dissertatio de Bibliothecarum ac Librorum Fatis, imprimis libris comestis.[1] This is nearly as tantalizing as the wooden-legged Britisher's explanation to the inquisitive Yankee, who solemnly engaged to ask not another question were he told how that leg was lost, and was accordingly told that "it was bitten off."

Religious and political intolerance has, as all the world knows, been a terrible enemy to literature, not only by absolute suppression, but by the restraints of the licenser. So little was literary freedom indeed understood anywhere until recent days, that it was only by an accident, after the Revolution, that the licensing of books was abolished in England. The new licenser, Edmond Bohun, happened in fact to be a Jacobite, and though he professed to conform to the Revolution settlement, his sympathies with the exiled house disabled him from detecting disaffection skilfully smothered, and the House of Commons, in a rage, abolished his office by refusing to renew the licensing act. Of the extent to which literature has suffered by suppression, there are no data for a precise estimate. It might bring out some curious results, however, were

[1] [The author's perplexity is caused by a mere shade of meaning. The good Oelrichs plainly refers to books which have been devoured; as we know, from the publishers' advertisements and the assurances of young ladies, that many books are, every year. This book, and particularly the pages on which these notes are written, will be eagerly devoured by an intelligent public, and so pass to a place among the *libri comesti.* — W.]

any investigator to tell us of the books which had been effectually put down after being in existence. It would, of course, be found that the weak were crushed, while the strong flourished. Among the valuable bibliographical works of Peignot, is a dictionary of books which have been condemned to the flames, suppressed, or censured. We do not require to go far through his alphabet to see how futile the burnings and condemnations have been in their effect on the giants of literature. The first name of all is that of Abelard, and so going on we pick up the witty scamp Aretin, then pass on to D'Aubigné, the great warrior and historian, Bayle, Beaumarchais, Boulanger, Catullus, Charron, Condillac, Crébillon, and so on, down to Voltaire and Wicliffe.

Wars and revolutions have of course done their natural work on many libraries, yet the mischief effected by them has often been more visible than real, since they have tended rather to dispersion than destruction. The total loss to literature by the dispersion of the libraries of the monastic establishments in England, is probably not nearly so great as that which has accompanied the chronic mouldering away of the treasures preserved so obstinately by the lazy monks of the Levant, who were found by Mr. Curzon at their public devotions laying down priceless volumes which they could not read to protect their dirty feet from the cold floor. In the wildest times the book repository often partakes in the good fortune of the humble student whom the storm passes over. In the hour of danger too, some friend who keeps a quiet eye upon its safety may interpose at the critical moment. The treasures of the French libraries were certainly in terrible danger when Robespierre had before him the draft of a decree, that "the books of the public libraries of Paris and the departments should no longer be permitted to offend the eyes of the republic by shameful marks of servitude." The word would have gone forth, and a good deal beyond the mere marks of servitude would have been doubtless destroyed, had not the emergency called forth the courage and energies of Renouard and Didot.[1]

There are probably false impressions abroad as to the susceptibility of literature to destruction by fire. Books are not good fuel, as, fortunately, many a housemaid has found, when, among other frantic efforts and failures in fire-lighting, she has reasoned from the false data of the inflammability of a piece of paper. In the days when heretical books were burned, it was necessary to place them on large wooden stages, and after all the pains taken to demolish them, considerable readable masses were sometimes found in the embers; whence it was supposed that the devil, conversant in fire and its effects, gave them his special protection. In the end it was found easier and cheaper to burn the heretics themselves than their books.

Thus books can be burned, but they don't burn, and though in great fires libraries have been wholly

[1] See Edwards on Libraries, vol. ii. p. 272.

or partially destroyed, we never hear of a library making a great conflagration like a cotton mill or a tallow warehouse. Nay, a story is told of a house seeming irretrievably on fire, until the flames, coming in contact with the folio Corpus Juris and the Statutes at Large, were quite unable to get over this joint barrier, and sank defeated. When anything is said about the burning of libraries, Alexandria at once flares up in the memory; but it is strange how little of a satisfactory kind investigators have been able to make out, either about the formation or destruction of the many famous libraries collected from time to time in that city. There seems little doubt that Cæsar's auxiliaries unintentionally burnt one of them; its contents were probably written on papyrus, a material about as inflammable as dried reeds or wood-shavings. As to that other burning in detail, when the collection was used for fuel to the baths, and lasted some six weeks — surely never was there a greater victim of historical prejudice and calumny than the "ignorant and fanatical" Caliph Omar al Raschid. Over and over has his act been disproved, and yet it will continue to be re-asserted with uniform pertinacity in successive rolling sentences, all as like each other as the successive billows in a swell at sea. [1]

[1] One of the latest inquirers who has gone over the ground concludes his evidence thus: — "Omar ne vint pas à Alexandrie; et s'il y fut venu, il n'eut pas trouvé des livres à brûler. La bibliothèque n'existait plus depuis deux siècles et demi." — Fournier, L'Esprit dans l'Histoire.

Apart, however, from violence and accident, there is a constant decay of books from what might be called natural causes, keeping, like the decay of the human race, a proportion to their reproduction, which varies according to place or circumstance; here showing a rapid increase where production outruns decay, and there a decrease where the morbid elements of annihilation are stronger than the active elements of reproduction. Indeed, volumes are in their varied external conditions very like human beings. There are some stout and others frail — some healthy and others sickly; and it happens often that the least robust are the most precious. The full fresh health of some of the folio fathers and schoolmen, ranged side by side in solemn state on the oaken shelves of some venerable repository, is apt to surprise those who expect mouldy decay; the stiff hard binding is as angular as ever, — there is no abrasion of the leaves, not a single dog-ear or a spot, or even a dust-border on the mellowed white of the margin. So, too, of those quarto civilians and canonists of Leyden and Amsterdam, with their smooth white vellum coats, bearing so generic a resemblance to Dutch cheeses, that they might be supposed to represent the experiments of some Gouda dairyman on the quadrature of the circle. An easy life and an established position in society are the secret of their excellent preservation and condition. Their repose has been little disturbed by intrusive readers or unceremonious investigators, and their repute for solid learning has given them a claim to attention and careful preservation.

Though this is dwindling away, like many other conventional distinctions of rank, yet are authors of the present day not entirely divested of the opportunity of taking their place on the shelf like these old dignitaries. It would be as absurd, of course, to appear in folio as to step abroad in the small-clothes and queue of our great-grandfathers' day, and even quarto is reserved for science and some departments of the law. But then, on the other hand, octavos are growing as large as some of the folios of the seventeenth century, and a solid roomy-looking book is still practicable. Whoever desires to achieve a sure, though it may be but a humble, niche in the temple of fame, let him write a few solid volumes, with respectably sounding titles, and matter that will rather repel the reader than court him to such familiarity as may beget contempt. Such books are to the frequenter of a library like country gentlemen's seats to travellers, something to know the name and ownership of in passing. The stage-coachman of old use to proclaim each in succession — the guide-book tells them now. So do literary guide-books, in the shape of library-catalogues and bibliographies, tell of these steady and respectable mansions of literature. No one speaks ill of them, or even proclaims his ignorance of their nature, and your "man who knows everything" will profess some familiarity with them, the more readily that the verity of his pretensions is not likely to be tested. A man's name may have resounded for a time through all the newspapers as the gainer of a great victory or the speaker of marvellous speeches — he may have been the most brilliant wit of some distinguished social circle — the head of a great profession — even a leading statesman, yet his memory has utterly evaporated with the departure of his own generation. Had he but written one or two of these solid books, now, his name would have been perpetuated in catalogues and bibliographical dictionaries; nay, biographies and encyclopædias would contain their titles, and perhaps the day of the author's birth and death. Let those who desire posthumous fame, counting recollection as equivalent to fame, think of this.

It is with no desire to further the annihilation or decay of the stout and long-lived class of books of which I have been speaking, that I now draw attention to the book-hunter's services in the preservation of some that are of a more fragile nature, and are liable to droop and decay. We can see the process going on around us, just as we see other things travelling towards extinction. Look, for instance, at school-books, how rapidly and obviously they go to ruin. True, there are plenty of them, but save of those preserved in the privileged libraries, or of any that may be tossed aside among lumber in which they happen to remain until they become curiosities, what chance is there of any of them being in existence a century hence? Collectors know well the extreme rarity and value of ancient school-books. Nor is their value by any means fanciful. The dominie will tell us that they are old-fashioned, and the pedagogue who keeps a school, "and ca's it a acaudemy," will sneer at them as "obsolete and incompatible with the enlightened adjuncts of modern tuition;" but if we are to consider that the condition of the human intellect at any particular juncture is worth studying, it is certainly of importance to know on what food its infancy is fed. And so of children's play-books as well as their work-books; these are as ephemeral as their other toys. Retaining dear recollections of some that were the favorites, and desiring to awaken from them old recollections of careless boyhood, or perhaps to try whether your own children inherit the paternal susceptibility to their beauties, you make application to the bookseller — but, behold, they have disappeared from existence as entirely as the rabbits you fed, and the terrier that followed you with his cheery clattering bark. Neither name nor description — not the announcement of the benevolent publishers, "Darton, Harvey, and Darton" — can recover the faintest traces of their vestiges. Old cookery-books, almanacs, books of prognostication, directories for agricultural operations, guides to handicrafts, and other works of a practical nature, are infinitely valuable when they refer to remote times, and also infinitely rare.

But of course the most interesting of all are the relics of pure literature, of poems and plays.

Whence have arisen all the anxious searches and disappointments, and the bitter contests, and the rare triumphs, about the early editions of Shakespeare, separately or collectively, save from this, that they passed from one impatient hand to another, and were subjected to an unceasing greedy perusal, until they were at last used up and put out of existence? True it was to be with him—

> "So sinks the day-star in the ocean bed,
> And yet anon repairs his drooping head,
> And tricks his beams, and with new spangled ore,
> Flames in the forehead of the morning sky."

But his tuneful companions who had less vital power have lain like some ancient cemetery or buried city, in which antiquaries have been for a long age digging and searching for some fragment of intellectual treasure.

One book, and that the most read of all, was hedged by a sort of divinity which protected it, so far as that was practicable, from the dilapidating effects of use. The Bible seems to have been ever touched with reverent gentleness, and, when the sordid effects of long handling had become inevitably conspicuous, to have been generally removed out of sight, and, as it were, decently interred. Hence it is that, of the old editions of the Bible, the copies are so comparatively numerous and in such fine preservation. Look at those two folios from the types of Guttenburg and Fust, running so far back into the earliest stage of the art of printing, that of them is told the legend of a combination with the devil, which enabled one man to write so many copies identically the same. See how clean and spotless is the paper, and how black, glossy, and distinct the type, telling us how little progress printing has made since the days of its inventors, in anything save the greater rapidity with which, in consequence of the progress of machinery, it can now be executed.

The reason of the extreme rarity of the books printed by the early English printers is that, being very amusing, they were used up — thumbed out of existence. Such were Caxton's book of the Ordre of Chyualry; his Knyght of the Toure; the Myrour of the World; and the Golden Legende; Cocke Lorell's Bote, by De Worde; his Kalender of Shepeherdes, and such like. If any one feels an interest in the process of exhaustion, by which such treasures were reduced to rarity, he may easily witness it in the *debris* of a circulating library; and perhaps he will find the phenomenon in still more distinct operation at any book-stall where lie heaps of school-books, odd volumes of novels, and a choice of Watts's Hymns and Pilgrim's Progresses. Here, too, it is possible that the enlightened onlooker may catch sight of the book-hunter plying his vocation, much after the manner in which, in some ill-regulated town, he may have beheld the *chiffonniers*, at early dawn, rummaging among the cinder-heaps for ejected treasures. A ragged morsel is perhaps carefully severed from the heap, wrapped in paper to keep its leaves together, and deposited in the purchaser's pocket. You would probably find it difficult to recognize the fragment, if you should see it in the brilliancy of its resuscitation. A skilled and cautious workman has applied a bituminous solvent to its ragged edges, and literally incorporated, by a sort of paper-making process, each mouldering page into a broad leaf of fine strong paper, in which the print, according to a simile used for such occasions, seems like a small rivulet in a wide meadow of margin. This is termed inlaying, and is a very lofty department in the art of binding. Then there is, besides, the grandeur of russia or morocco, with gilding, and tooling, and marbling, and perhaps a ribbon marker, dangling out with a decoration at its end — all tending, like stars, and garters, and official robes, to stamp the outer insignia of importance on the book, and to warn all the world to respect it, and save it from the risks to which the common herd of literature is liable.[1]

[1] There is something exceedingly curious, not only in its bearing on the matter of the text, but as a record of some peculiar manners and habits of the fourteenth century, in Robert of Bury's injunctions as to the proper treatment of the manuscripts which were read in his day, and the signal contrast offered by the practice both of the clergy and laity to his decorous precepts.

"We not only set before ourselves a service to God in preparing volumes of new books, but we exercise the duties of a holy piety, if we first handle so as not to injure them, then return them to their proper places and commend them to undefiling custody, that they may rejoice in their purity while held in the hand, and repose in security when laid up in their repositories.

I have recourse to our old friend Monkbarns again for a brilliant description of the bibliophile, as the French politely call him, in the performance of the function assigned to him in the dispensation

Truly, next to the vestments and vessels dedicated to the body of the Lord, holy books deserve to be most decorously handled by the clergy, upon which injury is inflicted as often as they presume to touch them with a dirty hand. Wherefore, we hold it expedient to exhort students upon various negligences which can always be avoided, but which are wonderfully injurious to books.

"In the first place, then, let there be a mature decorum in opening and closing of volumes, that they may neither be unclasped with precipitous haste, nor thrown aside after inspection without being duly closed; for it is necessary that a book should be much more carefully preserved than a shoe. But school-folks are in general perversely educated, and, if not restrained by the rule of their superiors, are puffed up with infinite absurdities; they act with petulance, swell with presumption, judge of everything with certainty, and are unexperienced in anything.

"You will perhaps see a stiff-necked youth, lounging sluggishly in his study, while the frost pinches him in winter time, oppressed with cold, his watery nose drops, nor does he take the trouble to wipe it with his handkerchief till it has moistened the book beneath it with its vile dew. For such a one, I would substitute a cobbler's apron in the place of his book. He has a nail like a giant's, perfumed with stinking filth, with which he points out the place of any pleasant subject. He distributes innumerable straws in various places, with the ends in sight, that he may recall by the mark what his memory cannot retain. These straws, which the stomach of the book never digests, and which nobody takes out, at first distend the book from its accustomed closure, and, being carelessly left to oblivion, at last become putrid. He is not ashamed to eat fruit and cheese over an open book, and to transfer his empty cup from side to side upon it; and because he has not his alms-bag at hand, he leaves the rest of the fragments in his books. He never ceases to chatter with eternal garrulity to his companions; and while he adduces a

of things, — renewing my already recorded protest against the legitimacy of the commercial part of the transaction : —

"'Snuffy Davie bought the Game of Chess,

multitude of reasons void of physical meaning, he waters the book, spread out upon his lap, with the sputtering of his saliva. What is worse, he next reclines with his elbows on the book, and by a short study invites a long nap; and by way of repairing the wrinkles, he twists back the margins of the leaves, to the no small detriment of the volume. He goes out in the rain, and now flowers make their appearance upon our soil. Then the scholar we are describing, the neglecter rather than the inspector of books, stuffs his volume with firstling violets, roses, and quadrifoils. He will next apply his wet hands, oozing with sweat, to turning over the volumes, then beat the white parchment all over with his dusty gloves, or hunt over the page, line by line, with his forefinger covered with dirty leather. Then, as the flea bites, the holy book is thrown aside, which, however, is scarcely closed in a month, and is so swelled with the dust that has fallen into it, that it will not yield to the efforts of the closer.

"But impudent boys are to be specially restrained from meddling with books, who, when they are learning to draw the forms of letters, if copies of the most beautiful books are allowed them, begin to become incongruous annotators, and wherever they perceive the broadest margin about the text, they furnish it with a monstrous alphabet, or their unchastened pen immediately presumes to draw any other frivolous thing whatever that occurs to their imagination. There the Latinist, there the sophist, there every sort of unlearned scribe tries the goodness of his pen, which we have frequently seen to have been most injurious to the fairest volumes, both as to utility and price. There are also certain thieves who enormously dismember books by cutting off the side margins for letter-paper (leaving only the letters or text), or the fly-leaves put in for the preservation of the book, which they take away for various uses and abuses, which sort of sacrilege ought to be prohibited under a threat of anathema.

1474, the first book ever printed in England, from a stall in Holland, for about two groschen, or twopence of our money. He sold it to Osborne for twenty pounds, and as many books as came to twenty pounds more. Osborne resold this inimitable windfall to Dr. Askew for sixty guineas. At Dr. Askew's sale,' continued the old gentleman, kindling as he spoke, 'this inestimable treasure blazed forth in its full value, and was purchased by royalty itself for one hundred and seventy pounds! Could a copy now occur, Lord only knows,' he ejaculated, with a deep sigh and lifted-up hands, — 'Lord only knows what would be its ransom! — and yet it was originally secured, by skill

"But it is altogether befitting the decency of a scholar that washing should without fail precede reading, as often as he returns from his meals to study, before his fingers, besmeared with grease, loosen a clasp or turn over the leaf of a book. Let not a crying child admire the drawings in the capital letters, lest he pollute the parchment with his wet fingers, for he instantly touches whatever he sees.

"Furthermore, laymen, to whom it matters not whether they look at a book turned wrong side upwards or spread before them in its natural order, are altogether unworthy of any communion with books. Let the clerk also take order that the dirty scullion, stinking from the pots, do not touch the leaves of books unwashed; but he who enters without spot shall give his services to the precious volumes.

"The cleanliness of delicate hands, as if scabs and postules could not be clerical characteristics, might also be most important, as well to books as to scholars, who, as often as they perceive defects in books, should attend to them instantly, for nothing enlarges more quickly than a rent, as a fracture neglected at the time will afterwards be repaired with increased trouble."— Philobiblion, p. 101.

and research, for the easy equivalent of twopence sterling. Happy, thrice happy, Snuffy Davie!—and blessed were the times when thy industry could be so rewarded!'"

In such manner is it that books are saved from annihilation, and that their preservers become the feeders of the great collections in which, after their value is established, they find refuge; and herein it is that the class to whom our attention is at present devoted perform an inestimable service to literature. It is, as you will observe, the general ambition of the class to find value where there seems to be none, and this develops a certain skill and subtlety, enabling the operator, in the midst of a heap of rubbish, to put his finger on those things which have in them the latent capacity to become valuable and curious. The adept will at once intuitively separate from its friends the book that either is or will become curious. There must be something more than mere rarity to give it this value, although high authorities speak of the paucity of copies as being everything. David Clement, the illustrious French bibliographer, who seems to have anticipated the positive philosophy by an attempt to make bibliography, as the Germans have named it, one of the exact sciences, lays it down with authority, that "a book which it is difficult to find in the country where it is sought ought to be called simply *rare;* a book which it is difficult to find in any country may be called *very rare;* a book of which there are only fifty or sixty copies existing, or which appears so seldom as if there never had been more at any time than that number of copies, ranks as *extremely rare;* and when the whole number of copies does not exceed ten, this constitutes *excessive rarity*, or rarity in the highest degree." This has been received as a settled doctrine in bibliography; but it is utter pedantry. Books may be rare enough in the real or objective sense of the term, but if they are not so in the nominal or subjective sense, by being sought after, their rarity goes for nothing. A volume may be unique — may stand quite alone in the world — but whether it is so, or one of a numerous family, is never known, for no one has ever desired to possess it, and no one ever will.

But it is a curious phenomenon in the old-book trade, that rarities do not always remain rare; volumes seeming to multiply through some cryptogamic process, when we know perfectly that no additional copies are printed and thrown off. The fact is, that the rumor of scarcity, and value, and of a hunt after them, draws them from their hiding-places. If we may judge from the esteem in which they were once held, the Elzevirs must have been great rarities in this country; but they are now plentiful enough — the heavy prices in the British market having no doubt sucked them out of dingy repositories in Germany and Holland — so that, even in this department of commerce, the law of supply and demand is not entirely abrogated. He who dashes at all the books called rare, or even very rare, by Clement and his brethren, will be apt to suffer the keen disappointment of finding that there are many who participate with him in the possession of the same treasures. In fact, let a book but make its appearance in that author's Bibliothèque Curieuse, Historique, et Critique, ou Catalogue Raisonné de Livres difficiles à trouver; or in Graesses's Tresor de Livres Rares et Précieux — let it be mentioned as a rarity in Eibert's Allgemeines Bibliographisches Lexicon, or in Debure, Clement, Osmond, or the Repertorium Bibliographicum, — such proclamation is immediate notice to many fortunate possessors who were no more aware of the value of their dingy-looking volumes than Monsieur Jourdain knew himself to be in the habitual daily practice of talking prose.

So are we brought again back to the conclusion that the true book-hunter must not be a follower of any abstract external rules, but must have an inward sense and literary taste. It is not absolutely that a book is rare, or that it is run after, that must commend it to him, but something in the book itself. Hence the relics which he snatches from ruin will have some innate merits to recommend them. They will not be of that unhappy kind which nobody has desired to possess for their own sake, and nobody ever will. Something there will be of original genius, or if not that, yet of curious, odd, out of the way information, or of quaintness of imagination, or of characteristics pervading some class of men, whether a literary or a polemical, — something, in short, which people desirous of information will some day or other be anxious to read — such are the volumes which it is desirable to save from annihilation, that they may find their place at last in some of the great magazines of the world's literary treasures.

Librarians.

T will often be fortunate for these great institutions if they obtain the services of the hunter himself, along with his spoils of the chase. The leaders in the German wars often found it an exceedingly sound policy to subsidise into their own service some captain of free lances, who might have been a curse to all around him. Your great game-preservers sometimes know the importance of taking the most notorious poacher in the district into pay as a keeper. So it is sometimes of the nature of the book-hunter, if he be of the genial sort, and free of some of the more vicious peculiarities of his kind, to make an invaluable librarian. Such an arrangement will sometimes be found to be like mercy twice blessed, — it blesseth him that gives and him that takes. The imprisoned spirit probably finds freedom at last, and those purchases and accumulations which, to the private purse, were profuse and culpable recklessness, may become veritable duty; while the

wary outlook and the vigilant observation, which before were only leading a poor victim into temptation, may come forth as commendable attention and zealous activity.

Sometimes mistakes have been made in selections on this principle, and a zeal has been embarked which has been found to tend neither to profit nor edification; for there have been known, at the head of public libraries, men of the cerberus kind who loved the books so dearly, as to be unable to endure the handling of them by the vulgar herd of readers and searchers — even by those for whose special aid and service they are employed. They who have this morbid terror of the profanation of the treasures committed to their charge suffer in themselves the direst torments — something like those of a cat beholding her kittens tossed by a dog — whenever their favorites are handled; and the excruciating extent of their agonies, when some ardent and careless student dashes right into the heart of some *editio princeps*, or tall copy, or, perhaps, lays it open with its face on the table while he snatches another edition that he may collate a passage, is not to be conceived. It is then the dog *worrying* the kittens. Such men will only give satisfaction in great private libraries little disturbed by their proprietors, or in monastic or other corporate institutions, where it is the worthy object of the patrons to keep their collection in fine condition, and, at the same time, to take order that it shall be of the least possible service to education or literature. Angelo

Mai, the great librarian of the Vatican, who made so many valuable discoveries himself, had the character of taking good care that no one else should make any within his own strictly-preserved hunting grounds.

In the general case, however, a bibliophile at the head of a public library is genial and communicative, and has a pleasure in helping the investigator through the labyrinth of its stores. Such men feel their strength; and the immense value of the service which they may sometimes perform by a brief hint in the right direction which the inquiry should take, or by handing down a volume, or recommending the best directory to all the learning on the matter in hand, has laid many men of letters under great obligations to them.

The most eminent type of this class of men was Magliabecchi, librarian to the Grand Duke of Tuscany, who could direct you to any book in any part of the world, with the precision with which the metropolitan policeman directs you to St. Paul's or Piccadilly. It is of him that the stories are told of answers to inquiries after books, in these terms: — "There is but one copy of that book in the world. It is in the Grand Seignior's library at Constantinople, and is the seventh book in the second shelf on the right hand as you go in."[1] His faculties

[1] [The ability to give directions for finding any book in the world, even if the assertion be received as hyperbolical, is so marvellous as to seem almost incredible. But Magliabecchi's marvellousness is well authenticated. Yet, is the instance here cited of his knowledge very striking? If there had been half a

were, like those of all great men, self-born and self-trained. So little was the impoverished soil in which he passed his infancy congenial to his pursuits in after-life, that it was not within the parental intentions to teach him to read, and his earliest labors were in the shop of a green-grocer. Had his genius run on natural science, he might have fed it here, but it was his felicity and his fortune to be transferred to the shop of a patronizing bookseller. Here he drank in an education such as no academic forcing machinery could ever infuse. He devoured books, and the printed leaves became as necessary to his existence as the cabbage-leaves to the caterpillars which at times made their not welcome appearance in the abjured green-grocery. Like these verdant reptiles, too, he became assimilated to the food he fed on, insomuch that he was in a manner hot-pressed, bound, marble-topped, lettered, and shelved. He could bear nothing but books around him, and would allow no space for aught else ; his furniture, according to repute, being limited to two chairs, the second of which was admitted in order that the two together might serve as a bed.

Another enthusiast of the same kind was Adrien Baillet, the author, or, more properly speaking, the compiler, of the "Jugemens des Savans." Some

dozen copies of the book, and he had been able to tell the exact whereabout of each one, it would have been strange indeed. But there being only one in the world, if Magliabecchi had ever seen it, taken it down, looked at it, and put it back again, how could he help being able to put his finger upon it in the dark forever after? — W.]

copies of this book, which has a quantity of valuable matter scattered through it, have Baillet's portrait, from which his calm scholarly countenance looks genially forth, with this appropriate motto, "Dans une douce solitude, à l'abri du mensonge et de la vanité, j'adoptai la critique, et j'en fis mon étude, pour découvrir la vérité." Him, struggling with poverty, aggravated with a thirst for books, did Lamoignon the elder place at the head of his library, thus at once pasturing him in clover. When the patron told his friend, Hermant, of his desire to find a librarian possessed of certain fabulous qualifications for the duty, his correspondent said, "I will bring the very man to you;" and Baillet, a poor, frail, attenuated, diseased scholar, was produced. His kind patron fed him up, so far as a man who could not tear himself from his books, unless when nature became entirely exhausted, could be fed up. The statesman and his librarian were the closest of friends; and on the elder Lamoignon's death, the son, still more distinguished, looked up to Baillet as a father and instructor.

Men of this stamp are generally endowed with deep and solid learning. For any one, indeed, to take the command of a great public library, without large accomplishments, especially in the languages, is to put himself in precisely the position where ignorance, superficiality, and quackery are subjected to the most potent test, and are certain of detection. The number of librarians who have united great learning to a love of books, is the best practical answer to all sneers about the two being incompatible. Nor, while we count among us such names as Pannizzi, Birch, Halket, Naudet, Laing, Cogswell, Jones, Pertz, and Tod, is the race of learned librarians likely to decay.

It will be worth while for the patrons of public libraries, even in appointments to small offices, to have an eye on bookish men for filling them. One librarian differs greatly from another, and on this difference will often depend the entire utility of the institution, and the question whether it is worth keeping it open or closing its door. Of this class of workmen it may be said quite as aptly as of the poet, *nascitur, non fit.* The usual testimonies to qualification — steadiness, sobriety, civility, intelligence, &c. — may all be up to the mark that will constitute a first-rate book-keeper in the mercantile sense of the term, while they are united in a very dreary and hopeless keeper of books. Such a person ought to go to his task with something totally different from the impulses which induce a man to sort dry goods or make up invoices, with eminent success. In short, your librarian would need to be in some way touched with the malady which has been the object of these desultory remarks.

PART III.—HIS CLUB.

Clubs in General.

N author of the last generation, professing to deal with any branch of human affairs, if he were ambitious of being considered philosophical, required to go at once to the beginning of all things, where, finding man alone in the world, he would describe how the biped set about his own special business, for the supply of his own wants and desires; and then finding that the human being was, by his instincts, not a solitary but a social animal, the ambitious author would proceed in well-balanced sentences to describe how men aggregated themselves into hamlets, villages, towns, cities, counties, parishes, corporations, select vestries, and so on. I find that, without the merit of entertaining any philosophical views, I have followed, unconsciously, the same routine. Having discussed the book-hunter as he individually pursues his object, I now propose to look in upon him at his club, and say something about its peculiarities, as the shape in which he takes up the pursuit collectively with others who happen to be like-minded to himself.

Those who are so very old as to remember the Episcopal Church of Scotland, in that brief period of stagnant depression, when the repeal of the penal laws had removed from her the lustre of martyrdom, and she had not yet attained the more secular lustre which the zeal of her wealthy votaries has since conferred on her, will be familiar with the name of Bishop Robert Jolly. To the ordinary reader, however, it may be necessary to introduce him more specifically. He was a man of singular purity, devotedness, and learning. If he had no opportunity of attesting the sincerity of his faith by undergoing stripes and bondage for the Church of his adoption, he developed in its fulness that unobtrusive self-devotion, not inferior to martyrdom, which dedicates to obscure duties the talent and energy that, in the hands of the selfish and ambitious, would be the sure apparatus of wealth and station. He had no doubt risen to an office of dignity in his own Church — he was a bishop. But to understand the position of a Scottish bishop in those days, one must figure Parson Adams, no richer than Fielding has described him, yet incumbered by a title ever associated with wealth and dignity, and only calculated, when allied with so much poverty and social humility, to deepen the incongruity of his lot, and throw him more than ever on the mercy of the scorner. The office was indeed conspicuous, not by its dignities or emoluments, but by the extensive opportunities it afforded for self-devotion. One may have noticed his successor of the present day figuring in newspaper paragraphs as "The Lord Bishop of Moray and Ross." It did not fall to the lot of him of whom I write to render his title so flagrantly incongruous. A lordship was not necessary, but it was the principle of his Church to require a bishop, and in him she got a bishop. In reality, however, he was the parish clergyman of the small and poor remnant of the Episcopal persuasion who inhabited the odoriferous fishing-town of Fraserburgh. There he lived a long life of such simplicity and abstinence as the poverty of the poorest of his flock scarcely drove them to. He had one failing to link his life with this nether world — he was a book-hunter. How with his poor income, much of which went to feed the necessities of those still poorer, he should have accomplished anything in a pursuit generally considered expensive, is among other unexplained mysteries. But somehow he managed to scrape together a curious and interesting collection, so that his name became associated with rare books, as well as with rare Christian virtues.

When it was proposed to establish an institution for reprinting the works of the fathers of the Episcopal Church in Scotland, it was naturally deemed that no more worthy or characteristic name could be attached to it than that of the venerable prelate who, by his learning and virtues, had so long adorned the episcopal chair of Moray and Ross, and who had shown a special interest in the department of literature to which the institution was to be devoted. Hence it came to pass that, through a perfectly natural process, the association for the purpose of reprinting the works of certain old divines was to be ushered into the world by the style and title of THE JOLLY CLUB.

There happened to be among those concerned, however, certain persons so corrupted with the wisdom of this world, as to apprehend that the miscellaneous public might fail to trace this designation to its true origin, and might indeed totally mistake the nature and object of the institution, attributing to it aims neither consistent with the ascetic life of the departed prelate, nor with the pious and intellectual objects of its founders. The counsels of these worldly-minded persons prevailed. The Jolly Club was never instituted, — at least as an association for the reprinting of old books of divinity, though I am not prepared to say that institutions more than one so designed may not exist for other purposes. The object, however, was not entirely abandoned. A body of gentlemen united themselves together under the name of another Scottish prelate, whose fate had been more distinguished, if not more fortunate; and the Spottiswoode Society was established. Here, it will be observed, there was a passing to the opposite extreme; and so intense seems to have been the anxiety to escape from all excuse for indecorous jokes or taint of joviality, that the word Club, wisely adopted by other bodies of the same kind, was abandoned, and this one called itself a Society.

To that abandonment of the *medio tutissimus* has been attributed its early death by those who contemn the taste of those other communities, essentially Book Clubs, which have taken to the devious course of calling themselves "Societies."

In fact, all our *societies*, from the broad-brimmed Society of Friends downwards, have something in them of a homespun, humdrum, plain, flat — not unprofitable, perhaps, but unattractive character. They may be good and useful, but they have no dignity or ornament, and are quite destitute of the strange meteoric power and grandeur which have accompanied the career of *Clubs*. Societies there are, indeed, which identify themselves through their very nomenclature with misfortune and misery, seeming proudly to proclaim themselves victims to all the saddest ills that flesh is heir to — as, for instance, Destitute Sick Societies, Indigent Blind Societies, Deaf and Dumb Societies, Burial Societies, and the like. The nomenclature of some of these benevolent institutions seems likely to test the etymological skill of the next generation of learned men. Perhaps some ethnological philosopher will devote himself to the special investigation and development of the phenomenon; and if such things are done then in the way in which they are now, the result will appear in something like the following shape: —

"Man, as we pursue his destiny from century to century, is still found inevitably to resolve himself into a connected and antithetic series of consecutive cycles. The eighteenth century having been an age of individuative, the nineteenth necessarily became an age of associative or coinonomic development. He, the man — to himself the *ego*, and to others the mere *homo* — ceased to revolve around the pivot of his own individual idiosyncrasy, and, following the instincts of his nature, resolved himself into associative community. In this necessary development of their nature all partook, from the congresses of mighty monarchs down to those humbler but not less majestic types of the predominant influence, which, in the expressive language of that age, were recognized as twopenny goes. It is known only to those whose researches have led them through the intricacies of that phase of human progress, how multifarious and varied were the forms in which the inner spirit, objectively at work in mankind, had its external subjective development. Not only did associativeness shake the monarch on his throne, and prevail over the councils of the assembled magnates of the realm, but it was the form in which each shape and quality of humanity, down even to penury and disease, endeavored to express its instincts; and so the blind and the lame, the deaf and dumb, the sick and poor, made common stock of their privations, and endeavored by the force of union to convert weakness into strength," &c.

When the history of clubs is fully written, let us hope that it will be in another fashion. If it sufficiently abound in details, such a history would be full of marvels, from the vast influences which it would describe as arising from time to time by silent obscure growth out of nothing, as it were. Just look at what clubs have been, and have done; a mere enumeration is enough to recall the impression. Not to dwell on the institutions which have made Pall Mall and its neighborhood a conglomerate of palaces, or on such lighter affairs as "the Four-in-Hand," which the railways have left behind, or the "Alpine," whose members they carry to the field of their enjoyment: there was the Mermaid, counting among its members Shakespeare, Raleigh, Beaumont, Fletcher, and Jonson;[1] then came the King's Head; the October; the Kit-Cat; the Beaf-Steak; the Terrible Calves Head; Johnson's club, where he had Bozzy, Goldie, Burke, and Reynolds; the Poker, where Hume, Carlyle, Ferguson, and Adam Smith took their claret.

In these, with all their varied objects — literary, political, or convivial — the one leading peculiarity was the powerful influence they exercised on the condition of their times. A certain club there was with a simple unassuming name, — differing, by the way, only in three letters from that which would have commemorated the virtues of Bishop Jolly.

[1] [This assertion, so often made as to be generally believed, has not an iota of evidence to sustain it. There is no proof whatever, direct or indirect, that Shakespeare was ever at the Mermaid. That Raleigh and Beaumont and Fletcher and Jonson left him out of their fellowship, is, indeed, incredible; and so in spite of the lack of proof, I with the rest devoutly believe that they all drank sack at the Mermaid together. — W.]

The club in question, though nothing in the eye of the country but an easy knot of gentlemen who assembled for their amusement, cast defiance at a sovereign prince, and shook the throne and institutions of the greatest of modern states. But if we want to see the club culminating to its highest pitch of power, we must go across the water and saturate ourselves with the horrors of the Jacobin clubs, the Breton, and the Feuillans. The scenes we will there find stand forth in eternal protest against Johnson's genial definition in his Dictionary, where he calls a club "an assembly of good fellows, meeting under certain conditions."

The Structure of the Book Clubs.

HERE has been an addition, by no means contemptible, to the influence exercised by these institutions on the course of events, in the book clubs, or printing clubs as they are otherwise termed, of the present day. They have within a few years added a department to literature. The collector, who has been a member of several, may count their fruit by the thousand, all ranging in symmetrical and portly volumes. Without interfering either with the author who seeks in his copyrights the reward of his genius and labor, or with the publisher who calculates on a return for his capital, skill, and industry, the book clubs have ministered to literary wants, which these legitimate sources of supply have been unable to meet.

I hope no one is capable of reading so far through this book who is so grossly ignorant as not to know that the book clubs are a set of associations for the purpose of printing and distributing among their members certain books, calculated to gratify the peculiar taste which has brought them together and united them into a club. An opportunity may perhaps be presently taken for indulging in some characteristic notices of the several clubs, their members, and their acts and monuments: in the mean time let me say a word on the utilitarian efficiency of this arrangement — on the blank in the order of terrestial things which the book club was required to fill, and the manner in which it has accomplished its function.

There is a class of books of which the production has in this country always been uphill work; — large solid books, more fitted for authors and students than for those termed the reading public at large — books which may hence, in some measure, be termed the raw materials of literature, rather than literature itself. They are eminently valuable; but, since it is to the intellectual manufacturer who is to produce an article of salable literature that they are valuable, rather than to the general consumer, they do not secure an extensive sale. Of this kind of literature the staple materials are old state papers and letters, old chronicles, specimens of poetic, dramatic, and other literature — more valuable as vestiges of the style and customs of their age than for their absolute worth as works of genius — massive volumes of old divinity, disquisitions on obsolete science, and the like.

It is curious, by the way, that costly books of this sort seem to succeed better with the French than with us, though we do not generally give that people credit for excelling us in the outlay of money. Perhaps it is because they enjoy the British market as well as their own that they are enabled to excel us; but they certainly do so in the publication, through private enterprise, of great costly works, having a sort of national character. The efforts to rival them in this country have been considerable and meritorious, but in many instances signally unfortunate. Take, for instance, the noble edition of Holingshed and the other chroniclers, published in quarto volumes by the London trade; the Parliamentary History, in thirty-six volumes, each containing about as much reading as Gibbon's Decline and Fall; The State Trials; Sadler's and Thurlow's State Papers; the Harleian Miscellany, and several other ponderous publications of the same kind. All of them are to be had cheap, some at just a percentage above the price of waste paper. When an attempt was made to publish in the English language a really thorough Biographical Dictionary, an improvement on the French Biographie Universelle, it stuck in letter A, after the completion of seven dense octavo volumes — an abortive fragment, bearing melancholy testimony to what such a work ought to be. Publications of this kind have, in several instances, caused great losses to some, while they have brought satisfaction to no one concerned in them. A publisher has just the same distaste as any other ordinary member of the human family to the loss of five or ten thousand pounds in hard cash. Then, as touching the purchasers, — no doubt the throwing of "a remnant" on the market may sometimes bring the book into the possession of one who can put it to good use, and would have been unable to purchase it at the original price. But the rich deserve some consideration as well as the poor. It will be hard to find the man so liberal and benevolent that he will joyfully see his neighbor obtain for thirty shillings the precise article for which he has himself paid thirty pounds; nor does there exist the descendant of Adam who, whatever he may say or pretend, will take such an antithesis with perfect equanimity. Even the fortunate purchasers of portions of "the remnant," or "the broken book," as another pleasant technicality of the trade has it, are not always absolutely happy in their lot. They have been tempted by sheer cheapness to admit some bulky and unwieldy articles into their abodes, and they look askance at the commodity as being rather a sacrifice to mammon than a monument of good taste.

It has been the object of the machinery here referred to, to limit the impressions of such works to those who want and can pay for them — an extremely simple object, as all great ones are. There is, however, a minute nicety in the adjustment of the machinery, which was not obvious until it came forth in practice — a nicety without which the whole system falls to pieces. It was to accomplish this nicety that the principle of the club was found to be so well adapted. A club is essentially a body to which more people want admission than can gain it; if it do not manage to preserve this characteristic, it falls to pieces for want of pressure from without, like a cask divested of its hoops. To make the books retain their value, and be an object of desire, it was necessary that the impressions should be slightly within the natural circulation — that there should be rather a larger number desirous of obtaining each volume than the number that could be supplied with it. The club effected this by its own natural action. So long as there were candidates for vacancies and the ballot-box went round, so long were the books printed in demand and valuable to their possessors. If there were 110 or 120 people willing to possess and pay for a certain class of books, the secret of keeping up the pressure from without and the value of the books was, to limit the number of members and participators to 100. There is nothing noble or disinterested in this. The arrangement has no pretension to either of these qualities; nor when we come to the great forces which influence the supply and demand of human wants, whether in the higher or the humbler departments, will we find these qualities in force, or indeed any other motive than common selfishness. It is a sufficient vindication of the arrangement that it produced its effect. If there were ten or twenty disappointed candidates, the hundred were possessed of the treasures which none could have obtained but for the restrictive arrangements. Scott used to say that the Bannatyne Club was the only successful joint-stock company he ever invested in — and the remark is the key-note of the motives which kept alive the system that has done so much good to literature.

To understand the nature and services of these valuable institutions, it is necessary to keep in view the limits within which alone they can be legitimately worked. They will not serve for the propagation of standard literature — of the books of established reputation, which are always selling. These are merchandise, and must follow the law of trade like other commodities, whether they exist in the form of copyright monopolies, or are open to all speculators. No kind of coöperation will bring the volumes into existence so cheaply as the outlay of trade capital, which is expected to replace itself with a moderate profit after a quick sale. The perfection of this process is seen in the production and sale of that book which is ever the surest of a market — the Bible; and when a printer requires the certain and instantaneous return of his outlay, that is the shape in which he is most secure of obtaining it.

On the other hand, the clubs will not avail for ushering into the world the books of fresh ambitious authors. That paradise of the geniuses, in which their progeny are to be launched full sail, where they are to encounter no risks, and draw all the profits without discount or percentage, as yet exists only in the imagination. It would not work very satisfactorily to have a committee decreeing the issues, and the remuneration to be paid to each aspirant — ten thousand copies of Poppleton's Epic, and a check for a thousand pounds handed over out of the common stock, to begin with — half the issue, and half the remuneration for the Lyrics of Astyagus, as a less robust and manful production, but still a pleasant, murmuring, meandering, earnest little dream-book, fresh with the solemn purpose of solitude and silence. No, it must be confessed our authors and men of letters would make sad work of it, if they had the bestowal of the honors and pecuniary rewards of literature in their hands, whether these were administered by an intellectual hierarchy or by a collective democracy. Hence the clubs have wisely confined their operations to books which are not the works of their members; and to keep clear of all risk of literary rivalries, they have been almost exclusively devoted to the promulgation of the works of authors long since dead, whether by printing from original manuscripts or from rare printed volumes.

It has been pleaded that this machinery might

have been rendered influential for the encouragement of living authorship. It has been, for instance, observed, with some plausibility, that he who has the divine fervor of the author in him, will sacrifice all he has to sacrifice — time, toil, and health — so that he can but secure a hearing by the world; and institutions of the nature of the book clubs might afford him this at all events, leaving him to find his way to wealth and honors, if the sources of these are in him. No doubt the history of book-publishing shows how small are the immediate inducements and the well-founded hopes that will set authors in motion, and, indeed, a very large percentage of valueless literature proves that the barriers between the author and the world are not very formidable, or become somehow easily removable. This, in fact, furnishes the answer to the pleading here alluded to; and it may further be safely said, where the book demanding an introduction professes to be a work of genius, addressing itself to all mankind, that if it really be what it professes, the market will get it. No production of the kind is liable to be lost to the world.

Here it is plaintively argued by Philemon, that the rewards of genius are very unequally distributed. Who can deny it? Nothing is distributed with perfect balance like chemical equivalents in this world, at least so far as mortal faculties are capable of estimating the elements of happiness and unhappiness in the lot of our fellow-men; nor can one imagine that a world, all balanced and squared off to perfection, would be a very tolerable place to live in. Genius must take its chance, like all other qualities, and, on the whole, in a civilized country it gets on pretty well. Is it not something in itself to possess genius? and is it seemly, or a good example to the uninspired world, that its owner should deem it rather a misfortune than a blessing because he is not also surrounded by plush and shoulder-knots? If all geniuses had a prerogative right to rank and wealth, and all the pomps and vanities of this wicked world, could we be sure that none but genuine geniuses would claim them, and that there would be no margin for disputation with "solemn shams"? Milton's fifteen pounds are often referred to by him who finds how hard it is to climb, &c.; but we have no "return," as the blue-books call it, of all the good opportunities afforded to intellects ambitious of arising as meteors but only showing themselves as farthing rush-lights. On the other hand, no doubt, the wide fame and the rich rewards of the popular author are not in every instance an exact measure of his superiority to the disappointed aspirant. His thousand pounds do not furnish incontrovertible evidence that he is a hundred times superior to the drudge who goes over as much work for ten pounds, and there may possibly be some one making nothing who is superior to both.

Such aberrations are incident to all human affairs; but in those of literature, as in many others, they are exceptional. Here, as in other spheres of exertion, merit will in the general case get its own in some shape. Indeed, there is a very remarkable economic phenomenon, never, as it occurs to me, fully examined, which renders the superfluous success of the popular author a sort of insurance fund for enabling the obscure adventurer to enter the arena of authorship, and show what he is worth. Political economy has taught us that those old bugbears of the statute law called forestallers and regraters are eminent benefactors, in as far as their mercenary instincts enable them to see scarcity from afar, and induce them to "hold on" precisely so long as it lasts but no longer, since, if they have stock remaining on hand when abundance returns, they will be losers. Thus, through the regular course of trade, the surplus of the period of abundance is distributed over the period of scarcity with a precision which the genius of a Joseph or a Turgot could not achieve.

The phenomenon in the publishing world to which I have alluded has some resemblance to this, and comes to pass in manner following. The confirmed popular author whose books are sure to sell is an object of competition among publishers. If he is absolutely mercenary, he may stand forth in the public market and commit his works to that one who will take them on the best terms for the author and the worst for himself, like the contractor who gives in the lowest estimate in answer to an advertisement from a public department. Neither undertaking holds out such chances of gain as independent speculation may open, and thus there is an inducement to the enterprising publisher to risk his capital on the doubtful progeny of some author unknown to fame, in the hope that it may turn out "a hit." Of the number of books deserving a better fate, as also of the still greater number deserving none better than the fate they have got, which have thus been published at a dead loss to the publisher, the annals of bookselling could afford a moving history.

When an author has sold his copyright for a comparative trifle, and the book turns out a great success, it is of course matter of regret that he cannot have the cake he has eaten. This is one side of the balance-sheet, and on the other stands the debit account of the author who, through a work which proved a dead loss to its publisher, has made a reputation which has rendered his subsequent books successful, and made himself fashionable and rich. There have been instances where publishers who have bought for little the copyright of a successful book have allowed the author to participate in their gains; and I am inclined to believe that these instances are fully as numerous as those in which an author, owing his reputation and success to a book which did not pay its expenses, has made up the losses of his first publisher.

If we go out of the hard market and look at the tendency of sympathies, they are all in the author's favor. Publishers, in fact, have, though it is not generally believed, a leaning towards good literature, and a tendency rather to over than to under estimate the reception it may meet with from the world. In considering whether they will take the risk of a new publication, they have nothing to judge of it by except its literary merit, for they cannot obtain the votes of the public until they are committed ; and, indeed, there have been a good many instances where a publisher, having a faith in some individual author and his star, has pushed and fought a way for him with dogged and determined perseverance, sometimes with a success of which, were all known, he has more of the real merit than the author, who seems to have naturally, without any external aid, taken his position among the eminent and fortunate.

There are, at the same time, special disquisitions on matters of science or learning intended for peculiar and limited audiences, which find their way to publicity without the aid of the publisher. For these there is an opening in certain institutions far older than the book clubs, and possessed of a far higher social and intellectual position, since they have the means of conferring titles of dignity on those they adopt into their circle — titles which are worn not by trinkets dangling at the button-hole, but by certain cabalistic letters strung to the name in the directory of the town where the owner lives, or in the numberless biographical dictionaries which are to immortalize the present generation. So the author of an essay, especially in scholarship or science, will, if it be worth anything, find a place for it in the Transactions of one or other of the learned societies. It will probably keep company with, if indeed it be not itself one of, a series of papers which appear in the quarto volumes of the learned corporation's Transactions, merely because they cannot get into the octavo pages of the higher class of periodicals; but there they are, printed in the face of the world, whose inhabitants at large may worship them if they so please, and their authors cannot complain that they are suppressed. Whether the authors of these papers may have been ambitious of their appearance in a wider sphere, or are content with their appearance in "The Transactions," it suffices for the present purpose to explain how these volumes are a more suitable receptacle than those printed by the book clubs for essays or disquisitions by men following up their own specialties in literature or science; and if it be the case that some of the essays which appear in the Transactions of learned bodies would have gladly entered society under the auspices of some eminent periodical, yet it is proper at the same time to admit that many of the most valuable of these papers, concerning discoveries or inventions which adepts alone can appreciate, could only be satisfactorily published as they have been. And so we find our way back to the proposition, that the book clubs have been judiciously restricted to the promulgation of the works of dead authors.

This has not necessarily excluded the literary contributions of living men, in the shape of editing and commenting; and it is really difficult to estimate the quantity of valuable matter which is thus deposited in obscure but still accessible places. A deal of useful work, too, has been done in the way of translation; and where the book to be dealt with is an Icelandic saga, a chronicle in Saxon, in Irish Celtic, or even in old Norman, one may confess to the weakness of letting the original remain, in some instances, unexamined, and drawing one's information with confiding gratitude from the translation furnished by the learned editor.

Let me offer one instance of the important service that may be done by affording a vehicle for translations. The late Dr. Francis Adams, a village surgeon by profession, was at the same time, from taste and pursuit, a profound Greek scholar. He was accustomed to read the old authors on medicine and surgery — a custom too little respected by his profession, of whom it is the characteristic defect to respect too absolutely the standard of the day. As a physician, who is an ornament to his profession and a great scholar, once observed to me, the writings of the old physicians, even if we reject them from science, may be perused with profit to the practitioner as a record of the diagnosis of cases stated by men of acuteness, experience, and accuracy of observation. Adams had translated from the Greek the works of Paul of Ægina, the father of obstetric surgery, and printed the first volume. It was totally unnoticed, for in fact there were no means by which the village surgeon could get it brought under the notice of the scattered members of his profession who desired to possess such a book. The remainder of his labors would have been lost to the world had it not been taken off his hands by the Sydenham Club, established for the purpose of reprinting the works of the ancient physicians.

The Roxburghe Club.

GREAT institutions and small institutions have each individually had a beginning, though it cannot always be discovered, distance often obscuring it before it has been thought worth looking after. There is an ingenious theory abroad, to the effect that every physical impulse, be it but a wave of a human hand, and that every intellectual impulse, whether it pass through the mind of a Newton or a brickmaker, goes, with whatever strength it may possess, into a common store of dynamic influences, and tells with some operative power, however imperceptible and infinitesimal, upon all subsequent events, great or small, so that everything tells on everything, and there is no one specific cause, primary or secondary, that can be assigned to any particular event. It may be so objectively, as the transcendentalists say, but to common apprehensions there are specific facts which are to them emphatic as beginnings, such as the day when any man destined for leadership in great political events was born, or that whereon the Cape of Good Hope was doubled, or America was discovered.

The beginning of the book clubs is marked by a like distinctness, both in date and circumstance. The institution did not spring in full maturity and equipment, like Pallas from the brain of Jove; it was started by a casual impulse, and remained long insignificant; but its origin and early progress are as distinctly and specifically its own, as the birth and infancy of any hero or statesman are his. It is to the garrulity of Dibdin writing before there was any prospect that this class of institutions would reach their subsequent importance and usefulness, that we owe many minute items of detail about the cradle of the new system. We first slip in upon a small dinner-party, on the 4th of June in the year 1813, at the table of "Hortensius." The day was one naturally devoted to hospitality, being the birthday of the reigning monarch, George III., but this the historian passes unnoticed, the object of all absorbing interest being the great conflict of the Roxburghe book sale, then raging through its forty-and-one days. Of Hortensius, it is needless to know more than that he was a distinguished lawyer, and had a fine library, which having described, Dibdin passes on thus to matters of more immediate importance. "Nor is the hospitality of the owner of these treasures of a less quality and calibre than his taste; for Hortensius regaleth liberally — and as the 'night and day champagnes' (so he is pleased humorously to call them) sparkle upon his Gottingen-manufactured table-cloth, 'the master of the revels,' or (to borrow the phraseology of Pynson) of the 'feste royalle,' discourseth lustily and loudly upon the charms — not of a full-curled or full-bottomed 'King's Bench' periwig — but of a full-margined Bartholomæus or Barclay like his own."[1]

After some forty pages of this sort of matter, we get another little peep at this momentous dinner-party. "On the clearance of the Gottingen-manufactured table-cloth, the Roxburghe battle formed the subject of discussion, when I proposed that we should not only be all present, if possible, on the day of the sale of the Boccaccio, but that we should meet at some 'fair tavern' to commemorate the sale thereof." They met accordingly on the 17th of June, some eighteen in number, "at the St. Albans Tavern, St. Albans Street, now Waterloo Place." Surely the place was symbolical, since on the 18th of June, three years afterwards, the battle of Waterloo was fought; and as the importance attributed to the contest at Roxburghe House on the 17th procured for it afterwards the name of the Waterloo of book-battles, it came to pass that there were two Waterloo commemorations treading closely one on the other's heels.

The pecuniary stake at issue, and the consequent excitement when the Valdarfer Boccaccio was knocked off, so far exceeded all anticipation, that at

1 Bibliographical Decameron, vol. iii. p. 28.

the festive board a motion was made and carried by acclamation, for meeting on the same day and in the same manner annually. And so the Roxburghe Club, the parent of all the book clubs, came into existence.

It must be admitted that its origin bears a curious generic resemblance to some scenes which produce less elevating results. On the day of some momentous race or cock-fight, a parcel of sporting devotees, "regular bricks," perhaps, agree to celebrate the occasion in a tavern, and when the hilarity of the evening is at its climax, some festive orator, whose enthusiasm has raised him to the table, suggests, amidst loud hurrahs and tremendous table-rapping, that the casual meeting should be converted into an annual festival, to celebrate the event which has brought them together. At such an assemblage, the list of toasts will probably include Eclipse, Cotherstone, Mameluke, Plenipo, the Flying Dutchman, and other illustrious quadrupeds, along with certain bipeds, distinguished in the second degree as breeders, trainers, and riders, and may perhaps culminate in "the turf and the stud all over the world." With a like appropriate reference to the common bond of sympathy, the Roxburghe toasts included the uncouth names of certain primitive printers, as Valdarfer himself, Pannartz, Fust, and Schoeffher, terminating in "The cause of Bibliomania all over the world."[1]

[1] As of other influential documents, there have been various versions of the Roxburghe list of toasts, and a corresponding

The club thus abruptly formed consisted of affluent collectors, some of them noble, with a sprinkling of zealous practical men, who assisted

amount of critical discussion, which leaves the impression common to such disputes, that this important manifesto was altered and enlarged from time to time. The version which bears the strongest marks of completeness and authenticity, was found among the papers of Mr. Hazlewood, of whom hereafter. It is here set down as nearly in its original shape as the printer can give it: —

The Order of ye Tostes.

The Immortal Memory of
John Duke of Roxburghe.
Christopher Valdarfer, Printer of the Decameron of 1471.
Gutemberg, Fust, and Schoeffher, the Inventors of the Art of Printing.
William Caxton, the Father of rhe British Press.
Dame Juliana Barnes, and the St. Albans Press.
Wynkyn de Worde, and Richard Pynson, the Illustrious Successors of William Caxton.
The Aldine Family, at Venice.
The Giunta Family, at Florence.
The Society of the Bibliophiles at Paris.
The Prosperity of the Roxburghe Club.
The Cause of Bibliomania all over the World.

It will be seen that this accomplished black letterer must have been under a common delusion, that our ancestors not only wrote, but pronounced the definite article "the" as "ye." Every blunderer ambitious of success in fabricating old writings is sure to have recourse to this trick, which serves for his immediate detection. The Gothic alphabet, in fact, as used in this country, had a Theta for expressing in one letter our present t and h conjoined. When it was abandoned, some printers substituted for it the letter y as most nearly resembling it in shape, hence the "ye"

them in their great purchases, while doing minor strokes of business for themselves. These who in some measure fed on the crumbs that fell from the master's table were in a position rather too closely resembling the professionals in a hunt or cricket club. The circle was a very exclusive one, however; the number limited to thirty-one members, "one black ball excluding;" and it used to be remarked, that it was easier to get into the Peerage or the Privy Council than into "The Roxburghe."

which occurs sometimes in old books, but much more frequently in modern imitations of them.*

The primitive Roxburgheians used to sport these toasts as a symbol of knowingness and high caste in book-hunting freemasonry. Their representative man happening on a tour in the Highlands to open his refreshment wallet on the top of Ben Lomond, pledged his guide in the potent *vin du pays* to Christopher Valdarfer, John Gutemberg, and the others. The Celt had no objection in the world to pledge successive glasses to these names, which he had no doubt belonged "to fery respectaple persons," probably to the chief landed gentry of his entertainer's neighborhood. But the best Glenlivet would not induce him to pledge "the cause of Bibliomania all over the world," being unable to foresee what influence the utterance of words so unusual and so suspiciously savoring of demonology might exercise over his future destiny.

* [The author must have forgotten for the moment his observations during his reading of old books. In not a few English books of the century 1500 the use of *y* for *th* is almost invariable, at the beginning of a monosyllable; and from this the usage varies to an only occasional substitution of the *y*. It seems to me that Hazlewood's list of the Roxburghe toasts (so dry and dusty that it is not surprising that such oceans of claret were needed to wash them down) shows that he knew just the nature and the reason of this custom, and not that he supposed "the" used to be pronounced *ye*. In the list the article occurs many times, and only once as "ye." How did he pronounce it in the other instances? Indeed, it is quite impossible that a man so familiar with old books as Hazlewood was, could have been ignorant upon such a point. — W.]

Nothing has done so much to secure the potent influence of clubs as the profound secrecy in which their internal or domestic transactions have generally been buried. The great safeguard of this secrecy will be found in that rigid rule of our social code which prohibits every gentleman from making public the affairs of the private circle; and if from lack of discretion, as it is sometimes gently termed, this law is supposed to have a lax hold on any one, he is picked off by the "one," "two," "three black balls." It is singular that a club so small and exclusive as the Roxburghe should have proved an exception to the rule of secrecy, and that the world has been favored with revelations of its doings which have made it the object of more amusement than reverence. In fact, through failure of proper use of the black ball, it got possession of a black sheep, in the person of a certain Joseph Hazlewood. He had achieved a sort of reputation in the book-hunting community by discovering the hidden author of Drunken Barnaby's Journal. In reality, however, he was a sort of literary Jack Brag. As that amusing creation of Theodore Hook's practical imagination mustered himself with sporting gentlemen through his command over the technicalities or slang of the kennel and the turf, so did Hazlewood sit at the board with scholars and aristocratic book-collectors through a free use of their technical phraseology. In either case, if the indulgence in these terms descended into a motley grotesqueness, it was excused as excessive fervor carrying the enthusiast off his feet. When Hazlewood's treasures — for he was a collector in his way — were brought to the hammer, the scraps and odds and ends it contained were found classified in groups under such headings as these — Garlands of Gravity, Poverty's Pot Pourri, Wallat of Wit, Beggar's Baldardash, Octagonal Olio, Zany's Zodiac, Noddy's Nuncheon, Mumper's Medley, Quaffing Quavers to Quip Queristers, Tramper's Twattle, or Treasure and Tinsel from the Tewksbury Tank, and the like. He edited reprints of some rare books — that is to say, he saw them accurately reprinted letter by letter. Of these one has a name which — risking due castigation if I betray gross ignorance by the supposition — I think he must certainly have himself bestowed on it, as it excels the most outrageous pranks of the alliterative age. It is called "Green-Room Gossip; or, Gravity Gallinipt; A Gallimaufry got up to guile Gymnastical and Gyneocratic Governments; Gathered and garnished by Gridiron Gabble, Gent., Godson to Mother Goose."

The name of Joseph Hazlewood sounds well; it is gentleman-like, and its owner might have passed it into such friendly commemoration as that of Bliss, Cracherode, Heber, Sykes, Utterson, Townley, Markland, Hawtrey, and others generally understood to be gentlemen, and, in virtue of their bookish propensities, scholars. He might even, for the sake of his reprints, have been thought an "able editor," had it not been for his unfortunate efforts to chronicle the doings of the club he had got into.[1] His history, in manuscript, was sold

[1] A voice from the other side of the Atlantic reveals the portentous nature of the machinery with which Mr. Hazlewood conducted his editorial labors. The following is taken from the book on the Private Libraries of New York, already so freely quoted.

"A unique book of unusual interest to the bibliophile in this department is the copy of Ancient and Critical Essays upon English Poets and Poesy, edited by Joseph Hazlewood, 2 vols. 4to, London, 1815. This is Hazlewood's own copy, and it is enriched and decorated by him in the most extravagant style of the bibliomaniac school in which he held so eminent a position. It is illustrated throughout with portraits, some of which are very rare; it contains all the letters which the editor received in relation to it from the eminent literary antiquarians of his day; and not only these, but all the collations and memoranda of any consequence which were made for him during its progress, frequently by men of literary distinction. To these are added all the announcements of the work, together with the impressions of twelve cancelled pages, printed four in one form and eight in another, apparently by way of experiment, with other cancelled matter; tracings of the fac-simile woodcuts of the title to Puttenham's Arte of English Poesie, with a proof of it on India paper, and three impressions of this title, one all in black, one with the letter in black and the device in red, and the third *vice versâ;* tracings for, and proofs of, other woodcuts; an impression of a leaf printed to be put into a single copy of the work, &c., &c.; for we must stop, although we have but indicated the nature rather than the quantity of the matter, all of it unique, which gives this book its peculiar value. But it should be remarked besides, that the editorial part of the work is interleaved for the purpose of receiving Mr. Hazlewood's explanations and corrections, and those that he received from literary friends, which alone would give this copy a singular interest. It is bound by Clarke, in maroon morocco."*

* [These volumes (which are in the collection of the editor of this book) certainly show a disposition on the part of the man who made them to have his

with his other treasures after his death, and was purchased by the proprietor of the Athenæum, where fragments of it were printed some fifteen years ago, along with editorial comments, greatly to the amusement, if not to the edification, of the public.

In these revelations we find how long a probation the system of book clubs had to pass through, before it shook off the convivial propensities which continued to cluster round the normal notion of a club, and reached the dry asceticism and attention to the duties of printing and editing, by which the greater number of book clubs are distinguished. It was at first a very large allowance of sack to the proportion

"nothings monstered." They exhibit a perfect picture in little of the fussy, finical way into which Dibdin had got book-loving people fifty years ago. And yet we must remember that they were got up only for Hazlewood's own private use and comfort. It is true, also, that the examination of them is a very entertaining process to those who take an interest in the making of books. We see how a date is hunted up and verified, a fact established; how one friend was working at Oxford in the Bodleian to help the editor upon this point, and another in his own antique library to furnish him information upon the other. We see how one of a humbler rank sat up all night to do the heavy task of writing out, *punctuatim et literatim*, a black-letter tract, that the press might not be stopped. We see the trying of experiments, the rejection of plans, and the reasons therefor; and in fact the working of the whole machinery which was set a-going to produce the book; — and, indeed, much else beside. Thus Hazlewood's folly, if we must call it so, affords us some not irrational pleasure. Hazlewood was an obscure but reputable solicitor, who, without any advantages of early education or of pecuniary success, worked his way to a very considerable knowledge of old English literature and a companionship with the eminent black-letter scholars of his day. He lived in a somewhat dependent position with a crusty old uncle, with whom he had not a feeling in common, and who allowed him two little closet-like rooms at the top of the house, which he managed to fill with books which after his death were sold for £2500. We owe to him, among other things, the reprints of the "Book of St. Albans," "The Mirrour for Magistrates," and "The Palace of Pleasure," together with the larger part of "The Censura Literaria." Let us be grateful to him for what he did, and treat his foibles as we would have others treat our own. — W.]

of literary food, and it was sarcastically remarked that the club had spent a full thousand pounds in guzzling before it had produced a single valuable volume. We have some of the bills of fare at the "Roxburghe Revels," as they were called. In one, for instance, there may be counted, in the first course, turtle cooked five different ways, along with turbot, john dory, tendrons of lamb, soutee of haddock, ham, chartreuse, and boiled chickens. The bill amounted to £5 14s. a head; or, as Hazlewood expresses it, "according to the long-established principles of 'Maysterre Cockerre,' each person had £5 14s. to pay." Some illustrious strangers appear to have been occasionally invited to attend the symposium. If the luxurious table spread for them may have occasioned them some surprise, they must have experienced still more in the tenor of the invitation to be present, which, coming in the name of certain "Lions of literature," as their historian and the author of the invitation calls them, was expressed in these terms—"The honor of your company is requested to dine with the Roxburghe dinner, on Wednesday the 17th instant."[1] One might be tempted to offer the reader a fuller speci-

[1] [The author has yielded himself too much to the guidance of the editorial comments of the "Athenæum" which he previously mentions,—an exceedingly dishonorable and malicious performance. It certainly would have become the distinguished members of this club, the "revered of the Roxburghe" as Scott calls them in "Woodstock," to look a little more carefully after the wording of the invitation to their dinners. But they had no hand in it; neither was "their historian," *i. e.* Hazlewood,

men of the historian's style; but unfortunately its characteristics, grotesque as they are, cannot be exemplified in their full breadth without being also given at full length. The accounts of the several dinners read like photographs of a mind wandering in the mazes of indigestion-begotten nightmare.[1]

When Dibdin protested against the publication of this record, he described it a great deal too attractively when he called it "the concoction of one in his gayer and unsuspecting moments — the repository of private confidential communications — a mere memorandum-book of what had passed at con-

the "author of the invitation," by which people were asked to dine with a dinner. The author was the keeper of the tavern at which the dinners were eaten! See Dibdin's "Reminiscences," 1836, Vol. I. p. 378, — "and Mr. Richolds, the master of the hotel, always filled up his printed circulars by asking us 'to *dine with the Roxburghe dinner*.'" — W.]

[1] It is but fair, however, to a reputation which was considerable within its own special circle, to let the reader judge for himself; so, if he think the opportunity worth the trouble of wading through small print, he may read the following specimen of Mr. Hazlewood's style. He would certainly himself not have objected to its being taken as a criterion of the whole, since he was evidently proud of it.

"Consider, in the bird's-eye view of the banquet, the trencher cuts, foh! nankeen displays: as intersticed with many a brilliant drop to friendly beck and clubbish hail, to moisten the viands or cool the incipient cayenne. No unfamished livery-man would desire better dishes, or high-tasted courtier better wines. With men that meet to commune, that can converse, and each willing to give and receive information, more could not be wanting to promote well-tempered conviviality — a social compound of mirth, wit, and wisdom; combining all that Anacreon was famed for, tempered with the reason of Demosthenes, and intersected

vivial meetings, and in which 'winged words' and flying notes of merry gentlemen and friends were obviously incorporated." No! certainly wings and flying are not the ideas that naturally associate with the historian of the Roxburghe, although, in one instance, the dinner is sketched off in the following epigrammatic sentence, which startles the reader like a plover starting up in a dreary moor:—"Twenty-one members met joyfully, dined comfortably, challenged eagerly, tippled prettily, divided regretfully, and paid the bill most cheerfully." On another occasion the historian's enthusiasm was too expan-

with the archness of Scaliger. It is true, we had not any Greek verses in praise of the grape; but we had, as a tolerable substitute, the ballad of the "Bishop of Hereford and Robin Hood," sung by Mr. Dodd, and it was of his own composing. It is true, we had not any long oration denouncing the absentees, the cabinet counsel, or any other set of men; but there was not a man present that at one hour and seventeen minutes after the cloth was removed but could have made a Demosthenic speech far superior to any record of antiquity. It is true, no trace of wit is going to be here preserved, for the flashes were too general, and what is the critical sagacity of a Scaliger compared to our chairman? Ancients believe it! We were not dead drunk, and therefore lie quiet under the table for once, and let a few moderns be uppermost."

The following chronicle of the third dinner and second anniversary records an interesting little personal incident:—

"After Lord Spencer left the chair, it was taken, I believe, by Mr. Heber, who kept it up to a late hour,—Mr. Dodd, very volatile and somewhat singular, at the same time quite novel, in amusing the company with Robin Hood ditties and similar productions. I give this on after report, having left the room very early from severe attack of sickness, which appeared to originate in some vile compound partook of at dinner."

sive to be confined to plain prose, and he inflated it in lyric verse: —

> "Brave was the banquet, the red, red juice,
> Hilarity's gift sublime,
> Invoking the heart to kindred use,
> And bright'ning halo of time."

This, and a quantity of additional matter of like kind, was good fun to the scorners, and, whether any of the unskilful laughed at it, scarcely made even the judicious grieve, for they thought that those who had embarked in such pompous follies deserved the lash unconsciously administered to them in his blunders by an unhappy member of their own order.

In, fact, however, this was the youthful giant sowing his wild oats. Along with them there lay also, unseen at first, the seed of good fruit. Of these was a resolution adopted at the second meeting, and thus set forth by the historian in his own peculiar style: — "It was proposed and concluded for each member of the club to reprint a scarce piece of ancient lore to be given to the members, one copy to be on vellum for the chairman, and only as many copies as members."

The earliest productions following on this resolution were on a very minute scale. One member, stimulated to distinguish himself by "a merry conceited jest," reprinted a French morsel called "La Contenance de la Table," and had it disposed of in such wise, that as each guest opened his napkin expecting to find a dinner-roll, he disclosed the typographical treasure; it stands No. 6 on the list of Roxburghe books, and is probably worth an enormous sum. The same enthusiast reprinted in a more formal manner a rarity called "News from Scotland, declaring the damnable life of Dr. Fian, a notable sorcerer," &c. This same morsel was afterwards reprinted for another club, in a shape calculated almost to create a contemptuous contrast between the infantine efforts of the Roxburghe and the manly labors of its robust followers. It is inserted as what the French call a *pièce justificative* in Pitcairn's Criminal Trials, edited for the Bannatyne, and there occupies ten of the more than 2000 pages which make up that solid book.

It was not until the year 1827 that a step was taken by the Roxburghe Club which might be called its first exhibition of sober manhood. Some of the members, ashamed of the paltry nature of the volumes circulated in the name of the club, bethought themselves of uniting to produce a book of national value. They took Sir Frederick Madden into their counsels, and authorized him to print eighty copies of the old metrical romance of Havelok the Dane. This gave great dissatisfaction to the historian, who muttered how "a MS. not discovered by a member of the club was selected, and an excerpt obtained, not furnished by the industry or under the inspection of any one member, nor edited by a member; but, in fact, after much *pro* and *con*, it was made a complete hireling concern, truly at the expense of the club, from the copying to the publishing."

The value of this book has been attested by the extensive critical examination it has received, and by the serviceable aid it has given to all recent writers on the infancy of English literature. It was followed by another interesting old romance, William and the Wer Wolf, valuable not only as a specimen of early literature, but for the light it throws on the strange wild superstition dealing with the conversion of men into wolves, which has been found so widely prevalent that it has received a sort of scientific title in the word Lycanthropy. These two books made the reputation of the Roxburghe, and proved an example and encouragement to the clubs which began to arise more or less on its model. It was a healthy protest against the Dibdinism which had ruled the destinies of the club, for Dibdin had been its master, and was the Gamaliel at whose feet Hazlewood and others patiently sat. Of the term now used, the best explanation I can give is this, that in the selection of books — other questions, such as rarity or condition, being set aside, or equally balanced — a general preference is to be given to those which are the most witless, preposterous, and in every literary sense valueless — which are, in short, rubbish. What is here meant will be easily felt by any one who chooses to consult the book which Dibdin issued under the title of "The Library Companion, or the Young Man's Guide and the Old Man's Comfort in the Choice of a Library." This, it will be observed, is not intended as a manual of rare or curious, or in any way peculiar books, but as the instruction of a Nestor on the best books for study and use in all departments of literature. Yet one will look in vain there for such names as Montaigne, Shaftesbury, Benjamin Franklin, D'Alembert, Turgot, Adam Smith, Malebranche, Lessing, Goethe, Schiller, Fenelon, Burke, Kant, Richter, Spinoza, Flechier, and many others. Characteristically enough, if you turn up Rousseau, in the index you will find Jean Baptiste, but not Jean Jacques. You will search in vain for Dr. Thomas Reid, the metaphysician, but will readily find Isaac Reed, the editor. If you look for Molinæus or Du Moulin, it is not there, but alphabetic vicinity gives you the good fortune to become acquainted with "Moule, Mr., his Bibliotheca Heraldica." The name Hooker will be found, not to guide the reader to the Ecclesiastical Polity, but to Dr. Jackson Hooker's Tour in Iceland. Lastly, if any one shall search for Hartley on Man, he will find in the place it might occupy, or has reference to, the editorial services of "Hazlewood, Mr. Joseph." [1]

[1] [The author is running *amok* against Dibdin, and I certainly shall not stand in his way. Dibdin's "Library Companion" is fairly open to all the fault he finds with it; though he omits saying that in spite of its defects and its offences it contains a great deal of information which is really valuable to the book-buyer. But there is yet none the less needed, and especially in this country, a hand-book which should be what Dibdin's work professes to be, and which should direct the young student, and protect the inexperienced buyer against worthless or inferior editions, guard him against superseded authors, inform him of current prices, and in fact enable him to obtain, without paying

Though the Roxburghe, when it came under the fostering care of the scholarly Botfield, and secured the services of men like Madden, Wright, and Taylor, outgrew the pedantries in which it had been reared, and performed much valuable literary work, yet its chief merit is in the hints its practice afforded to others. The leading principle, indeed, which the other clubs so largely adopted after the example of the Roxburghe, was not an entire novelty. The idea of keeping up the value of a book by limiting the impression, so as to restrain it within the number who might desire to possess it, was known before the birth of this the oldest book club. The practice was sedulously followed by Hearne the antiquary, and others, who provided old chronicles and books of the class chiefly esteemed by the book-hunter. The very fame of the restricted number, operating on the selfish jealousy of man's nature, brought out competitors for the possession of the book, who never would have thought of it but for the pleasant idea of keeping it out of the hands of some one else.

There are several instances on record of an un-

dearly on the way, the best books upon the subjects which interest him. Neither a Course of Reading, nor a Manual like Lowndes's will do this. The book, although it should of course be somewhat critical, might be of moderate size and price; for it should of course be limited to the wants of people generally who have literary tastes and purposes, but who have no time or inclination for bibliography. Such folk as have special hobbies, or those who design the collection of great libraries, would not need its help. — W.]

known book lying in the printer's warerooms, dead from birth and forgotten, having life and importance given to it by the report that all the copies, save a few, have been destroyed by a fire in the premises. This is an illustration in the sibylline direction of value being conferred by the decrease of the commodity; but by judiciously adjusting the number of copies printed, the remarkable phenomenon has been exhibited of the rarity of a book being increased by an increase in the number of copies. To understand how this may come to pass, it is necessary to look on rarity as not an absolute and objective quality, but as relative to the number who desire to possess the article. Ten copies which two hundred people want constitute a rarer book than two copies which twenty people want. A book may be the sole remaining copy — in technical language, may be unique — but nobody has heard of it, and nobody wants it, so it stands quietly on its own shelf uncoveted. But let its owner print, say, twenty copies for distribution — the book-hunting community have got the "hark-away," and are off after it. In this way, before the days of the clubs, many knowing people multiplied rarities; and at the present day there are reprints by the clubs themselves of much greater pecuniary value than the rare books from which they have been multiplied.

Some Book-Club Men.

O one probably did more to raise the condition of the book clubs than Sir Walter Scott. In 1823 the Roxburghe made proffers of membership to him, partly, it would seem, under the influence of a waggish desire to disturb his great secret, which had not yet been revealed. Dibdin, weighting himself with more than his usual burden of ponderous jocularity, set himself in motion to intimate to Scott the desire of the club that the Author of Waverley, with whom it was supposed that he had the means of communicating, would accept of the seat at the club vacated by the death of Sir Mark Sykes. Scott got through the affair ingeniously with a little coy fencing that deceived no one, and was finally accepted as the Author of Waverley's representative. The Roxburghe had, however, at that time, done nothing in serious book-club business, having let loose only the small flight of flimsy sheets of letterpress already referred to. It was Scott's own favorite club, the Bannatyne, that first projected the plan of printing substantial and valuable volumes.

At the commencement of the same year, 1823, when he took his seat at the Roxburghe (he did not take his bottle there, which was the more important object, for some time after), he wrote to the late Robert Pitcairn, the editor of the Criminal Trials, in these terms: — "I have long thought that a something of a bibliomaniacal society might be formed here, for the prosecution of the important task of publishing *dilettante* editions of our national literary curiosities. Several persons of rank, I believe, would willingly become members, and there are enough of good operatives. What would you think of such an association? David Laing was ever keen for it; but the death of Sir Alexander Boswell and of Alexander Oswald has damped his zeal. I think, if a good plan were formed, and a certain number of members chosen, the thing would still do well."[1]

Scott gave the Bannatyners a song for their festivities. It goes to the tune of "One Bottle More," and is a wonderful illustration of his versatile powers in the admirable bibulous sort of joviality which he distils, as it were, from the very dust of musty volumes. Two of the strangest characters that literature ever produced, or who ever joined the book-hunt, are hit off in the following stanzas — the snarling Pinkerton, and Ritson, who, though he had lived an unbeliever, in eternal quarrels with the rest of his kind, on his death-bed found just one sin to repent of — an act of apostasy to his vegetarian faith, in having, when tired and wet after a long pedestrian journey, eaten a potato fried in fat: —

[1] Notices of the Bannatyne Club, privately printed.

"John Pinkerton next, and I'm truly concerned
I can't call that worthy so candid as learned;
He rai'ed at the plaid, and blasphemed the claymore,
And set Scots by the ears in his one volume more.
One volume more, my friends, one volume more —
Celt and Scot shall be pleased with one volume more.

"As bitter as gall, and as sharp as a razor,
And feeding on herbs as a Nebuchadnezzar,
His diet too acid, his temper too sour,
Little Ritson came out with his two volumes more.
But one volume, my friends, one volume more —
We'll dine on roast beef, and print one volume more."

Scott printed, as a contribution to his favorite club, the record of the trial of two Highlanders for murder, which brought forth some highly characteristic incidents. The victim was a certain Sergeant Davis, who had charge of one of the military parties or guards dispersed over the Highlands to keep them in order after the '45. Davis had gone from his own post at Braemar up Glen Clunie to meet the guard from Glenshee. He chose to send his men back and take a day's shooting among the wild mountains at the head of the glen, and was seen no more. How he was disposed of could easily be divined in a general way, but there were no particulars to be had. It happened, however, that there was one Highlander who, for reasons best known to himself — they were never got at — had come to the resolution of bringing his brother Highlanders, who had made away with the sergeant, to justice. It was necessary for his own safety, however, that he should be under the pressure of a motive or impulse sufficient to justify so heartless and unnatural a proceeding, otherwise he would himself have been likely to follow the sergeant's fate. Any reference to his conscience, the love of justice, respect for the laws of the land, or the like, would of course have been received with well-merited ridicule and scorn. He must have some motive which a sensible Highlander could admit as probable in itself, and sufficient for its purpose.

Accordingly, the accuser said he had been visited by the sergeant's ghost, who had told him everything, and laid on him the heavy burden of bringing his slaughterers in the flesh to their account. If that were not done, the troubled spirit would not cease to walk the earth, and so long as he walked would the afflicted denouncer continue to be the victim of his ghostly visits. The case was tried at Edinburgh, and though the evidence was otherwise clear and complete, the Lowland jury were perplexed and put out by the supernatural episode. A Highland story with a ghost acting witness at second hand, roused all their Saxon prejudices, and they cut the knot of difficulties by declining to convict. A point was supposed to have been made, when the counsel for the defence asked the ghost-seer what language the ghost, who was English when in the flesh, spoke to the Highlander, who knew not that language; and the witness answered, through his interpreter, that the spectre spoke as good Gaelic as ever was heard in Lochaber. Sir Walter Scott, however, remarks that there was no incongruity in this, if we once get over the first step of the ghost's existence. It is curious that Scott does not seem to have woven the particulars of this affair into any one of his novels.

Among those who contributed to place the stamp of a higher character on the labors of the book clubs, one of the most remarkable was Sir Alexander Boswell. A time there was, unfortunately, when his name could not easily be dissociated from exasperating political events, but now that the generation concerned in them has nearly passed away, it becomes practicable, even from the side of his political opponents, to glance at his literary abilities and accomplishments without recalling exciting recollections. He was a member of the Roxburghe, and though he did not live to see the improvement in the issues of that institution, or the others which kept pace with it, he, alone and single-handed, set the example of printing the kind of books which it was afterwards the merit of the book clubs to promulgate. He gave them, in fact, their tone. He had at his paternal home of Auchinleck a remarkable collection of rare books and manuscripts; one of these afforded the text from which the romance of Sir Tristrem was printed. He reprinted from the one remaining copy in his own possession the disputation between John Knox and Quentin Kennedy, a priest who came forward against the great Reformer as the champion of the old religion. From the Auchinleck Press came also reprints of Lodge's Fig for Momus, Churchyard's Mirrour of

Man, the Book of the Chess, Sir James Dier's Remembrancer of the Life of Sir Nicholas Bacon, the Dialogus inter Deum et Evam, and others.

The possession of a private printing-press is, no doubt, a very appalling type of bibliomania. Much as has been told us of the awful scale in which drunkards consume their favored poison, one is not accustomed to hear of their setting up private stills for their own individual consumption. There is a Sardanapalitan excess in this bibliographical luxuriousness which refuses to partake with other vulgar mortals in the common harvest of the public press, but must itself minister to its own tastes and demands. The owner of such an establishment is subject to no extraneous caprices about breadth of margins, size of type, quarto or folio, leaded or unleaded lines; he dictates his own terms; he is master of the situation, as the French say; and is the true autocrat of literature. There have been several renowned private presses: Walpole's, at Strawberry Hill; Mr. Johnes's, at Hafod; Allan's, at the Grange; and the Lee Priory Press. None of these, however, went so distinctly into the groove afterwards followed by the book clubs as Sir Alexander Boswell's Auchinleck Press. In the Bibliographical Decameron is a brief history, by Sir Alexander himself, of the rise and progress of his press. He tells us how he had resolved to print Knox's Disputation: "For this purpose I was constrained to purchase two small fonts of black letter, and to have punches cut for eighteen or twenty double letters and contractions. I was thus enlisted and articled into the service, and being infected with the *type* fever, the fits have periodically returned. In the year 1815, having viewed a portable press invented by Mr. John Ruthven, an ingenious printer in Edinburgh, I purchased one, and commenced compositor. At this period, my brother having it in contemplation to present Bamfield to the Roxburghe Club, and not aware of the poverty and insignificance of my establishment, expressed a wish that his tract should issue from the Auchinleck Press. I determined to gratify him, and the portable press being too small for general purposes, I exchanged it for one of Mr. Ruthven's full-sized ones; and having increased my stock to *eight* small fonts, roman and italic, with the necessary appurtenances, I placed the whole in a cottage, built originally for another purpose, very pleasantly situated on the bank of a rivulet, and, although concealed from view by the surrounding wood, not a quarter of a mile from my house."[1]

To show the kind of man who coöperated with Scott in such frivolities, let me say a word or two more about Sir Alexander. He was the son, observe, of Johnson's Jamie Boswell, but he was about as like his father as an eagle might be to a peacock. To use a common colloquial phrase, he was a man of genius, if ever there was one. Had he been a poorer and socially humbler man than he was — had he had his bread and his position to

[1] Bibliographical Decameron, ii. 454.

make — he would probably have achieved immortality. Some of his songs are as familiar to the world as those of Burns, though their author is forgotten, — as, for instance, the song of parental farewell, beginning —

> "Good-night, and joy be wi' ye a';
> Your harmless mirth has cheered my heart,"

and ending with this fine and genial touch —

> "The auld will speak, the young maun hear;
> Be canty, but be good and leal;
> Your ain ills aye hae heart to bear,
> Another's aye hae heart to feel;
> So, ere I set I'll see you shine,
> I'll see you triumph ere I fa',
> My parting breath shall boast you mine.
> Good-night, and joy be wi' you a'."

His "Auld Gudeman, ye're a drucken carle," "Jenny's Bawbee," and "Jenny dang the Weaver," are of another kind, and perhaps fuller of the peculiar spirit of the man. This consisted in hitting off the deeper and typical characteristics of Scottish life with an easy touch that brings it all home at once. His lines do not seem as if they were composed by an effort of talent, but as if they were the spontaneous expressions of nature.

Take the following specimen of ludicrous pomposity, which must suffer a little by being quoted from memory; it describes a highland procession —

> "Come the Grants o' Tullochgorum
> Wi' their pipers on afore 'em;
> Proud the mithers are that bore 'em,
> Fee fuddle, fau fum.

"Come the Grants o' Rothiemurchus,
Ilka ane his sword and durk has,
Ilka ane as proud's a Turk is,
Fee fuddle, fau fum."

To comprehend the spirit of this, one must endow himself with the feelings of a Lowland Scot before Waverley and Rob Roy imparted a glow of romantic interest to the Highlanders. The pompous and the ludicrous were surely never more happily interwoven. One would require to go farther back still to appreciate the spirit of "Skeldon Haughs, or the Sow is Flitted." It is a picture of old Border feudal rivalry and hatred. The Laird of Bargainy resolved to humiliate his neighbor and enemy, the Laird of Kerse, by a forcible occupation of part of his territory. For the purpose of making this aggression flagrantly insulting, it was done by tethering or staking a female pig on the domain of Kerse. The animal was, of course, attended by a sufficient body of armed men for her protection. It was necessary for his honor that the Laird of Kerse should drive the animal and her attendants away, and hence came a bloody battle about the flitting of the sow. In the contest, Kerse's eldest son and hope, Jock, is killed, and the point or moral of the narrative is, the contempt with which the old laird looks on that event, as compared with the grave affair of flitting the sow. A retainer who comes to tell him the result of the battle stammers in his narrative on account of his grief for Jock, and is thus pulled up by the laird —

"'Is the sow flitted?' cries the carle,
'Gie me my answer, short and plain —
Is the sow flitted, yammerin' wean?'"

To which the answer is, —

"'The sow, deil tak her, 's ower the water,
And at their back the Crawfords clatter;
The Carrick couts are cowed and bitted.'"

Hereupon the laird's exultation breaks forth, —

"'My thumb for Jock — the sow's flitted.'"

Another man of genius and learning, whose name is a household one among the book clubs, is Robert Surtees, the historian of Durham. You may hunt for it in vain among the biographical dictionaries. Let us hope that this deficiency will be well supplied in the Biographia Britannica, projected by Mr. Murray. Surtees was not certainly among those who flare their qualities before the world — he was to a peculiar degree addicted, as we shall shortly see, to hiding his light under a bushel; and so any little notice of him in actual flesh and blood, such as this left by his friend, the Rev. James Tate, master of Richmond School, interests one: —

"One evening I was sitting alone — it was about nine o'clock in the middle of summer — there came a gentle tap at the door. I opened the door myself, and a gentleman said with great modesty, 'Mr. Tate, I am Mr. Surtees of Mainsforth. James Raine begged I would call upon you.' 'The master of Richmond School is delighted to see you,' said I; 'pray walk in.' 'No, thank you, sir; I have ordered a bit of supper; perhaps you will walk up with me?' 'To be sure I will;' and away we went. As we went along, I quoted a line from the Odyssey. What was my astonishment to hear from Mr. Surtees, not the next only, but line after line of the passage I had touched upon. Said I to myself, 'Good Master Tate, take heed; it is not often you catch such a fellow as this at Richmond.' I never spent such an evening in my life." What a pity, then, that he did not give us more of the evening, which seems to have left joyful memories to both; for Surtees himself thus commemorated it in Macaronics, in which he was an adept —

"Doctus Tatius hic residet,
Ad Coronam prandet ridet,
Spargit sales cum cachinno,
Lepido ore et concinno,
Ubique carus inter bonos
Rubei montis præsens honos."[1]

[1] [In macaronics? The author's memory must have failed him for a moment, or all other writers are wrong in supposing that a mixture of two languages, both being used as one, each being often subjected to the grammatical inflections of the other, is essential to the macaronic style. Thus, the lines beginning —

" Trumpeter unus erat
Qui scarletum coatum habebat,"

are macaronic. And perhaps this specimen of the style is good enough and not too well known to be quoted entire in illustration: —

"FELIS ET MURES.

" Felis sedit by a hole;
Intentus he, cum omni soul,
Prendere rats.

In the same majestic folio in which this anecdote may be found — the Memoir prefixed to the His-

Mice cucurrerunt over the floor,
In numero duo, tres, or more —
Obliti cats.

" Felis saw them, oculis,
I'll have them, inquit he, I guess —
Dum ludunt.
Tunc ille crept toward the group,
Habeam, dixit, good rat soup —
Pingues sunt.

" Mice continued all ludere,
Intenti they in ludum vere —
Gaudenter.
Tunc rushed the felis into them,
Et tore them omnes limb from limb —
Violenter.

MORAL.

" Mures omnes nunc be shy,
Et aurem præbe mihi —
Benigne.
Sic ho! facis, " verbum sat,"
Avoid a devilish big tomcat
Studiose! "

The lines quoted in the text from Surtees are mere dog Latin in the stanza and style of Drunken Barnaby. The reader who is at all curious about macaronic poetry cannot do better than to consult M. Octave Delepierre's *Macaronéa, ou Melanges de Litterature Macaronique des Differents Peuples de l'Europe.* 8vo. Paris, 1852. He will find in it some learning, but not much entertainment; which is the fault of the subject rather than of the author.

From macaronic verse to verse written for the sake of rhyme, is such an easy transition that I may be excused for adding here the following lines, which I owe to a friend. And although I must say that I think he might have been better employed than

tory of Durham — we are likewise told how, when at college, he was waiting on a Don on business; and, feeling coldish, stirred the fire. "Pray, Mr. Surtees," said the great man, "do you think that any other undergraduate in the college would have taken that liberty?" "Yes, Mr. Dean," was the reply — "any one as cool as I am!" This would have been not unworthy of Brummell. The next is not in Brummell's line. Arguing with a neighbor about his not going to church, the man said, "Why, sir, the parson and I have quarrelled about the tithes." "You fool," was the reply, "is that any reason why you should go to hell?" Yet another. A poor man, with a numerous family, lost his only cow. Surtees was collecting a subscription to replace the loss, and called on the Bishop of Lichfield, who was Dean of Durham, and owner of the great tithes in the parish, to ascertain what

in writing such stuff, yet the indulgent reader will perhaps pardon him for showing that the discussion in recent numbers of the London "Athenæum" upon the possibility of a rhyme to *step*, and the decision that none exists, are not well founded: —

HORSE-BREAKER AND GREY-MARE.

"Aurelia, prettiest of horse-breakers,
Caught Nobleigh, lord of many acres.
But this time, so it came to pass,
Instead of horse, she tamed an ass.
None of his friends will e'er dispute it;
For he, while struggling to refute it,
Was blindly led on, step by step,
To marry the fair demi-rep.
And seeking but a female Rarey,
He got a wife somewhat grey-mare-y." — W.]

he would give. "Give!" said the Bishop, "why, a cow, to be sure. Go, Mr. Surtees, to my steward, and tell him to give you as much money as will buy the best cow you can find." Surtees, astonished at this unexpected generosity, said—"My Lord, I hope you will ride to heaven upon the back of that cow." A while afterwards he was saluted in the college by the late Lord Barrington, with—"Surtees, what is the absurd speech that I hear you have been making to the dean?" "I see nothing absurd in it," was the reply; "when the dean rides to heaven on the back of that cow, many of your prebendaries will be glad to lay hold of her tail."

I have noted these innocent trifles concerning one who is chiefly known as a deep and dry investigator, for the purpose of propitiating the reader in his favor, since the sacred cause of truth renders it necessary to refer to another affair in which his conduct, however trifling it might be, was not innocent. He was addicted to literary practical jokes of an audacious kind, and carried his presumption so far as to impose on Sir Walter Scott a spurious ballad which has a place in the Border Minstrelsy. Nor is it by any means a servile imitation, which might pass unnoticed in a crowd of genuine and better ballads; but it is one of the most spirited and one of the most thoroughly endowed with individual character in the whole collection. This guilty composition is known as "The Death of Featherstonhaugh," and begins thus:—

"Hoot awa', lads, hoot awa';
Ha' ye heard how the Ridleys, and Thirlwalls, and a',
Ha' set upon Albany Featherstonhaugh,
And taken his life at the Dead Man's Haugh?
There was Williemoteswick
And Hardriding Dick,
And Hughie of Hawdon, and Will of the Wa',
I canna tell a', I canna tell a',
And many a mair that the deil may knaw.

"The auld man went down, but Nicol his son
Ran away afore the fight was begun;
And he run, and he run,
And afore they were done
There was many a Featherston gat sic a stun,
As never was seen since the world begun.
I canna tell a', I canna tell a',
Some got a skelp, and some got a claw,
But they gar't the Featherstons haud their jaw.
Some got a hurt, and some got nane,
Some had harness, and some got staen."

This imposture, professing to be taken down from the recitation of a woman eighty years old, was accompanied with some explanatory notes, characteristic of the dry antiquary, thus:—"Hardriding Dick is not an epithet referring to horsemanship, but means Richard Ridley of Hardriding, the seat of another family of that name, which, in the time of Charles I., was sold on account of expenses incurred by the loyalty of the proprietor, the immediate ancestor of Sir Matthew Ridley. Will o' the Wa' seems to be William Ridley of Walltown, so called from its situation on the great Roman wall. Thirlwall Castle, whence the clan of Thirlwalls derived their name, is situated on the small river of Tippell, near the western boundary of Northumberland. It is near the wall, and takes its name from the rampart having been *thirled* — that is, pierced or breached — in its vicinity."

In the Life of Surtees, the evidence of the crime is thus dryly set forth, in following up a statement of the transmission of the manuscript, and of its publication: — "Yet all this was a mere figment of Surtees's imagination, originating probably in some whim of ascertaining how far he could identify himself with the stirring times, scenes, and poetical compositions which his fancy delighted to dwell on. This is proved by more than one copy among his papers of this ballad, corrected and interlined, in order to mould it to the language, the manners, and the feelings of the period and of the district to which it refers. Mr. Surtees no doubt had wished to have the success of his attempt tested by the unbiassed opinion of the very first authority on the subject; and the result must have been gratifying to him."

In Scott's acknowledgment of the contribution, printed also in the Life of Surtees, there are some words that must have brought misgivings and fear of detection to the heart of the culprit, since Scott, without apparently allowing doubts to enter his mind, yet marked some peculiarities in the piece, in which it differed from others. "Your notes upon the parties concerned give it all the interest of authority, and it must rank, I suppose, among those half-serious, half-ludicrous songs, in which the poets of the Border delighted to describe what they considered as the *sport of swords*. It is perhaps remarkable, though it may be difficult to guess a reason, that these Cumbrian ditties are of a different stanza and character, and obviously sung to a different kind of music, from those on the northern Border. The gentleman who collected the words may perhaps be able to describe the tune."

There is perhaps no system of ethics which lays down with perfect precision the moral code on literary forgeries, or enables us to judge of the exact enormity of such offences. The world looks leniently on them, and sometimes sympathizes with them as good jokes. Allan Cunningham did not lose his designation of "honest Allan" by the tremendous "rises" which he took out of Cromek about those remains of Nithsdale and Galloway song — a case in point so far as principle goes, but differing somewhat in the intellectual rank of the victim to the hoax. The temptation to commit such offences is often extremely strong, and the injury seems slight, while the offender probably consoles himself with the reflection that he can immediately counteract it by confession. Vanity, indeed, often joins conscientiousness in hastening on a revelation. Surtees, however, remained in obdurate silence, and I am not aware that any edition of the Minstrelsy draws attention to his handiwork. Lockhart seems not only to have been ignorant of it, but to have been totally unconscious of the risk of such a thing, since he always speaks of its author as a respectable local antiquary, useful to Scott as a harmless drudge. Perhaps Surtees was afraid of what he had done, like that teller in the House of Commons who is said by tradition to have attempted to make a bad joke in the division on the Habeas Corpus Act by counting a fat man as ten, and, seeing that the trick passed unnoticed, and also passed the measure, became afraid to confess it.

The literary history of "The Death of Featherstonhaugh" naturally excited uneasiness about the touching ballad of "Barthram's Dirge," also contributed to the Minstrelsy as the fruit of the industrious investigations of Surtees. Most readers will remember this —

"They shot him dead at the Nine-Stone Rig,
Beside the headless cross,
And they left him lying in his blood,
Upon the moor and moss."

After this stanza, often admired for its clearness as a picture, there is a judicious break, and then come stanzas originally deficient in certain words, which, as hypothetically supplied by Surtees, were good-naturedly allowed to remain within brackets, as ingenious suggestions: —

"They made a bier of the broken bough,
The sauch and the aspine gray,
And they bore him to the Lady Chapel,
And waked him there all day.

"A lady came to that lonely bower,
And threw her robes aside;
She tore her ling [long] yellow hair,
And knelt at Barthram's side.

"She bathed him in the Lady Well,
His wounds sae deep and sair,
And she plaited a garland for his breast,
And a garland for his hair."

A glance at the reprint of the Life of Surtees for the book club called after his name, confirms the suspicions raised by the exposure of the other ballad — this also is an imposition.[1]

Altogether, such affairs create an unpleasant uncertainty about the paternity of that delightful department of literature, our ballad poetry. Where next are we to be disenchanted? Of the way in which ancient ballads have come into existence, there is one sad example within my own knowledge. Some mad young wags, wishing to test the critical powers of an experienced collector, sent him a new-made ballad, which they had been enabled to secure only in a fragmentary form. To the surprise of its fabricator, it was duly printed; but what naturally raised his surprise to astonishment, and revealed to him a secret, was, that it was no longer a fragment, but a complete ballad, — the collector, in the course of his industrious inquiries among the peasantry, having been so fortunate as to recover the missing fragments! It was a case where neither

[1] The editor of the Life prints the following note by Mr. Raine, the coadjutor of Surtees in his investigations into the history of the North of England: — "I one evening in looking through Scott's Minstrelsy wrote opposite to this dirge *aut Robertus aut Diabolus*. Surtees called shortly after, and, pouncing upon the remark, justified me by his conversation on the subject, in adding to my note *ita, teste seipso*," p. 87.

could say anything to the other, though Cato might wonder, *quod non rideret haruspex, haruspicem cum vidisset.* This ballad has been printed in more than one collection, and admired as an instance of the inimitable simplicity of the genuine old versions!

It may perhaps do something to mitigate Surtees's offence in the eye of the world, that it was he who first suggested to Scott the idea of improving the Jacobite insurrections, and, in fact, writing Waverley. In the very same letter, quoted above, where Scott acknowledges the treacherous gift, he also acknowledges the hints he has received; and, mentioning the Highland stories he had imbibed from old Stewart of Invernahyle, says, "I believe there never was a man who united the ardor of a soldier and tale-teller — or man of talk, as they call it in Gaelic — in such an excellent degree; and as he was as fond of telling as I was of hearing, I became a violent Jacobite at the age of ten years old; and even since reason and reading came to my assistance, I have never got rid of the impression which the gallantry of Prince Charles made on my imagination. Certainly I will not renounce the idea of doing something to preserve these stories, and the memory of times and manners which, though existing as it were yesterday, have so strangely vanished from our eyes."

So much for certain men of mark whose pursuits or hobbies induced them to cluster round the cradle of this new literary organization. When it was full grown it gathered about it a large body of systematic workers, who had their own special departments in the great republic of letters. To offer a just and discriminating account of these men's services would draw me through an extensive tract of literary biography.

There is a shallow prejudice very acceptable to all blockheads, that men who are both learned and laborious must necessarily be stupid. It is best to meet the approach of such a prejudice at once, by saying that the editors of club books are not mere dreary drudges, seeing the works of others accurately through the press, and attending only to dates and headings. Around and throughout the large library of volumes issued by these institutions, there run prolific veins of fresh literature pregnant with learning and ability. The style of work thus set a-going has indeed just the other day been incorporated into a sort of department of state literature, since the great collection called "The Chronicles and Memorials of Great Britain and Ireland during the Middle Ages," of which the Master of the Rolls accepts the responsibility, is carried out in the very spirit of the book clubs, in which indeed most of the editors of the Chronicles have been trained.

Without prejudice to others, let me just name a few of those to whom the world is under obligation for services in this field of learned labor. For England, there are James Orchard Halliwell, Sir Frederic Madden, Beriah Botfield, Sir Henry Ellis, Alexander Dyce, Thomas Stapleton, William J.

Thoms, Crofton Croker, Albert Way, Joseph Hunter, John Bruce, Thomas Wright, John Gough Nichols, Payne Collier, Joseph Stevenson, and George Watson Taylor, who edited that curious and melancholy book of poems, composed by the Duke of Orleans while he was a prisoner in England after the battle of Agincourt — poems composed, singularly enough, in the English language, and at a period extremely deficient in native vernacular literature.

In Scotland, it was in the earlier issues of the Bannatyne that Thomas Thomson, too indolent or fastidious to commit himself to the writing of a book, left the most accessible vestiges of that power of practically grasping historical facts and conditions, which Scott admired so greatly, and acknowledged so much benefit from. He was followed by Professor Innes, who found and taught the secret of extracting from ecclesiastical chartularies, and other early records, the light they throw upon the social condition of their times, and thus collected matter for the two pleasant volumes which have become so popular. The Bannatyne Club lately finding no more to do, wound up with a graceful compliment to David Laing, the man to whom, after Scott, it has been most indebted. And, lastly, it is in the Scotch book clubs that Joseph Robertson has had the opportunity of exercising those subtle powers of investigation and critical acumen, peculiarly his own, which have had a perceptible and substantial effect in raising archæology out of that quackish repute which it had long to endure under the name of antiquarianism. For Ireland, of which I have something further to say at length, let it suffice in the mean time to name Dean Butler, Dr. Reeves, Mr. O'Donovan, Mr. Eugene Curry, and Dr. Henthorn Todd.

There is another and distinct class of services which have been performed through the medium of the club books. The Roxburghe having been founded on the principle that each member should print a volume, to be distributed among his colleagues, an example was thus set to men of easy fortune and scholarly tastes, which has been followed with a large liberality, of which the public have probably but a faint idea. Not only in those clubs founded on the reciprocity system of each member distributing and receiving, but in those to be presently noticed, where the ordinary members pay an annual sum to be expended in the printing of their books, have individual gentlemen came forward and borne the expense of printing and distributing costly volumes.[1] In some instances valuable works have thus

[1] [The author's remark, that the British public "have probably but a faint idea" of the liberality with which individuals among his countrymen have printed and distributed costly volumes, makes it proper to observe that there is probably here, and certainly abroad, a similar ignorance of a similar generous and public-spirited practice among men of some means (though not always of wealth) and of literary tastes in this country. The books thus printed as gifts generally refer to the early history of our nation, or to the antiquities of the land in which it has fallen to our lot to supplant barbarism by civilization. Of course very small editions are printed; and these are given ex-

been presented to the members at the cost of those who have also undergone the literary labor of editing them.

There is something extremely refined and gentlemanlike in this form of liberality. The recipient of the bounty becomes the possessor of a handsome costly book without being subjected in any way to the obligation of receiving a direct gift at the hands of the munificent donor; for the recipient is a sort of corporation — a thing which the lawyers say has no personal responsibility and no conscience, and which all the world knows to have no gratitude.

clusively to students, public institutions, and collectors. For collecting books upon the history of our nation, of our people during their colonial condition, and of the American races whom we have displaced, has so long been a special literary object, and has been so eagerly pursued, that the demand has created a special department of the book-trade, and scarce books upon America, the English colonies in America, the United States, or the several States, bring prices which seem absurd when compared with their intrinsic value. So directly at variance with the truth is Sir Archibald Alison's assertion that we are "wholly regardless of historical records or monuments," and that future historians will therefore be obliged "to write the history of the present generation from the archives of other lands;" for which thought, by the way, he is indebted to one of the few errors of the candid and philosophical De Tocqueville. But these historical reprints do not include all the privately printed books, among which are even occasional reproductions of some very rare old English book, and monographs upon important questions in literature. And this in a country where, according to the same grave historian, "literature receives but little encouragement." For our own sakes it would not be worth while to notice these matters. We can afford to pass them by. But it is curious and instructive to observe with how much ignorance people can enable themselves to write about us. — W.]

PART IV.—BOOK-CLUB LITERATURE.

Generalities.

EARLY a quarter of a century after the birth of the first book club, a new era was ushered in by its brother, the Camden, established for the printing of books and documents connected with the early civil, ecclesiastical, and literary history of the British Empire. It discarded the rule which threw on each member the duty of printing and distributing a book, and tried the more equitable adjustment of an annual subscription to create a fund for defraying the expense of printing volumes to be distributed among the members. These, at first limited to 1000, expanded to 1200. Clubs with various objects now thickly followed. Any attempt to classify them as a whole, is apt to resemble Whately's illustration of illogical division —"*e. g.*, if you were to divide 'book' into 'poetical, historical, folio, quarto, French, Latin,'" &c. One of the systems of arrangement is topographical, as the Chetham, "for the purpose of publishing biographical and historical books connected with the counties palatine of Lancaster and Chester."[1] The Surtees, again, named after our friend the ballad-monger, affects "those parts of England and Scotland included in the east between the Humber and the Firth of Forth, and in the west between the Mersey and the Clyde — a region which constituted the ancient kingdom of Northumberland." The Maitland, with its head-quarters in Glasgow, gives a preference to the west of Scotland, but has not been exclusive. The Spalding Club, established in Aberdeen, the granite capital of the far north, is the luminary of its own district, and has produced fully as much valuable historical matter as any other club in Britain. Then there is the Irish Archæological — perhaps the most learned of all — with its casual assistants, the Ossianic, the Celtic, and the Iona. The Ælfric may be counted their ethnical rival, as dealing with the productions of the Anglo-Saxon enemies of the Celt. The Camden professes, as we have seen, to be general to the British Empire. The name of the club called "The Oriental Translation Fund" tells its own story.

There are others, too, with no topographical connection, which express pretty well their purpose in their names — as the Shakespeare, for the old drama — the Percy, for old ballads and lyrical pieces. The Hakluyt has a delightful field — old voyages

[1] Among other volumes of interest, the Chetham has issued a very valuable and amusing collection of documents about the siege of Preston, and other incidents of the insurrection of 1715 in Lancashire.

and travels. The Rae Society sticks to zoölogy and botany; and the Wernerian, the Cavendish, and the Sydenham, take the other departments in science, which the names given to them readily indicate.

In divinity and ecclesiastical history we have the Parker Society, named after the archbishop. Its tendencies are "low," or, at all events, "broad;" and as it counted some seven thousand members, it could not be allowed the run of the public mind without an antidote being accessible. Hence, "The Library of Anglo-Catholic Theology," the tendency of which was not only shown in its name, but in its possessing among its earliest adherents the Rev. E. B. Pusey and the Rev. John Keble. The same party strengthened themselves by a series of volumes called the "Library of the Fathers of the Holy Catholic Church anterior to the Division of the East and West, translated by Members of the English Church." In Scotland, the two branches which deny the supremacy of Rome (it would give offence to call them both Protestant) are well represented by the Spottiswoode, already referred to as the organ of Episcopacy; and the more prolific Wodrow, which, named after the zealous historian of the Troubles, was devoted to the history of Presbyterianism, and the works of the Presbyterian fathers.

Thus are the book clubs eminently the republic of letters, in which no party or class has an absolute predominance, but each enjoys a fair hearing. And whereas if we saw people for other purposes than literature combining together according to ecclesiastical divisions, as High Church or Low, Episcopalian or Presbyterian, we should probably find that each excluded from its circle all that do not spiritually belong to it, we are assured it is quite otherwise in the book clubs — that High Churchmen or Romanists have not been excluded from the Parker, or evangelical divines prohibited from investing in the Library of Anglo-Catholic Theology. Nay, the most zealous would incline to encourage the communication of their own peculiar literary treasures to their avowed theological opponents, as being likely to soften their hearts, and turn them towards the truth. Some adherents of these theological clubs there also are of slightly latitudinarian propensities, to whom the aspirations of honest religious zeal, and the records of endurance and martyrdom for conscience' sake, can never be void of interest, or fail in summoning up feelings of respectful sympathy, whatever be the denominational banner under which they have been exhibited. Some of these clubs now rest from their labors, the literary strata in which they were employed having been in fact worked out. Whether dead or living, however, their books are now a considerable and varied intellectual garden, in which the literary busy bee may gather honey all the day and many a day.

It will be readily supposed from the different and utterly separate grooves in which they run, and is very well known to the prowler among club books, that although these volumes profess to be printed from old manuscripts, or to be mere reprints of rare books, they take a considerable portion of their tone and tendency from the editor. In fact, the editor of a club book is, in the general case, a sort of literary sportsman, who professes to follow entirely his own humor or caprice, or, say, his own taste and enjoyment, in the matter which he selects, and the manner in which he lays it before his friends. Hence, many of these volumes, heavy and unimpressible as they look, yet are stamped strongly with the marks of the individuality, or of the peculiar intellectual cast, of living men. Take down, for instance, the volume of the Camden called "De Antiquis Legibus Liber, otherwise, Cronica Majorum et Vicecomitum Londoniarum," printed from "a small folio, nine inches and a half in length and seven inches in breadth, the binding of white leather covering wooden backs, and containing 159 leaves of parchment, paged continuously with Arabic cyphers." It is partly a record of the old municipal laws of the city of London, partly a chronicle of events. Had it fallen to be edited by a philosophical inquirer into the origin and principles of jurisprudence, or an investigator of the rise and progress of cities, or a social philosopher of any kind, it is hard to say what might have been made of it — easy to say that it would have been made something very different from what it is. The editor was an illustrious genealogist. Accordingly, early in his career as expositor of the character of the volume, he alights upon a proper name, not entirely isolated, but capable of being associated with other names. Thus, he is placed on a groove, and off he goes travelling in the fashion following over 220 pages of printed quarto: "Henry de Cornhill, husband of Alice de Courcy, the heiress of the Barony of Stoke Courcy Com. Somerset, and who, after his decease, re-married Warine Fitz-Gerald the king's chamberlain, leaving by each an only daughter, co-heirs of this Barony, of whom Joan de Cornhill was the wife of Hugh de Neville, Proto Forester of England, wife first of Baldwine de Reviers, eldest son and heir-apparent of William de Vernon, Earl of Devon, deceased in his father's lifetime; and, secondly, of the well-known favourite of King John, Fulk de Breauté, who had name from a commune of the Canton of Goderville, arrondissement of Le Havre, department of La Seine Inférieure, rendered accompt of this his debt in the same roll;" and so on over the remainder of the 220 pages. If you turn over a few of them you will find the same sort of thing: "Agnes, the first daughter, was married to William de Vesey, of whom John de Vesey, issueless, and William de Vesey, who had issue, John de Vesey, who died before his father; and afterwards the said William de Vesey, the father, without heir of his body;" and so on.

The reader whose fortune it has been to pass a portion of his early days among venerable Scottish gentlewomen of the old school, will perhaps experience an uneasy consciousness of having encountered matter of this description before. It may recall to him misty recollections of communications which followed a course something like this: "And so ye see, auld Pittoddles, when his third wife deed, he got married upon the laird o' Blaithershin's aughteenth daughter, that was sister to Jemima, that was married intil Tam Flumexer, that was first and second cousin to the Pittoddleses, whase brither became laird afterwards, and married Blaithershin's Baubie — and that way Jemima became in a kind o' way her ain niece and her ain aunty, an' as we used to say, her gude-brither was married to his ain grannie."

But there is the deep and the shallow in genealogy, as in other arts and sciences, and, incoherent as it may sound to the uninitiated, the introduction to the Liber de Antiquis Legibus is no old woman's work, but full of science and strange matter.[1] It all grows, however, in genealogical trees, these being the predominant intellectual growth in the editor's mind. In fact, your thorough genealogist

[1] I remember hearing of an instance at a jury trial in Scotland, where counsel had an extremely subtle point of genealogy to make out, and no one but a ploughman witness, totally destitute of the genealogical faculty, to assist him to it. His plan — and probably a very judicious one in the general case — was to get the witness on a table-land of broad unmistakable principle, and then by degrees lure him farther on. Thus he got the witness readily to admit that his own mother was older than himself, but no exertion or ingenuity could get his intellect a step beyond that broad admission.

is quite a peculiar intellectual phenomenon. He is led on by a special and irresistible internal influence or genius. If he should for some time endeavor to strive after a more cosmopolite intellectual vitality, the ruling spirit conquers all other pursuits. The organism of the tree resumes its predominance, and if he have healthy sturdy brains, whatever other matter they may have collected is betimes dragged into the growth, and absorbed in the vitality of the majestic bole and huge branches. There is perhaps no pursuit more thoroughly absorbing. The reason is this: No man having yet made out for himself an articulate pedigree from Adam — Sir Thomas Urquhart, the translator of Rabelais, to be sure, made one for himself, but he had his tongue in his cheek all the while — no clear pedigree going back to the first of men, every one, whether short or long, Celtic or Saxon, comes into the clouds at last. It is when a pedigree approaches extinction that the occasion opens for the genealogist to exercise his subtlety and skill, and his exertions become all the more zealous and exciting that he knows he must be baffled somewhere. The pursuit is described as possessing something like the same absorbing influence which is exercised over certain minds by the higher mathematics. The devotees get to think that all human knowledge centres in their peculiar science and the cognate mysteries and exquisite scientific manipulations of heraldry, and they may be heard talking with compassionate contempt of some one so grossly ignorant as not to know a bar-dexter from a bend-sinister, or who asks what is meant by a cross potent quadrate party per pale.

These are generally great readers—reading is absolutely necessary for their pursuit ; but they have a faculty of going over literary ground, picking up the proper names, and carrying them away, unconscious of anything else, as pointers go over stubble fields and raise the partridges, without taking any heed of the valuable examples of cryptogamic botany or palæozoic entomology they may have trodden over. A certain writer on logic and metaphysics was once as much astonished as gratified by an eminent genealogical antiquary's expression of interest in a discovery which his last book contained. The philosopher thought his views on the quantification of the predicate or on bifurcate analysis had at last been appreciated ; but the discovery was merely this, that the name of a person who, according to the previously imperfect science of the genealogist, ought not to have existed then and there, was referred to in a letter from Spinoza, cited in defence of certain views upon the absolute.

The votaries of this pursuit become powers in the world of rank and birth, from the influence they are able to bring upon questions of succession and inheritance. Hence they are, like all great influences, courted and feared. Their ministry is often desired, sometimes necessary ; but it is received with misgiving and awe, since, like the demons of old summoned by incantation, they may destroy the audacious mortal who demands their services. The most sagacious and sceptical men are apt to be mildly susceptible to conviction in the matter of their own pedigrees, and, a little conscious of their weakness, they shrink from letting the sacred tree be handled by relentless and unsympathizing adepts. One of these intellectual tyrants, a man of great ability, when he quarrelled with any one, used to threaten to "bastardize" him, or to find the bend-sinister somewhere in his ancestry; and his experience in long genealogies made him feel assured, in the general case, of finding what he sought if he went far enough back for it.

The next volume you lay hand on is manifestly edited by an Ecclesiologist, or a votary of that recent addition to the constituted "ologies," which has come into existence as the joint offspring of the revival of Gothic architecture and the study of primitive-church theology. Through this dim religious light he views all the things in heaven and earth that are dealt with in his philosophy. His notes are profusely decorated with a rich array of rood screens, finial crockets, lavatories, aumbries, lecterns, lych sheds, albs, stoups, sedilia, credence tables, pixes, hagioscopes, baudekyns, and squenches. It is evident that he keeps a bestiary, or record of his experiences in bestiology, otherwise called bestial eikonography; and if he be requested to give a more explicit definition of the article, he will perhaps inform you that it is a record of the types of the ecclesiological symbolization of beasts. If you prevail on him to exhibit to you this solemn record, which he will open with befitting reverence, the faintest suspicion of a smile curling on your lip will suffuse him with a lively sorrow for your lost condition, mixed with righteous indignation towards the irreverent folly whereof you have been guilty. He finds a great deal beyond sermons in stones, and can point out to you a certain piece of rather confused-looking architecture, which he terms a symbolical epitome of all knowledge, human and divine — an eikonographic encyclopædia.

If you desire an antidote to all this, you may find it in the editor in true blue who so largely refers to the Book of the Universal Kirk, The Hynd Let Loose, The Cloud of Witnesses, Naphtali, and Faithful Witness-Bearing Exemplified, and is great in his observations on the Auchinshauch Testimony, the Sanquhar Declaration, and that fine amalgamation of humility and dogmatism, the Informatory Vindication.[1]

There is no occasion for quarrelling with these specialties. They are typical of a zeal often prolific both in amusement and instruction; and when a man has gone through the labor of rendering many hundreds of pages from a crabbed old manuscript, or of translating as much from a nearly unknown tongue, it would be hard to deny him the recreation of a few capers on his own hobby. Keep in mind

[1] "An Informatory Vindication of a poor, wasted, misrepresented remnant of the suffering anti-popish, anti-prelatic, anti-erastian, anti-sectarian, *only true* church of Christ in Scotland."

that everything of this kind is outside the substance of the book. The editor has his swing in the introduction and appendix, and the notes; perhaps also in the title and index, if he can make anything of them. But it is a principle of honor throughout the clubs that the purity of the text shall not be tampered with, and so, whether dark or light, faint or strong, it is a true impression of the times, as the reader will perhaps find in the few specimens I propose to show him. As touching the literary value of what is thus restored, there are some who will say, and get applause for doing so, that there are too many bad or second-rate books in the world already; that every work of great genius finds its way to the world at once; and that the very fact of its long obscurity proves a piece of literature to be of little value. For all this, and all that can be added to it, there are those who love these recovered relics of ancestral literature, and are prepared to give reasons for their attachment. In the first place, and apart from their purely literary merits, they are records of the intellect and manners of their age. Whoever desires really to be acquainted with the condition of a nation at any particular time — say with that of England during Elizabeth's reign, or the Commonwealth — will not attain his object by merely reading the most approved histories of the period. He must endeavor as far as he can to live back into the times, and to do this most effectually he had better saturate himself to the utmost with its fugitive literature, reading every scrap he may lay hand on until he can find no more.

Looking at these relics, on the other hand, as pure literature, no doubt what is recalled out of the past loses the freshness and the fitness to surrounding conditions which gave it pungency and emphasis in its own day, while it has not that hold on our sympathies and attachment possessed by the household literature which generation after generation has been educated to admire, and which, indeed, has made itself a part of our method of thought, and our form of language. But precisely because it wants this qualification has resuscitated literature a peculiar value of its own. It breaks in with a new light upon the intellect of the day, and its conventional forms and colors. There is not in the intellectual history of mankind any so effective and brilliant an awakening as the resuscitation of classical literature. It was not one solitary star arising after another at long intervals and far apart in space, but a sudden blazing forth of a whole firmament of light. But that is a phenomenon to all appearance not to be repeated, or, more correctly speaking, not to be completed, since it broke up unfinished, leaving the world in partial darkness. Literature has been ever since wailing the loss of the seventy per cent. of Livy's History, of the eighty per cent. of Tacitus and of Euripides, of the still larger proportion of Æschylus and Sophocles, of the mysterious triumphs of Menander, and of the whole apparatus of the literary renown of Varro and of

Atticus. What would the learned world give for the restoration of these things? It may safely offer an indefinite reward, for so well has its surface been ransacked for them that their existence is hardly possible, though some sanguine people enjoy the expectation of finding them in some obscure back-shelves in the Sultan's library. The literary results of the costly and skilful scientific process for restoring the baked books found in Herculaneum were so appallingly paltry, as to discourage the pursuit of the lost classics. The best thing brought to light during the present century, indeed, is that institute of Gaius which cost Angelo Maï such a world of trouble, and was the glory and boast of his life; but it is not a very popular or extensively read book after all. The manuscripts that have been extracted from the dirty greedy fingers of the Armenian and Abyssinian monks, are the most valuable pieces of literature that have been rescued from the far past. Important light on the early history of eastern Christianity will no doubt be extracted from them; but they are written in those oriental tongues which are available only to the privileged few.

Unlikely as the treasures opened by the revival of classic literature are to be to any extent increased, let us not despise the harvest of our own home gleaners. They do not find now and then a buried Hamlet, or Paradise Lost, or Hudibras — though, by the way, the Poetical Remains of Butler, which in wit and sarcasm are second only to his great work, were rescued from oblivion by the drudging antiquary Thier, who was so conceited of the performance that he had the portrait of his own respectable and stupid face engraved beside that of Butler, in order perhaps that all men might see how incapable he was of fabricating the pieces to which it is prefixed. There is a good deal of the poetry of the club books of which it may at least be said, that worse is printed and praised as the produce of our contemporaries.[1]

[1] Take, for instance, the Hymns or Sacred Songs of Alexander Hume, a poet of the end of the sixteenth century, resuscitated by the Bannatyne. One of them called "The Day Estival, or Thanks for a Summer Day," though rounded off with a few established pastoralities, yet shows a keen observation of pleasing natural objects, and a ready capacity for describing them. After a short peroration we have the morning twilight announced.

"The shadow of the earth anon
Removes and drawes by,
Then in the east, when it is gone,
Appears a clearer sky."

Then the sunrise —

"The golden globe incontinent
Sets up his shining head,
And o'er the earth and firmament
Displays his beams abraid.

"For joy the birds with bolden throats,
Against his visage sheen,
Take up their kindly music notes
In woods and gardens green.

"Up braids the careful husbandman,
His corns and vines to see,
And every timeous artisan
In booth works busily.

It is not so much, however, in Poetry or the Drama as in Historical literature that the clubs develop their strength. It is difficult to estimate the greatness of the obligations of British history to these institutions. They have dug up, cleansed, and put in order for immediate inspection and use, a multitude of written monuments bearing on the greatest events and the most critical epochs in the progress of the empire. The time thus saved to

"The pastor quits the slothful sleep,
And passes forth with speed,
His little camow-nosed sheep
And rowting kie to feed."

And so the day goes on until we have this pleasant picture of a sultry noon: —

"The time so tranquil is and still,
That nowhere shall ye find,
Save on an high and barren hill,
The air of peeping wind.

"All trees and simples great and small,
That balmy leaf do bear,
Nor they were painted on a wall,
No more they move or stir.

"Calm is the deep and purpure see,
Yea, smoother than the sand;
The wells that weltering wont to be
Are stable like the land.

"So silent is the cessile air,
That every cry and call
The hills and dails and forest fair
Again repeat them all.

"The rivers fresh, the caller streams,
Doun rocks can softly rin,
The water clear like crystel seems,
And makes a pleasant din."

investigators is great and priceless. In no other department of knowledge can the intellectual laborer more forcibly apply the Latin proverb which warns him that his work is indefinite but his life brief. In the ordinary sciences the philosopher may and often does content himself with the well-rounded and professedly completed system of the

Then follow a variety of sketches of still and active life, appropriate to the several periods of the day's progress; and at last evening brings its own peculiar beauties: —

"The gloaming comes, the day is spent,
The sun goes out of sight,
And painted is the Occident
With purpour sanguine bright.

"The scarlet nor the golden thread,
Who would their beauties try,
Are nothing like the colour red
And beauty of the sky.

"Our west horizon circular,
Fra time the sun be set,
Is all with rubies, as it were,
Or roses red o'erset.

"What pleasure were to walk and see,
Endlong a river clear,
The perfect form of every tree
Within the deep appear!

"The salmon out of cruives and creels,
Uphalled into skoutts,
The bells and circles on the wells
Through louping of the trouts.

"O then it were a seemly thing,
While all is still and calm,
The praise of God to play and sing,
With cornet and with pscham."

day. But no one can grapple with history without feeling its inexhaustibleness. Its final boundaries seem only to retreat to a farther distance the more ground we master, as Mr. Buckle found, when he betook himself, like another Atlas, to grapple with the history of the whole world.

The more an investigator finds his materials printed for him, the farther he can go. No doubt it is sometimes desirable, even necessary, to look to some manuscript authority for the clearing-up of a special point; but too often the profession of having perused a great mass of manuscript authorities is an affectation and a pedantry. He who searches for and finds the truth in any considerable portion of history, performs too great an achievement to care for the praise of deciphering a few specimens of difficult handwriting, and revealing the sense hidden in certain words couched in obsolete spelling. If casual discoveries of this kind do really help him to great truths, it is well; but it too often happens that he exaggerates their value, because they are his own game, shot on his own manor. Until he has exhausted all that is in print, the student of history wastes his time in struggling with manuscripts. Hence the value of the services of the book clubs in immensely widening the arena of his immediate materials. To him their volumes are as new tools to the mechanic, or new machinery to the manufacturer. They economize, as it is termed, his labor; more correctly speaking, they increase its productiveness.

These books are fortunately rich in memorials of the great internal contest of the seventeenth century. Take, for instance, the notes of the proceedings of the Long Parliament, by Sir Ralph Verney, edited for the Camden by Mr. Bruce. They come upon us fresh from that scene of high debate, carrying with them the very marks of strife. The editor informs us that the manuscript is written almost entirely in pencil on slips of foolscap paper, which seem to have been so folded as to be conveniently placed on the knee, and transferred to the pocket as each was completed. "They are," he says, "full of abrupt terminations, as if the writer occasionally gave up the task of following a rapid speaker who had got beyond him, and began his note afresh. When they relate to resolutions of the House, they often contain erasures, alterations, or other marks of the haste with which the notes were jotted down, and of the changes which took place in the subject-matter during the progress towards completion. On several important occasions, and especially in the instance of the debate on the Protestation [as to the impeachment of Strafford], the confusion and irregularity of the notes give evidence to the excitement of the House; and when the public discord rose higher, the notes become more brief and less personal, and speeches are less frequently assigned to their speakers, either from greater difficulty in reporting, or from an increased feeling of the danger of the time, and the possible use that might be made of notes of violent remarks.

On several of the sheets there are marks evidently made by the writer's pencil having been forced upwards suddenly, as if by some one, in a full House, pressing hastily against his elbow while he was in the act of taking his note."

John Spalding.

OOKING from the opposite end of the island, and from a totally different social position, another watchful observer recorded the events of the great contest. This was John Spalding, commonly supposed to have been Commissary-Clerk of Aberdeen, but positively known in no other capacity than as author of the book aptly entitled The Troubles, or, more fully, "Memorials of the Troubles in Scotland and in England," from 1624 to 1645. Little, probably, did the Commissary-Clerk imagine, when he entered on his snug quiet office, where he recorded probates of wills and the proceedings in questions of marriage law, that he was to witness and record one of the most momentous conflicts that the world ever beheld — that contest which has been the prototype of all later European convulsions. Less still could he have imagined that fame would arise for him after two hundred years — that vehement though vain efforts should be made to endow the simple name of John Spalding with the antecedents and subsequents of a biographical existence, and that the far-off descendants of many of those lairds and barons, whose warlike deeds he noticed at humble distance, should raise a monument to his memory in an institution called by his name. He was evidently a thoroughly retiring man, for he has left no vestige whatever of his individuality. Some specimens of his formal official work might have been found in the archives of his office — these would have been especially valuable for the identification of his handwriting and the settlement of disputed questions about the originality of manuscripts; but these documents, as it happens, were all burnt early in last century with the building containing them. So ardent and hot has been the chase after vestiges of this man, that the fact was once discovered that with his own hand he had written a certain deed concerning a feu-duty or rent-charge of £25 7s. 4d., bearing date 31st January, 1663; but in spite of the most resolute efforts, this interesting document has not been found.

It is probably to this same unobtrusive reserve, which has shrouded his very identity, that we owe the valuable peculiarities of the Commissary-Clerk's chronicle. He sought no public distinctions, took no ostensible side, and must have kept his own thoughts to himself, otherwise he would have had to bear record of his own share of troubles. In this calm serenity, folding the arms of resignation on the bosom of patience as the Persians say, he took his notes of the wild contest that raged around him, setting down each event, great or small, with systematic deliberation, as if he were an experimental philosopher watching the phenomena of an eclipse or an eruption. Hence nowhere, perhaps, has it been permitted to a mere reader to have so good a peep behind the scenes of the mighty drama of war. We have plenty of chroniclers of that epoch — marching us with swinging historic stride on from battle unto battle — great in describing in long sentences the musterings, the conflicts, and the retreats. In Spalding, however, we shall find the numbers and character of the combatants, their arms, their dresses, the persons who paid for these, and the prices paid — the amount they obtained in pay, and the amount they were cheated out of — their banners, distinguishing badges, watchwords, and all other like particulars, set down with the minuteness of a bailiff making an inventory of goods on which he has taken execution. He is very specific in what one may term the negative side of the characteristics of war — the misery and desolation it spreads around. The losses of this "gudeman" and that lone widow are stated as if he were their law agent, making up an account to go to a jury for damages for the "spulzie of outside and inside plenishing, nolt, horse, sheep, cocks and hens, hay, corn, peats, and fodder." He specifies all the items of mansions and farm-houses attacked and looted, or "harried," as he calls it — the doors staved in, the wainscoting pulled down — the windows smashed — the furniture made firewood of —

the pleasant plantations cut down to build sleeping-huts — the linen, plate, and other valuables carried off: he will even, perchance, tell how they were distributed — who it was that managed to feather his nest with the plunder, and who it was that was disappointed and cheated.

He had opportunities of bestowing his descriptive powers to good purpose. Besides its ordinary share in the vicissitudes and calamities of the war, his town of Aberdeen was twice pillaged by Montrose, with laudable impartiality — once for the Covenanters and once for the Royalists. Here is his first triumphant entry: —

"Upon the morne, being Saturday, they came in order of battle, being well armed both on horse and foot, ilk horseman having five shot at the least, whereof he had ane carbine in his hand, two pistols by his sides, and other two at his saddle-torr; the pikemen in their ranks with pike and sword; the musketeers in their ranks with musket, musket-staff, bandelier, sword, powder, ball, and match. Ilk company, both horse and foot, had their captains, lieutenants, ensigns, sergeants, and other officers and commanders, all for the most part in buff coats and goodly order. They had five colors or ensigns, whereof the Earl of Montrose had one having his motto drawn in letters, 'For Religion, the Covenant, and the Countrie.' The Earl Marechal had one, the Earl of Kinghorn had one, and the town of Dundee had two. They had trumpeters to ilk company of horsemen, and drummers to ilk company of footmen. They had their meat, drink, and other provisions, bag and baggage, carried with them, done all by advice of his Excellency Field-Marshal Leslie, whose counsel General Montrose followed in this business. Then, in seemly order and good array, this army came forward and entered the burgh of Aberdeen, about ten hours in the morning, at the Over Kirk gateport, syne came down through the Broadgate, through the Castlegate, over at the Justice Port to the Queen's Links directly. Here it is to be noted that few or none of this haill army wanted ane blue ribbon hung about his craig [viz., neck] under his left arm, whilk they called 'the Covenanters' ribbon,' because the Lord Gordon and some other of the Marquis's bairns had ane ribbon, when he was dwelling in the toun, of ane red flesh color, which they wore in their hats, and called it 'the royal ribbon,' as a sign of their love and loyalty to the King. In dispite or dirision whereof this blue ribbon was worn and called 'the Covenanters' ribbon' by the haill soldiers of this army."

The well-ordered army passed through, levying a fine on the Malignants, and all seemed well; but because the citizens had not resisted Montrose, the loyal barons in the neighborhood fell on them and plundered them; and because they had submitted to be so plundered, the Covenanting army came back and plundered them also. "Many of this company went and brack up the Bishop's yetts, set on good fires of his peats standing within the close:

they masterfully broke up the haill doors and windows of this stately house; they brake down beds, boards, aumries, glassen windows, took out the iron staucheons, brake in the locks, and such as they could carry had with them, and sold for little or nothing; but they got none of the Bishop's plenishing to speak of, because it was all conveyed away before their coming." On Sunday, Montrose and the other leaders duly attended the devotional services of the eminent Covenanting divines they had brought with them. "But," says Spalding, "the renegate soldiers, in time of both preachings, is abusing and plundering New Aberdeen pitifully, without regard to God or man;" and he goes on in his specific way, describing the plundering until he reaches this climax: "No foul — cock or hen — left unkilled. The haill house-dogs, messens, and whelps within Aberdeen felled and slain upon the gate, so that neither hound nor messen or other dog was left that they could see." But there was a special reason for this. The ladies of Aberdeen, on the retiring of Montrose's army, had decorated all the vagabond street-dogs with the blue ribbon of the Covenant.

This was in 1639. Five years afterwards Montrose came back on them in more terrible guise still, to punish the town for having yielded to the Covenant. In Aberdeen, Cavalier principles generally predominated; but after being overrun and plundered successively by either party, the Covenanters, having the acting government of the country at their back, succeeded in establishing a predominance in the councils of the exhausted community. Spalding had no respect for the civic and rural forces they attempted to embody, and speaks of a petty bailie "who brought in ane drill-master to learn our poor bodies to handle their arms, who had more need to handle the plough and win their livings." Montrose had now with him his celebrated army of Highlanders — or Irish, as Spalding calls them — who broke at a rush through the feeble force sent out of the town to meet them. Montrose "follows the chase to Aberdeen, his men hewing and cutting down all manner of men they could overtake within the town, upon the streets, or in their houses, and round about the town, as our men were fleeing, with broadswords, but mercy or remeid. These cruel Irish, seeing a man well clad, would first tyr [*i. e.*, strip] him and save the clothes unspoiled, then kill the man; . . . nothing heard but pitiful howling, crying, weeping, mourning, through all the streets. . . . It is lamentable to hear how thir Irishes, who had gotten the spoil of the town, did abuse the samin. The men that they killed they would not suffer to be buried, but tirled them of their clothes, syne left their naked bodies lying above the ground. The wife durst not cry nor weep at her husband's slaughter before her eyes, nor the mother for her son — which if they were heard, then they were presently slain also, . . . and none durst bury the dead. Yea, and I saw two corpses carried to the burial through the old town with women only, and not ane man amongst them, so that the naked corpses lay unburied so long as these limmers were ungone to the camp."

The Commissary-Clerk was on Montrose's side, but he had the hatred of a Lowlander of that day for the Highlanders. He has a great many amusing episodes describing the light-handed lads from the hills coming down, and in the general confusion of the times plundering Cavalier and Covenanter alike; and on these occasions he drops his usual placidity and becomes rabid and abusive, as the best-tempered Americans are said to become when they speak of niggers, and deals out to them the terms—limmers, thieves, robbers, cut-throats, masterful vagrants, and so forth, with great volubility.[1] Of some of their

[1] [It would be more satisfactory if this statement were somewhat more specific; if we knew who were meant by "the Americans," and by whom they are said to become "rabid and abusive when they speak of niggers." If by the Americans are meant the fire-eating slaveholders and the poor-white trash which lives upon their refuse and does their dirty work, the justice of the remark must be admitted. This sort of American is rabid and abusive enough upon the subject of "niggers." The London "Morning Herald" itself upon the subject of "Yankees" can hardly surpass the richness and pungency of his vocabulary; the style of every true Briton a few years ago when he spoke of Frenchmen went little beyond it, even in profanity. But outside of the fellowship above named are about twenty millions of people sometimes designated as Americans, for want of a better name, among whom this book will find its readers, and who will be surprised and doubtless gratified to learn how very foul-mouthed they become when they speak of a subject in which their concern is not at all of a personal, but purely of a public and philanthropic nature. — W.]

chiefs, renowned in history, he speaks as mere robber-leaders, and when they are known by one name in their own country and another in the Lowlands, he puts an *alias* between the two. The very initial words of his chronicle are, "Efter the death and burial of Angus Macintosh of Auldterlie, *alias* Angus Williamson."

Montrose having departed, Argyle's troops commenced to plunder the district for having submitted to his enemy, and these, being doubly offensive as Covenanters and Highlanders, are treated accordingly. But it is necessary to be impartial; and having bestowed so much on the Cavalier annalist, let us take a glimpse at the other side.

Robert Wodrow.

FROM the collections of the Reverend Robert Wodrow, the historian of The Sufferings of the Church of Scotland, a rich harvest has been reaped by the northern clubs, one of which appropriately adopted his name. He was a voluminous writer and an inexhaustible collector. It is generally classed among the failings of the book-hunter that he looks only to the far past, and disregards the contemporary and the recent. Wodrow was a valuable exception to this propensity. Reversing the spirit of the selfish bull which asks what posterity has done for us, he stored up contemporary literature for subsequent generations; and he thus left, at the commencement of the eighteenth century, such a library as a collector of the nineteenth, could he have sent a caterer before him, would have prepared to await his arrival in the world. The inestimable value of the great collection of the civil-war pamphlets made by George Thomason, and fortunately preserved in the British Museum, is very well known. Just such another of its kind is Wodrow's, made up of the pamphlets, broadsides, pasquinades, and other fugitive pieces of his own day, and of the generation immediately preceding. These are things easily obtained in their freshness, but the term fugitive is too expressive of their nature, and after a generation or two they have all flown away, save those which the book-hunter has exorcised into the vaults of some public collection. There is perhaps too little done in our own day in preserving for posterity these mute witnesses of our sayings and doings. They are too light and volatile to be caught by the Copyright Act, which so carefully deposits our quartos and octavos in the privileged libraries. It is pleasant, by the way, at this moment, to observe that the eminent scholar who has charge of the chief portion of Wodrow's gatherings, as keeper of the Advocates' Library, is following his example, by preserving a collection of the pamphlets of the present century which will keep our posterity in employment, if they desire to unwind the intricacies of all our civil and ecclesiastical sayings and doings.

Wodrow carried on an active correspondence about matters of contemporary policy, and the special inquiries connected with his History: selections from this mass have furnished three sturdy volumes. Besides pamphlets, he scraped together quantities of other people's manuscripts — some of them rising high enough in importance to be counted State papers. How the minister of the quiet rural parish of Eastwood could have got his hands on them is a marvel, but it is fortunate that they were saved from destruction; and it is nearly equally fortunate that they have been well ransacked by zealous club-book makers, who have by this time probably exhausted the better part of their material. In the next place, Wodrow left behind several biographies of eminent members of his own Church, its saints and martyrs; and goodly masses out of this storehouse have also been printed.

But by far the most luxurious morsel in the worthy man's intellectual larder was not intended to reach the profane vulgar, but destined for his own special rumination. It consists in the veritable contents of his private note-books, containing his communings with his own heart and his imagination. They were written on small slips of paper, in a hand direly cramped and minute; and lest this should not be a sufficient protection to their privacy, a portion was committed to certain ciphers, which their ingenious inventor deemed, no doubt, to be utterly impregnable. In stenography, however, the art of lock-picking always keeps ahead of the art of locking, as that of inventing destructive missiles seems to outstrip that of forging impenetrable plates. Wodrow's trick was the same as that of Samuel Pepys, and productive of the same consequences—the excitement of a rabid curiosity, which at last found its way into the recesses of his secret communings. They are now printed, in the fine type of the Maitland Club, in four portly quartos, under the title, Wodrow's Analecta. Few books would hold out so much temptation to a commentator, but their editor is dumb, faithfully reprinting the whole, page by page, and abstaining both from introduction and explanatory foot-note.

Perhaps in the circumstances this was a prudent measure. Those who enjoy the weaknesses of the enthusiastic historian have them at full length. As to others partially like-minded with him, but more worldly, who would rather that such a tissue of absurdities had not been revealed, they are bound over to silence, seeing that a word said against the book is a word of reproach against its idolized author—for as to the editor, he may repeat after Macbeth, "Thou canst not say I did it."

Mr. Buckle's ravenous researches into the most distant recesses of literature revealed to him this pose. He has taken some curious specimens out of it, but he might have made his anthology still richer had he been in search of the picturesque and ludicrous, instead of seeking solid support for his great theory of positivism. What he chiefly amuses one with in this part of the world, however, is the solemn manner in which he treats the responsibility of giving increased publicity to such things, and invokes the Deity to witness that his objects are sincere, and he is influenced by no irreverence. This feeling may arise from a very creditable source, but a native of Scotland has difficulty in understanding it. In this country, being, as many of us have been, within the very skirts of the great contests that have shaken the realm — Jacobitism on the one hand and Covenantism on the other — we are roughened and hardened, and what shocks our sensitive neighbors is very good fun to ourselves.

It appears that Wodrow had intended to publish a book on remarkable special providences — something of a scientific character it was to be, containing a classification of their phenomena, perhaps a theory of their connection with revealed religion. The natural laws by which they are ruled, he could not, of course, have sought to discover, since the principle on which he set out predicated the non-existence of such laws. The advantage of the peep enjoyed into his private note-book is, that we have his incompleted inquiries containing the stories as to which even he — a very poor adept at scepticism — required some confirmation. It is quite evident that we thus have something more valuable to philosophy, and infinitely more amusing, than his completed labors would have been. Here, for instance, is one of his break-downs — an interesting phenomenon, but not irrefragably proved: —

" This day I have an accompt from Marion Stevenson, who says she had it from one who was witness to it, that near Dunglass there was a child found upon the highway by some shearers, to their uptaking lately born; and they brought it to the next house, where the woman putting on the pan to make some meat for it, the pan filled full of corn; and when she turned it out and put it on the second time, it filled full of bear; and when put on the third time, it filled full of blood; and upon this the child began to alter its shapes some way, and to speak, and told them this year should have great plenty, and the next year also, but the third the land should be filled with blood and fire and sword! and the child desired it might be taken to the place where it was found, and left there. I hear not yet what was done with it. This is so incredible, that I set it down only for after trial and inquiry about it — no confirmation."

His wife tells him a story which in her youth she had heard narrated by Mr. Andrew Reid, minister of Kirkbean. It is a case of true love crossed by the interference of cruel relations. The swain leaves the country for several years — gets on — remembers the old love, and returns to fulfil his vows. It happens that on the day of his return the loved one dies. He is on his way to her house in the dusk of eve when he meets an old man, who tells him that he is going on a bootless errand — he will find a dead corpse for the warm living heart he expected. The stranger, however, pitying his distress, tells him there is a remedy — hands to the lover certain pills, and says, "If you will give her these, she will recover." So it turned out, and they were happily married. A certain visitor at the house, however, "a very eminent Christian," refused to salute the lady with the usual courtesies. He takes the husband aside, "and tells him that he was very much persuaded his wife was a devil, and indeed he could not salute her; and after some discourse prevailed so far with him as to follow his advice, which was to go with her and take her to that room where he found her, and lay her down upon the bed where he found her, and quit her of a devil. Which he did, and immediately she became a dead corpse half consumed." "This had need," says cautious Wodrow, "to be weel attested, and I have writ to Mr. Reid anent it." Curiosity urged me to look for and find among Wodrow's manuscripts Mr. Reid's answer. He says he often heard the story from his father as a truth, but had been unaccountably negligent in noting the particulars of it; and then he favors his correspondent with some special providences anent himself, which appear not to have been sufficiently pungent for Wodrow's taste.

A philosophical investigator of the established national superstitions would find excellent types of all of them in the Analecta. In the department of second-sight, for instance, restricted, with due observance to geographical propriety, within the Highland line, a guest disturbs a convivial meeting at Blair-Athol by exclaiming that he beholds a dirk sticking in the breast of their entertainer. That night he is stabbed to the heart; and even while the seer beheld the visionary dagger, a bare-legged gilly was watching outside to execute a long-cherished Highland vengeance. The Marquess of Argyle, who was afterwards beheaded, was playing with some of his clan at bowls, or bullets, as Wodrow calls them, for he was not learned in the nomenclature of vain recreations. "One of the players, when the Marquess stooped down to lift the bullet, fell pale, and said to them about him, 'Bless me! what is that I see? — my Lord with the head off, and all his shoulders full of blood.'"

In the department of fairy tricks, the infant of Thomas Paton, "a very eminent Christian," in its first use of speech, rattles out a volley of terrific oaths, then eats two cheeses, and attempts to cut its brother's throat. This was surely sufficient evidence to satisfy the most sceptical that it was a changeling, even had it not, as the result of certain well-applied prayers, "left the house with an extraordinary howling and crying."

Ghost and witch stories abound. The following is selected on account of the eminence of its hero, Gilbert Rule, the founder and first Principal of the University of Edinburgh: He was travelling on the dreary road across the Grampians, called the Cairn o' Mont, on which stood a lone desolate inn. It has now disappeared, but I remember it in its dreary old age, standing alone on the moor, with its grim gables and its loupin'-on stane, — just the sort of place where, in the romances, the horrified traveller used to observe a trap-door in his bedroom floor, and at supper picked the finger of a murdered man out of a mutton pie. There Rule arrived late at night seeking accommodation, but he could get none — the house was crammed. The only alternative was to make a bed for him in an empty house close by; it had been unoccupied for thirty years, and had a bad repute. He had to sleep there alone, for his servant would not go with him. Let Wodrow himself tell what came to pass.

"He walked some time in the room, and committed himself to God's protection, and went to bed. There were two candles left on the table, and these he put out. There was a large bright fire remaining. He had not been long in bed till the room door is opened, and an apparition, in shape of a country tradesman, came in and opened the curtains without speaking a word. Mr. Rule was resolved to do nothing till it should speak or attack him, but lay still with full composure, committing himself to the Divine protection and conduct. The apparition went to the table, lighted the two candles, brought them to the bedside, and made some steps towards the door, looking still to the bed, as if he would have Mr. Rule rising and following. Mr. Rule still lay still, till he should see his way further cleared. Then the apparition, who the whole time spoke none, took an effectual way to raise the doctor. He carried back the candles to the table, and went to the fire, and with the tongues[1] took down the kindled coals, and laid them on the deal chamber floor. The doctor then thought it time to rise and put on his clothes, in the time of which the spectre laid up the coals again in the chimney, and going to the table, lifted the candles and went to the door, opened it, still looking to the Principal as he would have him following the candles, which he now, thinking there was something extraordinary in the case, after looking to God for direction, inclined to do. The apparition went down some

1 [This will seem to most readers a typographical error; to some, merely an obsolete spelling. It is neither: it represents a common provincial pronunciation, which is heard even among the best-born and best-bred people in England. I remember a case in point which is amusing and significant. A friend of mine, whose manners and speech are those of cultivated people in this country, during a passage along the Mediterranean eastward, some years ago, was thrown much in company with a party consisting of a middle-aged Englishman of high official position, his young wife of noble family, and a young man of like social standing; all on their way to India. The lady was bright and lively, and of unexceptionable manners, though somewhat too much given to good-humored sarcasm. Finding my friend, to her surprise, though a "Yankee," yet not a salvage man in a full black dress-suit with satin waistcoat and cravat, (which we all know is the usual style of dress here in the morning and on a journey,) she graciously accepted his fellow-traveller attentions, and soon, with frank good-nature, he was tacitly installed of their party. But her young countryman was of course her favorite and her firm ally. Especially was this the case in a series of good-humored but often pungent attacks upon Yankees, combined with traps and contrivances to catch this particular one in offences against English speech and breeding. That these were all in vain did not of course diminish the watchfulness of the fair censor. Now it so happened that the

steps with the candles, and carried them into a long trance, at the end of which there was a stair which carried down to a low room. This the spectre went down, and stooped, and set down the lights on the lowest step of the stair, and straight disappears."

The learned Principal, whose courage and coolness deserve the highest commendation, lighted himself back to bed with the candles, and took the remainder of his rest undisturbed. Being a man of great sagacity, on ruminating over his adventure,

young gentleman who was going among the Sepoys to exchange his liver for a fortune, although of a high county family, and Eton and Oxford bred, was still infected, as many such men are, with some provincial taint upon his purity of speech, — quite unknown to himself. At breakfast one morning, no other persons being by, he asked my friend for the "sugar tongues." They were placed at his hand, with the mild query, "Do you say tongues?" "Tongues? To be sure. Why not? everybody says tongues." "In America we say tongs." There was a dispute, a bet; and the decision was left to Lady ——, whose English both parties admitted to be irreproachable. They tossed up for the question. It fell to my friend. The two approached her together, and he, who even in small matters is the soul of honor and punctilio, holding up the forceps, said, "Lady ——, don't you call these things tongues?" Her eyes flashed merry malice, and laughing, she cried out, "Ah, now I have you. Do you Yankees call 'em tongues? *Tawngs*, man, (broadening it out) *tawngs* is English." The chapfallen visage of her own true knight showed her instantly the pit into which she had flung herself. But she was sensible and really good-natured. Her eyes were opened. Gibing at Yankeeism was stopped; and for the rest of their companionship my friend was treated just as if he had not had the misfortune to be born on this side of the water, — a course which oddly enough proved to be the most convenient and agreeable that could have been devised for all parties. — W.]

he informed the sheriff of the county "that he was much of the mind there was murder in the case." The stone whereon the candles were placed was raised, and there "the plain remains of a human body were found, and bones, to the conviction of all." It was supposed to be an old affair, however, and no traces could be got of the murderer. Rule undertook the functions of the detective, and pressed into the service the influence of his own profession. He preached a great sermon on the occasion, to which all the neighboring people were summoned; and behold, "in the time of his sermon, an old man near eighty years was awakened, and fell a-weeping, and before all the whole company acknowledged that, at the building of that house, he was the murderer."

In Wodrow's note-book the devil often cuts a humiliating figure, and is treated with a deal of rude and boisterous jeering. A certain "exercised Christian," probably during a fit of indigestion, was subjected to a heavy wrestling with doubts and irreconcilable difficulties, which raised in his mind horrible suggestions. The devil took occasion to put in a word or two for the purpose of increasing the confusion, but it had the directly opposite effect, and called forth the remark that, "on the whole, the devil is a great fool, and outshoots himself oft when he thinks he has poor believers on the haunch." On another occasion the devil performed a function of a very unusual kind, one would think. He is known to quote Scripture for his purposes, but who ever before heard of his writing a sermon — and, as it seems, a sound and orthodox one? There was, it appears, a youth in the University of St. Andrews, preparing to undergo his trials as a licentiate, who had good reason to fear that he would be plucked. He found he could make nothing whatever of the trial sermon, and was wandering about by lonely ways, seeking in vain for inspiration. At last, "there came up to him a stranger, in habit like a minister, in black coat and band, and who addressed the youth very courteously." He was mighty inquisitive, and at length wormed out the secret grief. "I have got a text from the Presbytery. I cannot for my life compose a discourse on it, so I shall be affronted." The stranger replied — "Sir, I am a minister; let me hear the text?" He told him. "Oh, then, I have an excellent sermon on that text in my pocket, which you may peruse and commit to your memory. I engage, after you have delivered it before the Presbytery, you will be greatly approven and applauded." The youth received it thankfully; but one good turn deserves another. The stranger had an eccentric fancy that he should have a written promise from the youth to do him afterwards any favor in his power; and there being no other liquid conveniently at hand for the signature of the document, a drop of the young man's blood was drawn for the purpose. Note now what followed. "Upon the Presbytery day the youth delivered an excellent sermon upon the text appointed him, which pleased and amazed the Presbytery to a degree; only Mr. Blair smelt out something in it which made him call the youth aside to the corner of the church, and thus he began with him: 'Sir, you have delivered a nate sermon, every way well pointed. The matter was profound, or rather sublime; your style was fine and your method clear; and, no doubt, young men at the beginning must make use of helps, which I doubt not you have done.' So beginning, Blair, who was a man of mighty gifts and repute, pressed on so close with repeated questions that the awful truth at last came out. There was nothing for it but that the Presbytery must engage in special exercise for the penitent youth. They prayed each in succession to no purpose, till it came to Blair's turn. "In time of his prayer there came a violent rushing of wind upon the church — so great that they thought the church should have fallen down about their ears — and with that the youth's paper and covenant drops down from the roof of the church among the ministers."

A large proportion of Wodrow's special providences are performed for the benefit of the clergy, either to provide them with certain worldly necessaries of which they may happen to be in want, or to give effect to their pious indignation, or, as some might be tempted to call it, their vindictive spite, against those who revile them. Perhaps an interdicted pastor, wandering over the desolate moors where he and his hunted flock seek refuge, is sorely impeded by some small want of the flesh, and gives expression to his wishes concerning it; when forthwith he is miraculously supplied with a shoulder of mutton or a pair of trousers, according to the nature of his necessities. He encounters ridicule or personal insult, and instantly the blasphemer is struck dead, or idiotic, or dumb, after the example of those who mocked Elisha's bald head; and Wodrow generally winds up these judgments with an appropriate admonitory text, as, for instance, "Touch not His anointed, and do His prophets no harm." As the persons for whom these special miracles are performed generally happen to be sorely beset by worldly privations and dangers, which are at their climax at the very time when they are able to call in supernatural intervention, a logician might be inclined to ask why, if the operations, and, as it were, the very motives, of the Deity are examined in respect of those events which are propitious to His favorite, they should not also be examined with the same critical pertinacity as to the greatly predominating collection of events which are decidedly unpropitious to him, so as to bring out the reason why the simpler course of saving him from all hardships and persecution had not been followed, instead of the circuitous plan of launching heavy calamities against him, and then issuing special miraculous powers to save him from a small portion of these calamities. But such logic would probably be unprofitably bestowed, and it is wiser to take the narratives as they stand and make the best use of them.

Whoever looks at them with a cold scientific eye will at once be struck by the close analogy of Wodrow's vaticinations and miracles to those of other times and places, and especially to those credited to the saints of the early Catholic Church, to which many of them, indeed, bear a wonderfully exact resemblance.

The Early Northern Saints.

ARRIED on by the power of association, we are thus brought to the door of an exceedingly interesting department of book-club literature, — the restoration of the true text of the early lives of the saints — a species of literature now recognized and separated from others by the title of Hagiology. Everybody knows, or ought to know, that the great library of this kind of literature, published by the Bollandists, begins with the beginning of the year, and gives the life of each saint successively according to his day in the calendar. Ignorance is more excusable on the question what constitutes saintship, and, supposing you to have found your saint, on the criterion by which the day of his festival should be adjusted in the calendar. Technically, to make a saint, there should be an act of pontifical jurisdiction, all the more solemn than any secular judicial act as the interests affected are more momentous; but only a small number of the saints stand on record in the proceedings of the Vatican. In fact, the great body of them were in the enjoyment of their honors hundreds of years before the certifying process was adopted, and to investigate all their credentials was far too weighty a task to be attempted. It is taken for granted that they have been canonized, and if it be difficult to prove that they have gone through this ceremony, they hold their ground through the still greater difficulty of proving that they have not. Some of those whose sanctity is established by this kind of acclamation are so illustrious that it would be ludicrous to suppose even the Vatican capable of adding to their eminence—more so, to imagine any process by which they could be unsanctified—such are St. Patrick, St. George, and St. David. But there is a vast crowd of village or parochial saints firmly established within their own narrow circles, but as unknown at the court of Rome as any obscure curate working in some distant valley, or among the poor of some great city. In such a crowd there will naturally be questionable personages. St. Valentine, St. Fiacre, St. Boniface, St. Lupus, St. Maccesso, St. Bobbio, and St. Jingo, have names not endowed with a very sanctimonious sound, but they are well-established respectable saints. Even Alban Butler, however, has hard work in giving credit to St. Longinus, St. Quirinus, St. Mercurius, St. Hermes, St. Virgil, St. Plutarch, and St. Bacchus. It is the occurrence of such names that makes Moreri speak of the Bollandist selection as rather loose, since it contains "vies des saintes bonnes, médiocres, mauvaises, vrayes, douteuses, et fausses."

The saint's festival-day is generally the anniversary of his death, or "deposition," as it is technically termed; but this is by no means an absolute rule. Few compilers deserve more sympathy than those who try to adjust saints' days by rule and chronology, since not only does one saint differ from another in the way in which his feast is established, but for the same saint there are different days in different countries, and even in different ecclesiastical districts — the diocese of Paris having, for instance, some special saints' days of its own, which differ from the practice throughout the rest of Catholic Christendom. Some saints, too, have been shifted about from day to day by authority. Queen Margaret of Scotland, the wife of Malcolm, whose real source of influence was that she represented the old Saxon line of England, had two great days, — that of her deposition on July the 8th, and that of her translation on July the 19th; but, by a papal ordinance immediately after the Revolution, her festival was established upon the 10th of June. This was rather a remarkable day in Britain, being that on which the poor infant son of the last of the Jameses, afterwards known in Parliamentary language as the Pretender, was born. The adjustment of Queen Margaret's day to that event was a stroke of policy for the purpose of rendering the poor child respectable, and removing all doubts about warming-pans and other disagreeables; but it is not known that the measure exercised the slightest influence on the British Parliament.

Bollandus, who was the first seriously to lay his hand to the great work called after him, was a Belgian Jesuit. He had got through January and February in five folio volumes, when he died in 1658. Under the auspices of his successor, Daniel Papebroch, March appeared in 1668 and April in 1675, each in three volumes. So the great work crept on day by day and year by year, absorbing the whole lives of many devoted laborers, conspicuous among whom are the unmelodious names of Peter Bosch, John Stilting, Constantine Suyskhen, Urban Sticken, Cornelius Bye, James Bue, and Ignacius Hubens. In 1762, a hundred and four years after January, September was completed. It filled eight volumes, for the work accumulated like a snowball as it rolled, each month being larger than its predecessor. Here the ordinary copies stop in forty-seven volumes, for the evil days of the Jesuits were coming on, and the new literary oligarchy, where Voltaire, Montesquieu, and D'Alembert held sway, had not been propitious to hagiology. A part of October was accomplished under the auspices of Maria Theresa, the Empress Queen, but for some reason or other it came within the category of rare books, and was not to be easily obtained until it was lately reprinted.

Whatever effect such a phenomenon may have on some denominations of the religious world, it can afford nothing but pure satisfaction to all historical investigators to know that this great work has been resumed in this middle of the nineteenth century. I have before me the ninth volume for October, embracing the twentieth and twenty-first days of that month, and containing about as much matter as the five volumes of Macaulay's History. On the 21st of October there is, to be sure, a very heavy job to be got through in St. Ursula and her eleven thousand virgins, whose bones may be seen in musty presses in the Church of the Ursulines in Cologne; but still as it moves forward, it is evident that the mighty work continues to enlarge its proportions. The winter is coming on too, a period crowded with the memorials of departed saints, as being unpropitious to men of highly ascetic habits, so that those who have undertaken the completion of the Bollandist enterprise have their work before them.

There is a marvellous uniformity in all the arrangements of this array of volumes which have thus appeared at intervals throughout two centuries. They dealt with matter too sublimely separated from the temporal doings of men to be affected by political events, yet could they not entirely escape some slight touches from the convulsions that had recast the whole order and conditions of society. When October was begun, Belgium, where the work is published, was attached to the Austrian Empire, and the French Revolution had not yet come. The Jesuits, though not favorites among monarchs, profess a decorous loyalty, and the earlier volumes of the month have portraits of the Empress Queen, and others of the Imperial family, in the most elaborate court costume of the days before the Revolution; while the later volumes, still loyal, are illustrated by the family circle of the Protestant king of constitutional Belgium, whose good-humored face and plain broadcloth coat are those doubtless of the right man, though one cannot help imagining that he feels himself somehow in the wrong place.

The crowds of saints who come sometimes swarming in on a single day to these teeming volumes, give one an almost oppressive notion of the quantity of goodness that must have after all existed in this wicked world. The labors of the Bollandists, not only in searching through all available literature, but in a special correspondence established with their Jesuit brethren throughout the world, are absolutely astounding. Their conscientious minuteness is wonderful; and many a one who thinks he is master of the ecclesiastical lore of his own parish, which he has made his specialty, has been petrified to find what he thought his discoveries all laid down with careful precision as matters of ordinary knowledge in some corner of these mighty volumes. The Bollandists obtained their information from the spot, and it is on the spot that this kind of literature must be worked out. A thoroughly accomplished antiquary, working within a limited district, will thus bring forth more full and satisfactory results, so far as they go, than even the Bollandists have achieved, and hence the great value of the services of the book clubs to hagiology.

The writer of the letters bearing the signature "Veritas" in all the newspapers, would, of course, specially object to the resuscitation of this class of literature, because it is full of fabulous accounts of miracles and other supernatural events which can only minister to credulity and superstition. But even in the extent and character of this very element there is a great significance. The size of a current falsehood is the measure of the size of the human belief that has swallowed it, and is a component part of the history of man.

The best critical writers on ancient history have agreed not to throw away the cosmogony and the hierology of Greece. It is part of Grecian history that the creed of the people was filled with a love of embodied fancies, so graceful and luxuriant. No less are the revel rout of Valhalla part of the virtual history of the Scandinavian tribes. But the lives of our saints, independently altogether of the momentous change in human affairs and prospects which they ushered in, have a substantial hold on history, of which neither the classical nor the northern hierology can boast. Poseidon and Aphrodite, Odin and Freya, vanish into the indefinite and undiscoverable at the approach of historical criticism. But separately altogether from their miracles, Cuthbert and Ninian, Columba and Kentigern, had actual existences. We know when they lived and when they died. The closer that historical criticism dogs their steps, the clearer it sees them, and the more it knows about their actual lives and ways. Even if they were not the missionaries who introduced Christianity among us, — as men who, in the old days before Britain became populous and affluent in the fruits of advanced civilization, trod the soil that we tread, it would be interesting to know about them — about the habitations they lodged in, the garments they wore, the food they ate, the language they spoke, their method of social intercourse among each other, and the sort of government under which they lived.

That by investigation and critical inquiry we can know more of these things than our ancestors of centuries past could know, is still a notion comparatively new which has not been popularly realized. The classic literature in which our early training lies has nothing in it to show us the power of historical inquiry, and much to make us slight it. The Romans, instead of improving on the Greeks, fell in this respect behind them. Father Herodotus, credulous as he was, was a better antiquary than any who wrote in Latin before the revival of letters. Occupied entirely with the glory of their conquests, and blind to the future which their selfish tyranny was preparing for them, the Romans were equally thoughtless of the past, unless it were exaggerated and falsified into a narrative to aggrandize their own glory. Their authors abdicated the duty of leaving to the world the true narrative of the early struggles and achievements out of which the Republic and the Empire arose. It is easy to be sceptical at any time. We can cut away Romulus and Remus from accepted history now, hundreds of years after the Empire has ceased to govern or exist. But the golden opportunity for sifting the genuine out of the fabulous has long passed away. It is seldom possible to construct the infant histories of departed nationalities. The difference between the facilities which a nation has for finding out its own early history, and those which strangers have for constructing it when the nationality has allowed its death-bed to pass over without the performance of that patriotic task, is nearly as great as a man's own facilities for writing the history of his youth, and those of the biographer who makes inquiries about him after he is buried.

We are becoming wiser than the Romans in this as in other matters, and are constructing the infant histories of the various European nations, out of the materials which each possesses. The biographies of those saints or missionaries who first diffused the light of the Gospel among the various communities of the Christian north, form a very large element in these materials; and no wonder, when we remember that the Church possessed all the literature of the age, such as it was. In applying, however, to the British Empire, this new source of historical information, there arose the difficulty that it was chiefly supplied from Ireland. If all hagiology were under a general suspicion of the fabulous,

Irish history was known to be a luxuriant preserve of fables, and these causes of dubiety being multiplied by each other in the mind, it seemed almost impossible to obtain a hearing for the new voice. In fact, during a long period the three nations were engaged in a competition which should carry its history through the longest track of fictitious glory, and this was a kind of work in which Ireland beat her neighbors entirely. Hence, when all were pressing pretty close upon the Deluge, Ireland took the leap at once and cleared that gulf. As a fairish record of these successful efforts, I would recommend to the reader's notice a very well-conditioned and truly learned-looking folio volume, called "The General History of Ireland, collected by the learned Jeffrey Keating, D. D., faithfully translated from the original Irish Language, with many curious Amendments taken from the Psalters of Tara and Cashel, with other authentic Records, by Dermod O'Connor, Antiquary to the Kingdom of Ireland." Opposite to the title-page is a full-length portrait of Brian Boroomh, whose fame has been increased of late years by the achievements of his descendant in the cabbage-garden. The monarch is in full burnished plate armor, with scarf and surcoat — all three centuries at least later in fashion than the era attributed to him. But that is a trifle. It would involve much hard and useless work to make war on the anachronisms of historical portraits, and we are not to judge of historical works by their engraved decorations. Here, however, the picture is sober truth itself to what the inquiring reader finds in the typography. After the descriptive geographical introduction common in old histories, the real commencement comes upon us in this form: —

"Of the first invasion of Ireland before the Flood!" "Various," the author tells us, "are the opinions concerning the first mortal that set a foot upon this island. We are told by some that three of the daughters of Cain arrived here, several hundred years before the Deluge. The White Book, which in the Irish is called Leabhar Dhroma Sneachta, informs us that the oldest of these daughters was called Banba, and gave a name to the whole kingdom. After these, we are told that three men and fifty women arrived in the island; one of them was called Ladhra, from whom was derived the name of Ardladhan. These people lived forty years in the country, and at last they all died of a certain distemper in a week's time. From their death, it is said that the island was uninhabited for the space of an hundred years, till the world was drowned. We are told that the first who set foot upon the island were three fishermen that were driven thither by a storm from the coast of Spain. They were pleased with the discovery they had made, and resolved to settle in the country; but they agreed first to go back for their wives, and in their return were unfortunately drowned by the waters of the Deluge at a place called Tuath Inbhir. The names of these three fishermen were Capa,

Laighne, and Luasat. Others, again, are of opinion that Ceasar, the daughter of Bith, was the first that came into the island before the Deluge. . . . When Noah was building the ark to preserve himself and his family from the Deluge, Bith, the father of Ceasar, sent to desire an apartment for him and his daughter, to save them from the approaching danger. Noah, having no authority from Heaven to receive them into the ark, denied his request. Upon this repulse, Bith Fiontan, the husband of Ceasar, and Ladhra her brother, consulted among themselves what measures they should take in this extremity."

The result was, that, like the Laird of Macnab, they "built a boat o' their ain," but on a much larger scale, being a fair match with the ark itself. But justice must be done to every one. The learned Dr. Keating does not give us all this as veritable history; on the contrary, being of a sceptical turn of mind, he has courage enough to stem the national prejudice, and throw doubt on the narrative. He even rises up into something like eloquent scorn when he discusses the manner in which some antediluvian annals were said to be preserved. Thus: —

"As for such of them who say that Fiontan was drowned in the Flood, and afterwards came to life, and lived to publish the antediluvian history of the island — what can they propose by such chimerical relations, but to amuse the ignorant with strange and romantic tales, to corrupt and perplex the original annals, and to raise a jealousy that no manner of credit is to be given to the true and authentic chronicles of that kingdom ?"

I shall quote no more until after the doctor, having exhausted his sceptical ingenuity about the antediluvian stories, finds himself again on firm ground, prepared to afford his readers, without any critical misgivings, "an account of the first inhabitants of Ireland after the Flood." He now tells us with simple and dignified brevity that "the kingdom of Ireland lay waste and uninhabited for the space of three hundred years after the Deluge, till Partholanus, son of Seara, son of Sru, son of Easru, son of Framant, son of Faathochda, son of Magog, son of Japhet, son of Noah, arrived there with his people." From such a patriarchal nomenclature the reader of Keating is suddenly introduced to a story of domestic scandal, in which a "footman" and a "favorite greyhound" make their frequent appearance. Then follow many great epochs — the arrival of the Firbolgs, the dynasty of the Tuatha de Danans, with revolutions and battles countless, before we come to the commencement of a settled dynasty of kings, of whom more than ninety reigned before the Christian era. It is, after all, more sad than ridiculous to remember that within the present generation many historians believed not only what Keating thus tells as truth, but also what he ventured to doubt; and if the English antiquaries, according to their wont, called for records, — did these not exist abundantly, if they could be got at, in those authentic genealogies, which were from time to time adjusted and collated with so much skill and scrupulous accuracy by the official antiquaries who met in the Hall of Tara? The reader unacquainted with this out-of-the-way and rather weedy corner of literature, may think this vague exaggeration, and I shall finish it by quoting the latest printed, so far as I know, of the numerous solemn and methodical statements about the manner in which the records of these very distant matters were authenticated.

"When the said princes got the kingdom into their hands, they assigned large territories to their antiquaries and their posterity to preserve their pedigree, exploits, actions, &c.; and so very strict they were on this point, that they established a triennial convention at Tara, where the chief kings of Ireland dwelt, where all the antiquaries of the nation met every third year to have their chronicles and antiquities examined before the king of Ireland, the four provincial kings, the king's antiquary-royal, &c.; the least forgery in the antiquary was punished with death, and loss of estate to his posterity forever — so very exact they were in preserving their venerable monuments, and leaving them to posterity truly and candidly; so that even at this day (though our nation lost estate and all almost) there is not an ancient name of Ireland, of the blood-royal thereof descended, but we can bring, from father to father, from the present man in being to Adam — and I, Thaddy O'Roddy, who wrote this, have written all the families of the Milesian race from this present age to Adam."[1]

To all this preposterous, and now scarcely credible extravagance of fiction, there attaches a melancholy political moral. Poor Ireland, trodden by a dominant party whose hand was strengthened by her potent neighbor, sought relief from the gloom of the present, by looking far back into the fabulous glories of the past — and it seemed the last drop in her cup of bitterness when this pleasant vista was also to be closed by the hard utilitarian hand of the unsympathizing Saxon.

After "this sort of thing" it was naturally difficult to get sensible men to listen to proposals for opening valuable new sources of early history in Ireland. In fact, down to the time when Moore wrote his History in 1835, no one could venture to look another in the face when speaking of the early Irish annals, and the consequence was that that accomplished author wilfully shut his eyes to the rich supply of historical materials in which he might have worked to brilliant effect.

Yet, upon the general face of history, it must on examination have been fairly seen that Ireland is the natural place where a great proportion of whatever is to be known about the primitive Church in the British Islands was to be found. Indeed, in the history of Christianity, not the least wonderful chapter contains the episode of the repose in the West, where a portion of the Church, having settled down,

[1] Miscel. of Irish Arch. Soc., i. 120.

grew up in calm obscurity, protected by distance from the desolating contest which was breaking up the Empire of the world, and raged more or less wherever the Roman sway had penetrated. Of the southern Britons it could no longer be said, as in the days of Augustus, that they were cut off from all the world. England was an integral part of the Empire, where if the proconsul or legionary commander had not the hot sun and blue sky of Italy, there were partial compensations in the bracing air which renewed his wasted strength, the new and peculiar luxuries in the shape of shell-fish and wild-fowl that enriched his table, and the facilities which his insular authority afforded him for strengthening his political position, and plotting for a fragment of the disintegrating Empire. An admiral of the Roman fleet had at one time established his power in Britain, where he set up as Cæsar, and sought to create a new imperial centre. Thus the southern part of Britain was a province of the true Roman Empire awaiting the coming of the wild hordes who were gathering for the general overthrow, and was not the place where either the Christian Church or Italian civilization could find permanent refuge. The destined destroyer was indeed close at hand. Though the Romans had their walls, their roads, their forts, and even a few villas in Scotland, yet one going northward at that time through the territories of the Gadeni and the Otadeni, would observe the Romanized character of the country gradually decreasing, until he found himself among those rough independent northern tribes who, under the name of Picts and Scots, drove the Romanized Britons into the sea, and did for the insular portion of the Empire what the hordes who were called Goths, Franks, and Alemanni, were doing in the Roman provinces of the Continent.

Behind the scene of this destructive contest, Christianity, having been planted, flourished in peaceful poverty. It grew here and there over Ireland, and in a small portion of the remote part of Scotland; and the distance from the scene of warfare necessary for its safety is shown by the fate of St. Ninian's little church in the Mull of Galloway. It was too near the field of strife to live. The isolation in which the western Christians thus arose, was productive of ecclesiastical conditions very remarkable in themselves, but perfectly natural as the effects of their peculiar causes. The admirable organization for carrying out the civil government of the Roman empire, was a ready-made hierarchy for carrying out the ecclesiastical supremacy of the Bishop of Rome. It was far from the object of those who seized on the power of the Cæsars to abolish that power. On the contrary, they desired to work it on their own account, and thus the machinery of the Empire lived, exercising more or less vitality and power, down to the first French Revolution.

No part of its civil organization, however, retained the comprehensive vitality which the learning and subtlety of the priesthood enabled them to preserve, or rather restore, to its spiritual branch. Hence, wherever the conquerors of Rome held sway, there the priests of Rome obtained a sway also. But the one little fragment of the primitive Church, which had been so curiously cut off during the great contest, was beyond the sway of the conquerors of Rome, as it had been beyond the sway of the Emperors themselves. Hence, while the Church, as united to Rome, grew up in one great uniform hierarchy, the small, isolated Church in the West grew up with different usages and characteristics; and when afterwards those who followed them were charged with schism, they asserted that they had their canons and usages directly from the apostles, from whom they had obtained the Gospel and the regulations of the Church pure and undefiled. Thus arose the renowned contest between the early Scottish Church and the rest of Christendom about the proper period of observing Easter, and about the form of the tonsure. Hence, too, arose the debates about the peculiar discipline of the communities called Culdees, who, having to frame their own system of church government for themselves, humble, poor, and isolated as they were, constructed it after a different fashion from the potent hierarchy of Rome. The history of these corporations possesses extreme interest, even to those who follow it without a predetermined design to identify every feature of their arrangements with a modern English diocese, or with a modern Scottish presbytery; and not the least interesting portion of this history is its conclusion, in the final absorption, not without a struggle, of these isolated communities within the expanding hierarchy of the popes.

In a few humble architectural remains, these primitive bodies have left vestiges of their peculiar character to the present day. Neither deriving the form of their buildings nor their other observances from Rome, they failed to enter with the rest of the Church on that course of construction which led towards Gothic architecture. The earliest Christian churches on the Continent were constructed on the plan of the Roman basilica, or court of justice, and wherever the Church of Rome spread, this method of construction went with her. The oldest style of church-building — that which used to be called Saxon, and is now sometimes termed Norman, and sometimes Romanesque — degenerated directly from the architecture of Rome. There are ecclesiastical buildings in France and Italy, of which it might fairly be debated, from their style, whether they were built by the latest of the classical, or the earliest of the Gothic architects. The little Church in the West had not the benefit of such models. Places of worship, and cells, or oratories, were built of timber, turf, or osiers. The biographer of Columba describes his followers as collecting wattles for the construction of their first edifice. But they had also a few humble dwellings of stone, which, naturally enough, had no more resemblance to the proud fanes of the Romish hierarchy, than the primitive edifices of Mexico and New Zealand had to those of modern Europe. They were first found in Ireland; more lately, they have been traced in the Western Isles. They are small rude domes of rough stone; and if it may seem strange that the form adapted to the grandest of all architectural achievements should be accomplished by those rude masons who could not make a Roman arch, it must be remembered, that while the arch cannot be constructed without artificial support or scaffolding, a dome on a small scale may, and is indeed the form to which rude artists, with rude stones, and no other materials, would naturally be driven. It is that in which boys build their snow-houses. I shall not easily forget how, once, accompanying a piscatorial friend on the Loch of Curaan, near Ballyskelligs, in Kerry, I stepped on a small island to visit a Norman ruin there, and saw, besides the ruin and a stone cross, one of these small rough domes, testifying, by its venerable simplicity, that it had stood there centuries before the Norman church beside it. But the peculiar characteristics of the architecture of the West did not stop short with these simple types. It advanced, carrying in its advance its own significant character, until it became mingled with the architecture propagated from Rome, as the Christian community which worshipped within the buildings became absorbed in the hierarchy. The Oratory of Galerus, in Kerry, is a piece of solid, well-conditioned masonry, built after a plan of no mean symmetry and proportion, yet with scarcely a feature in common with the early Christian churches of the rest of Europe. Like the ruder specimens, it struggles for as much solidity and spaciousness as it can obtain in stone-work without the help of the arch, and it makes a good deal out of the old Egyptian plan of gradually narrowing the courses of stones inwards, until they come so near that large slabs of stone can be thrown across the opening. Some buildings of the same sort have been lately revealed in the island of Lewis: one named Teampul Rona, and another, which is dedicated to St. Flannan, Teampul Beannachadh.[1] The specialty of both these, as well as of the Irish buildings, is that they are edifices beyond all question raised for Christian worship, that they have been built with pains and skill, and yet that they have no vestige of that earlier type of Christian architecture which Europe in general obtained from Rome.

In offering a few stray remarks on the lives of the saints, or, more properly speaking, the missionaries, whose labors lay in the British Isles, it would be pedantic to cite the precise document, printed generally for one or other of the book clubs, which supplies the authority for each sentence. I must, however, mention one authority which stands superior among its brethren — the edition of Adamnan's Life of St. Columba, edited by Dr. Reeves, under

[1] See Mr. Mure's very curious volume on "Characteristics of Old Church Architecture in the Mainland and Western Islands of Scotland."

the joint patronage of the Irish Archæological and the Bannatyne Clubs. The original work has long been accepted as throwing a light on the Christianizing of the North, second only to that shed by the invaluable morsels in Bede. With wonderful industry and learning, the editor has incorporated the small book of Adamnan in a mass of new matter, every word of which is equally instructive and interesting to the student.

There is no doubt that the saints of Irish origin supply by far the more important portion of our hagiology. They are countless. Taking merely a topographical estimate of them — looking, that is, to the names of places which have been dedicated to them, or otherwise bear their names — we find them crowding Ireland, and swarming over the Highlands of Scotland and the North of England into London itself, where St. Bride's Well has given a gloomy perpetuity to the name of the first and greatest of Irish female saints. Some people would be content to attribute the frequentness of saintship among the Irish and the Highlanders to the opportunities enjoyed by them from the early Church having found a refuge in Ireland. Others would attribute the phenomenon to the extreme susceptibility of the Celtic race to religious enthusiasm, and would illustrate their views by referring to the present Celtic population in Ireland under the dominion of the priests, and their brethren of the west of Scotland equally under the dominion of the doctrinal antipodes of the priests ; while the parallel might be illustrated by a reference to those Highland Franciscans called "The Men," whose belcher neckcloths represent the cord, and their Kilmarnock bonnets the cowl.

At the commencement of Christianity the difference between the religious Celt and the religious Saxon was naturally far more conspicuous than it is now. Bede's description of the thoughtful calmness with which Ethelbert studied the preaching of Augustin, with all the consequences which the adoption of the new creed must bring upon his kingdom, is still eminently characteristic of the Saxon nature. In the life of St. Wilbrord a scene is described which is not easily alluded to with due reverence. The saint had prevailed on a Frisian Prince to acknowledge Christianity, and be baptized. Standing by the font, with one foot in the water, a misgiving seized on him, and he inquired touching his ancestors, whether the greater number of them were in the regions of the blessed, or in those of the spirits doomed to everlasting perdition. On being abruptly told by the honest saint that they were all, without exception, in the latter region, he withdrew his foot — he would not desert his race — he would go to the place where he would find his dead ancestors.

The conversion of the Picts by Columba seems to have proceeded deliberately. We find him, in the narrative of his life, exercising much influence on Brud their king, and occasionally enjoying a visit to the royal lodge on the pleasant banks of Loch-ness. There he is seen commending his friend and fellow-laborer St. Cormac to the good offices of the Regulus of the Orkney Islands, who is also at the court of Brud, to whom he owes something akin to allegiance; for Columba looks to Brud as well as to the Orcadian guest for the proper attention being paid to Cormac. Still, honored and respected as he is in the court of the Pictish monarch, Columba is not that omnipotent person which he finds himself to be in Dalriada and in Ireland. There still sits an unpleasant personage at the king's gate. A Magus, as he is called — a priest of the old heathen religion — is in fact well received at court, where, although doomed to be superseded by the Christian missionary, he yet seems to have been retained by the king, as a sort of protest that he had not put himself entirely under the control of the priests of the new doctrine.

It was indeed among their own people, the Celts of Ireland and of the Irish colony in the west of Scotland, that the reign of these saints was absolute. But if we count this ecclesiastical influence a feature of the Celtic nation, either the Welsh must not be counted as Celts, or they must be looked on as exceptions from this spiritual dominion. They were the people among whom, of all the tribes who inhabited Britain between the days of Julius Cæsar and those of William of Normandy, it might have been primarily expected that we would find the most vital Christianity and the greatest missionary force. They professed to have carried with them into their mountains the traditions and the nationality of that very important portion of the Christianized Roman Empire which was called Britannia. When the heart of the Empire became paralyzed, this branch, doubtless after a long harassing contest with the Picts and the Irish of the North, was broken, and partly subjected, partly driven away by the Saxons. That they should have failed, through all their revolutions and calamities, to preserve any remnants of Roman social habits, is not perhaps wonderful. But that they should have failed to preserve enough of Christian influence to second and support the missions sent to the Saxons, so soon after these had superseded the British power, looks like an exception to the usual rule of Christian progress. The Welsh antiquaries, through meritorious efforts, strive in vain to establish the existence of Welsh ecclesiarchs during the time when the countless saints of Ireland were swarming over Scotland and penetrating into England. They point to a stone said to commemorate a victory gained over the Picts and the Saxons by the Britons, not through their courage or their skill in fight, but by the Halleluiahs raised by two saints who were present in their host. These saints, however, Garmon and Lupus, were, as Bede tells us, Frenchmen, missionaries from the Gallican Church to correct the errors of the Britons. The venerable Bede scolds these Britons roundly for not having kept up the faith planted among them, and for not having been prepared to help Augustin and his followers in the very hard task of converting the Saxons. It is a pity that we do not know something more of Roman Christianity, and indeed of Roman civilization generally in Britain, before the Saxon days. There appears to have been among the Romanized British Christians little zeal and a good deal of controversy and dissent, and we hear a great deal more of the influence of the Pelagian heresy among them than of the influence of Christianity itself.

The scantiness of our acquaintance with Roman Christianity in Britain is the more to be regretted, because it would have been very interesting to compare its manifestations with those of the Church which found refuge in the West during the dark days of Rome — the days when the temporal empire was crushed, and the spiritual empire had not arisen. As we might expect from the ecclesiastical conditions already noticed, the persons who first exercised ecclesiastical authority in the two islands did not derive their strength from any foreign hierarchy, and had no connection with Rome. Any reference, indeed, to the influence of a Roman pontiff, either actual or prospective, in the life of any of our early saints, will prepare the critic for finding that the life has been written centuries after the era of the saint, or has been tampered with. In Adamnan's Life of Columba, Rome is mentioned once or twice as a very great city, but there is no allusion throughout that remarkable biography to any spiritual central authority exercised by the bishop there over the presbyters in Scotland and Ireland. This is, of course, nothing more than the statement of what the reader of a book has not found in it. Any other reader may find allusions to the supremacy of the popedom over these early Christian communities, if he can. But I think he is likely to find none; and any one who desires to study the real history of the rise and progress of the spiritual dominion of Rome would, with more profit, take up the books and records referring to events three or four hundred years after the age of Columba.

Self-sustained as they were, these isolated communities had a very strong vitality. The picture exhibited in the hagiographies is truly the reign of the saints. Their power was of an immediate, abrupt, and purely despotic kind, which would have been neutralized or weakened by anything like a central control. Prompt and blind obedience to the commands of the saint-superior was the rule of Hy or Iona, and of all the other religious communities of the West. Perhaps there were even here feuds, disputes, and mutinies of which no record has been preserved. The hagiographer can only commemorate those which were suppressed by some terrible manifestation of Divine power, for the person whose life he commemorates is only conventionally and nominally to be spoken of as a mortal; he is in reality superhuman, wielding, whenever he pleases, the thunderbolts of the Deity, annihilating dissent and disobedience to himself, as if it were blasphemy in the Deity's own presence, and crushing by an immediate miracle any effort to oppose his will, were it even about the proper hour of setting off on a journey, or the dinner to be ordered for the day.

The rank which those primitive clergy of Ireland and the Highlands occupy is almost invariably that of the saint, a rank as far separated from that which can be conferred by any human hierarchy as heaven is from earth. They were, as we have seen, independent of Rome from the beginning, and this great host of saints had lived and left their biographies to the world long before the system of judicial canonization. How a boundary is professed to be drawn between the genuine and the false among these saints of the North, cannot be easily understood. No one seems to object to any of them as spurious. Many of them are so very obscure that only faint and fragmentary traces of them can be found, yet it seems never to be questioned that they occupied the transcendent spiritual rank usually attributed to them. Of others nothing is known but the bare name, yet it is never doubted that the owner was entitled to his attribute of saint.

The brethren at Iona seem sometimes to have lived well, for we hear of the killing of heifers and oxen. A pragmatical fellow declines to participate in the meal permitted on the occasion of a relaxation of discipline — the saint tells him that since he refuses good meat at a time when he is permitted to have it, it is to be his doom to be one of a band of robbers who will be glad to appease their hunger on putrid horse-flesh. The ruling spirit, however, of this first Christian mission, as we find it recorded, is undoubtedly asceticism. The mortification of the flesh is the temporal source of spiritual power. Some incidents occur which put this spirit in a shape bordering on the ludicrous. A saint is at a loss to know how his power is waning. There is some mysterious countervailing influence acting against him, which manifests itself in the continued success of an irreverent king or chief, whom he thought he had taken the proper spiritual methods to humble. He at last discovers the mystery; the king had been *fasting* against him — entering the field of asceticism with him, in short, and not without success.

The biography of an Asiatic despot, so far as other persons are concerned, is merely the history of his commands and their obedience. It is only incidentally, therefore, that one is likely to acquire any information from it about the people over whom he rules. In like manner, the life of an Irish saint is the history of commanding and obeying; yet a few glimpses of social life may be caught through occasional chinks. The relation which the spiritual held towards the temporal powers is sufficiently developed to give ground for considerable inquiry and criticism. The more eminent of the saints had great influence in state affairs, ruling in some measure the monarchs themselves. Some monarch is occasionally mentioned as the friend of Columba, much as a bishop might allude to this or that lay lord as among his personal friends. We find him settling the succession of Aidan, the king of the Dalriadic Scots, through an influence to which any opposition was utterly hopeless. Send your sons to me, he says to Aidan, and God will show me who is to be your successor. The sign falls on Eochoid Buidh, and the saint tells the king that all his other sons will come to a premature end, and they drop off accordingly, chiefly in battle. This power of fixing the evil eye, of prophesying death, is found in perpetual use among the early saints. It is their ultimate appeal in strife and contest, and their instrument of vengeance when thwarted or affronted; and a terrible instrument it must have been. Who could gainsay those believed to hold in their hands the issues of life and death?

In our conceptions of the kings with whom these saints were familiar, it may be well not to be misled by words. We shall realize them better at the present day by looking to Madagascar or the Marquesas Islands than among the states of Europe. The palace was a shanty of log or wattle, protected, perhaps, by a rampart of earth or uncemented stones, and the king had a stone chair with a few mystic decorations scratched on it, which served for his throne on state occasions. The prospect of acquiring a gold torque or a silver drinking-cup would have a material influence over his imperial policy. Were we to believe the fabulous historians, Ireland was for centuries a compact kingdom under one imperial sovereign, who presided over subsidiary rulers in the provinces. But although sometimes one provincial king was powerful enough to keep the others in subjection, old Celtic Ireland never was a kingdom, properly speaking, for it never had a nationality. Some people maintain, not without reason, that the facility with which a nationality resolves itself into existence depends much, not only on race, but on geological conditions. The Celtic Irish seem to have always been too busy with local feuds and rivalries to achieve any broad nationality. And the nature of their country — a vast plain intersected by morasses and rivers, and here and there edged with mountain ranges — is unfavorable to the growth of a nationality, since it presents no general centre of defence against a foreign enemy, like that great central range of mountains in Scotland, which Columba's biographers call the Dorsum Britanniæ — the Backbone of Britain. Ireland, indeed, seems to have had no conception of a nationality until such a thing was suggested by the Normans and the Saxons, after they had been long enough there to feel patriotic. And so it has generally happened that any alarming outbreaks against the imperial government have been led by people of Norman or Saxon descent.

Still there is no doubt, difficult as it may be to realize the idea, that at the times with which we are dealing, Ireland enjoyed a kind of civilization, which enabled its princes and its priests to look down on Pictland, and even on Saxon England, as barbarian. The Roman dominion had not penetrated among them, but the very remoteness which kept the island beyond the boundaries of the Empire also kept it beyond the range of the destroyers of the Empire, and made it in reality the repository of the vestiges of imperial civilization in the north. Perhaps the difference between the two grades of civilization might be about the same as we could have found ten years ago between Tahiti and New Zealand.

An extensive and minute genealogical ramification, when it is authentic, is a condition of a pretty far advanced state of civilization. Abandoning the old fabulous genealogies which went back among the Biblical patriarchs, the rigid antiquaries of Ireland find their way through authentic sources to genealogical connections of a truly marvellous extent. Such illustrious men as the saints can of course be easily traced, as all were proud to establish connection with them, while Columba himself and several others were men of royal descent. But of the casual persons mentioned in the Life of Columba, Dr. Reeves hunts out the genealogy — fully as successfully, one would say, as that of any persons of the country-gentleman class in Britain, living at the beginning of this century, could be established. There are, indeed, many characteristics in the hagiologic literature bearing an analogy to modern social habits so close as to be almost ludicrous; and it is not easy to deal with these conditions of a very distant age, brought to us as they are through the vehicle of a language which is neither classical nor vernacular, but conventional — the corrupt Latin in which the biographers of the saints found it convenient to write. It would appear that when he was in Ireland, St. Columba kept his carriage, and the loss of the lynch-pin on one occasion is connected with a notable miracle. Dr. Reeves, as appropriate to this, remarks that "the memoirs of St. Patrick in the Book of Armagh make frequent mention of his chariot, and even name his driver." It is difficult to suppose such a vehicle ever becoming available in Iona; but there Columba seems to have been provided with abundance of vessels, and he could send for a friend, in the way in which MacGillicallum's "carriage," in the form of a boat, was sent for Johnson and Boswell.

There are many other things in these books which have a sound more familiar to us than any sense which they really convey. Here the saint blesses the store of a "homo plebeius cum uxore et filiis" — a poor man with a wife and family — a term expressively known in this day among all who have to deal with the condition of their fellow-men, from the chancellor of the exchequer to the relieving-officer. In the same chapter we are told, "de quodam viro divito tenacissimo" — of a very hard-fisted rich fellow — a term thoroughly significant in civilized times. He is doomed, by the way, to become bankrupt, and fall into such poverty that his offspring will be found dead in a ditch — a fate also intelligible in the nineteenth century. In another place we have among the saint's suitors "plebeius pauperrimus, qui in ea habitabat regione quæ Stagni litoribus Aporici est contermina." The "Stagnum Aporicum" is Lochaber; so here we have a pauper from the neighborhood of Lochaber — a designation which I take to be familiarly known at "the Board of Supervision for the Relief of the Poor in Scotland." We are told, too, of the saint being at a plebeian feast, and of a plebeius in the island of Raghery quarrelling with his wife.

The thoughtful student will find a more distinguished analogy with the habits of later civilization in the literature of these early churchmen. The subject of the introduction of letters into Ireland, and the very early literature of that country, is too large to be handled here. It is certain that in Columba's era, the middle of the sixth century, books were written and used in Ireland. The respect paid to a book in that age was something beyond that of the most ardent book-hunter. Many of the most exciting of the saintly miracles have for their end the preservation of a book in fire or in water. The custody of the Book of Armagh containing St. Patrick's canons was a great hereditary office; and the princely munificence which provided the book with a suitable case or shrine in the tenth century is recorded in Irish history. Besides their costly shrines already referred to, these books often had for an outer covering a bag or satchel, in which the sacred deposit was carried from place to place. The heart must be dead to all natural sensations that does not sympathize with Dr. Reeves in the following triumphant announcement: —

"Of leather cases the cover of the Book of Armagh is the most interesting example now remaining. It came, together with its inestimable inclosure, into the writer's possession at the end of 1853, and is now lying before him. It is formed of a single piece of strong leather, 36 inches long and 12 broad, folded in such a way as to form a six-sided case 12 inches long, 12¾ broad, and 2¾ thick, having a flap which doubles over in front, and is furnished with a rude lock and eight staples, admitted through perforations in the flap, for short iron rods to enter and meet at the lock. The whole outer surface, which has become perfectly black from age, is covered with figures and interlacings of the Irish pattern in relief, which appear to have been produced by subjecting the leather, in a damp state, before it was folded, to pressure upon a block of the whole size, having a depressed pattern, and allowing it to remain until the impression became indelible."

A pleasing peculiarity in the personal habits of these recluses is their frequent communion with birds and the gentler kind of beasts. Their legendary histories speak of these animals as apt mediums of vaticination and miraculous intervention; but we must be content, in the present age, to suppose that their frequent appearance, their familiar intercourse with the saints, and the quaint and amiable incidents in which they figure, are in reality characteristic memorials of the kindly feelings and the innocent pursuits natural to men of gentle disposition and retired life. Thus Columba one day gives directions to a brother to be on the watch at a certain point in the island of Iona, for there, by nine o'clock on that day, a certain stranger stork will alight and drop down, utterly fatigued with her journey across the ocean. That stork the brother is enjoined to take up gently, and convey to the nearest house, and feed and tend for three days, after which she will take wing and fly away to the sweet spot of her native Ireland, whence she had wandered. And this the brother is to do because the bird is a guest from their own beloved native land. The brother departs, and returns at the proper time. Columba asks no questions — he knows what has taken place, and commends the obedient piety of the brother who had sheltered and tended the wanderer.

Another saint, Ailbhe, had a different kind of intercourse with certain cranes. They went about in a large body, destroying the corn in the neighborhood, and would not be dispersed. The saint went and delivered an oration to them on the unreasonableness of their conduct, and forthwith, penitent and somewhat ashamed, they soared into the air and went their way. "St. Cuthbert's ducks" acquired a long celebrity. When that reverenced ascetic went to take up his residence in the wave-bounded solitude of the Farne Islands, he found the solan-geese there imbued with the wild habits common to their storm-nurtured race, and totally unconscious of the civilization and refinement of their kinsmen who graze on commons, and hiss at children and dogs. St. Cuthbert tamed them through his miraculous powers, and made them as obedient and docile a flock as abbot ever ruled. The geese went before him in regular platoons, following the word of command, and doing what he ordered — whether it might be the most ordinary act of the feathered biped, or some mighty miracle. Under his successors their conduct seems to have been less regular, though certainly not less peculiar; for we are told that they built their nests on the altar, and around the altar, and in all the houses of the island; further, that, during the celebration of mass, they familiarly pecked the officiating priest and his assistants with their bills. It is curious enough that the miraculous education of the birds makes its appearance in a Scottish legal or official document at the close of the fifteenth century. It is an instrument recording an attestation to the enormous value of the down of these renowned birds; and seems, indeed, to be an advertisement or puff by merchants dealing in the ware, though its ponderous Latinity is in curious contrast with the neat examples of that kind of literature to which we are accustomed in these days.[1]

[1] "Instrumentum super Aucis Sancti Cuthberti." — Spalding Club.

One of the prettiest of the stories about birds is divided between St. Serf, the founder of a monastery on Loch Leven, and St. Kentigern, the patron of Glasgow, where he is better known as St. Mungo. Kentigern was one among a parcel of neophyte boys whom the worthy old Serf, or Servanus, was perfecting in the knowledge of the truth. Their teacher had a feathered pet — "quædam avicula quæ vulgo ob ruborem corpusculi rubisca nuncupatur" — a robin-redbreast in fact, an animal whose good fortune it is never to be mentioned without some kindly reference to his universal popularity, and the decoration which renders him so easily recognized wherever he appears. St. Serf's robin was a wonderful bird; he not only took food from his master's hand and pecked about him according to the fashion of tame and familiar birds, but took a lively interest in his devotions and studies by flapping his wings and crowing in his own little way, so as to be a sort of chorus to the acts of the saint. The old man enjoyed this extremely; and his biographer, with more geniality than hagiographers usually show, sympathizes with this innocent recreation, applying the example of the bow that was not always bent in a manner suggestive of suspicions that he was not entirely unacquainted with profane letters. One day, when the saint had retired to his devotions, the boys amused themselves with his little pet; and a struggle arising among them for its possession, the head was torn from the body — altogether a natural incident. Thereupon, says the narrator, fear was turned to grief, and the avenging birch — "plagas virgarum quæ puerorum gravissima tormenta esse solent" — arose terribly in their sight. It was at this moment that an unpopular pupil, named Kentigern — a new boy, apparently — a stranger who had not taken in good-fellowship to the rest of the school, but was addicted to solitary meditation, entered the guilty conclave. Their course was taken — they threw the fragments of the bird into his hands and bolted. St. Serf enters, and the crew are awaiting in guilty exultation the bursting of his wrath. The consecrated youth, however, fitting the severed parts to each other, signs the cross, raises his pure hands to heaven, and breathes an appropriate prayer — when lo! robin lifts his little head, expands his wings, and hops away to meet his master. In the eucharistic office of St. Kentigern's day, this event, along with the restoration to life of a meritorious cook, and other miracles, inspired a canticle which, for long subsequent ages, was exultingly sung by the choristers in the saint's own cathedral of Glasgow, thus: —

> "Garrit ales pernecatus.
> Cocus est resuscitatus.
> Salit vervex trucidatus
> Amputato capite."

A bird proper, on the shield argent of the city of Glasgow, has been identified with the resuscitated pet of the patron saint. The tree on which it is there perched is a commemoration of another of the saint's miracles. In a time of frost and snow his enemies had extinguished his fire; but immediately drawing on the miraculous resources ever at the command of his class on such emergencies, he breathed fire into a frozen branch from the forest; and it was centuries afterwards attested that the green branches of that forest made excellent firewood.

Another element in the blazon of the Venice of the west is a fish, laid across the stem of the tree, "in base," as the heralds say, but not, as generally depicted, conformable either to their science, or that of the ichthyologist. This fish holds in its mouth something like a dish — in reality a ring, and thus commemorates a miraculous feat of the same saint, which has found its way into the romances of the juvenile portion of the reading public, where it is a standard nuisance. Queen Cadyow, whose conduct was of such a character that it is wonderful how any respectable saint could have prevailed on himself to serve her, gives her bridal ring to a paramour. Her husband lures the rival away to the bank of the Clyde, to sleep after the fatigues of the chase, and there, furtively removing the ring, pitches it into the river. The reader knows the result by instinct. St. Kentigern, appealed to, directs the first salmon that can be caught in the Clyde to be opened, and there, of course, is the ring in the stomach. This miracle is as common in the "Acta Sanctorum" as in the juvenile romances. It served St. Nathalan in such a manner as to preclude the supposition that the saint had invoked it on the occasion. He locked himself into iron chains, and threw their key into the river Dee, in order that he might be unable to open the fetterlock before he had made a pilgrimage to the tombs of St. Peter and St. Paul; but the water did its duty, and restored the key in the stomach of a fish.

We have naturally many fishing anecdotes connected with the northern saints. Columba is described as out a-fishing one day[1] with a parcel of his disciples, who are characterized as "strenui piscatores," a term which would be highly applicable to many a Waltonian of the present day. The saint, desirous of affording them a pleasant surprise, directs them to cast their net where a wonderful fish was prepared for them; and they drag out an "esox" (whatever that may mean) of wonderful size.

Some of the inhabitants of the deep familiar to these saints were animals of a formidable kind. Columba and a band of his disciples are going to

1 [What a comfortable thing is this genuine bit of English, — out a-fishing! Why is it that the men who really have the power to mould the language will not make a stand in favor of this fine idiom, in which, as Ben Jonson says, "the participle hath the force of a gerund"? Why shall we not continue to say, while this thing was a-doing, instead of, while this thing was being done; while the wall was a-building, instead of, while the wall was being built? The one is simple, idiomatic English, that a child or a wayfaring man can understand; and yet it is set aside by exquisites in grammar in favor of the other complex, illogical barbarism. — W.]

cross the river Ness, when they meet those who bear on their shoulders the body of one who, endeavoring to swim across the same river, had been bitten to death by a monster of the deep. The saint, in the face of this gloomy procession, requires that one of his disciples shall swim across the Ness, and bring over a boat which is on the other side. A disciple named Mocumin, whom the saint had miraculously cured of a bleeding of the nose, confident in the protecting power of his master, pulls off all his clothes save his tunica (whatever that may be — coat, kilt, or leathern shirt), and takes to the water. The monster, who is reposing deep down in the stillness of the profoundest pool, hears the stir of the water above, and is seen to rise with a splash on the surface, and make with distended jaws for the swimmer. The saint, of course, orders the beast back just at the moment when all seemed over, and is instantly obeyed. The characteristics of the monster could not be more closely identical with those of the crocodile or alligator, had the incident been narrated in Egypt or America.

Adventures with such monsters in our northern waters supply many of the triumphs attributed to the saints. St. Colman of Drumore actually extracted a young girl alive from the stomach of an "aquetalis bestia." She had been swallowed while standing on the edge of a lake, "camisiam suam lavantem" — washing her chemise, poor simple soul. St. Molua saw a monster, the size of a large boat, in pursuit of two boys swimming unconscious of danger in a lake in the county of Monaghan. He showed good worldly sense and presence of mind on the occasion ; for, instead of alarming them with an announcement of their perilous condition, he called out to them to try a race and see which would reach the bank first. The beast, balked of his prey, took in good part an admonition by the saint, and returned no more to frighten boys.

From fishes and aquatic monsters the law of association naturally leads us to the waters themselves. There are throughout the United Kingdom multitudes of wells, still bearing the names of the saints to whom they were dedicated. Some of these, remote from cities and advanced opinions, are still haunted by people, who believe them to be endowed with supernatural healing virtues. It is in Romish Ireland, of course, that this belief has its most legitimate seat, but even in the most orthodoxly-Presbyterian districts of Scotland, a lingering dubious trust in the healing virtues of sanctified fountains has given much perplexity to the clergy.

Some of these fountains are in caverns, and if in any one of these the well falls into a rude-hewn basin like a font, we may be sure that a hermit frequented the cave, and that it was the place of worship of early converts. Such a cave was the hiding-place, after the '45, of the worthy single-minded Lord Pitsligo, no bad prototype of the Baron of Bradwardine. It is entered by a small orifice like a fox's hole, in the face of the rugged cliffs which front the German Ocean near Troup-head. Gradually it rises to a noble arched cavern, at the end of which stands the stone font, filled with clear living water, which, save when it was the frugal drink of the poor Jacobite refugee, has probably been scarcely disturbed since the early day when heathen men and women went thither to throw off their idolatry and enter the pale of Christendom. The unnoticeable smallness of many of these consecrated wells makes their very reminiscence and still semi-sacred character all the more remarkable. The stranger hears rumors of a distinguished well miles on miles off. He thinks he will find an ancient edifice over it, or some other conspicuous adjunct. Nothing of the kind — he has been lured all that distance over rock and bog to see a tiny spring bubbling out of the rock, such as he may see hundreds of in a tolerable walk any day. Yet, if he search in old topographical authorities, he will find that the little well has ever been an important feature of the district — that, century after century, it has been unforgotten; and, with diligence, he may perhaps trace it to some incident in the life of the saint, dead more than 1200 years ago, whose name it bears. Highlanders still make pilgrimages to drink the waters of such fountains, which they judiciously mix with the other aqua to which they are attached. They sometimes mimic the spirit of the old pilgrimage, by leaving behind them an offering at the fountain. I have seen such offerings by the brink of remote Highland springs. The market value of them would not afford an alarming estimate of the intensity of the superstition still lingering in this form in the land. The logic of the depositors probably suggests, that the spiritual guardians of the fountain, though amenable to flattery and propitiation by gift, are not really well informed about the market value of worldly chattels, and are easily put off with rubbish.

A historical inquiry into the worship or consecration of wells and other waters would be interesting. In countries near the tropics, where sandy deserts prevail, a well must ever have been a thing of momentous importance; and we find among the tribes of Israel the digging down a well spoken of as the climax of reckless, heartless, and awful destructiveness. To find, however, how in watery Ireland and Scotland a mere driblet of the element so generally abounding should have been an object of veneration for centuries, we must look to something beyond physical wants and their supply.

The principal cause of the sanctification of springs must, of course, be explained by the first of Christian ordinances. The spring close by the dwelling or cell of the saint—the spring on account of which he probably selected the centre of his mission—had not only washed the forefathers of the district from the stain of primeval heathenism, but had applied the visible sign by which all, from generation to generation, had been admitted into the bosom of the Church. This might seem to afford a cause sufficient in itself for the effect, yet it appears to have been aided by other causes more recondite and mysterious. Notwithstanding all the trash talked about Druids and other persons of this kind, we know extremely little of the heathenism of the British Isles. The little that we do know is learned from the meagre notices which the biographers of the saints have furnished of that which the saints superseded. It is not their function to commemorate the abominations of heathenism; they would rather bury it in eternal oblivion—*premat nox alta* — but they cannot entirely tell the triumphs of their spiritual heroes without some reference, however faint, to the conquered enemies.

The earliest recorded conflicts between the new and the old creed are connected with fountains. In one page of the Life of Columba we find the saint, on a child being brought to him for baptism, in a desert place where no water was, striking the rock like Moses, and drawing forth a rill, which remained in perennial existence — a fountain surrounded by a special sanctity. In the next page he deals with a well in the hands of the Magi. They had put a demon of theirs into it to such effect, that any unfortunate person washing himself in the well or drinking of its water, was forthwith stricken with paralysis, or leprosy, or blindness of an eye, or some other corporeal calamity. The malignant powers with which they had inspired this formidable well spread far around the fear of the Magi, and consequently their influence. But the Christian missionaries were to show a power of a different kind — a power of beneficence, excelling and destroying the power of malignity. The process adopted is fully described. The saint, after a suitable invocation, washed his hands and feet in the water, and then drank of it with his disciples. The Magi looked on with a malignant smile to see the accursed well produce its usual effect; but the saint and his followers came away uninjured: the demon was driven out of the well, and it became ever afterwards a holy fountain, curing many of their infirmities. Another miracle, bearing against the Magi, introduces us to one of their number by name, and gives a little of his domestic history. His name is Broichan, and he is tutor to Brud, king of the Picts, with whom he dwells on the banks of the Ness. It might have relieved the mind of the historical inquirer to be told that Brud built for himself the remarkable vitrified fort of Craig-Phadric, which rises high above the Ness, and to be informed of the manner in which its calcined rampart was constructed; but nothing is said on the subject, and Craig-Phadric stands on its own isolated merits, still to be guessed at, without one tangible word out of record or history to help any theory about its object or construction home to a conclusion. One is free, however, to imagine Brud, the heathen king of the Picts, living on the scarped top of the hill, in a lodging of wattled or wooden houses, surrounded by a rampart of stones fused by fire, as the only cement then known. Such we may suppose to have been the "domus regia," whence the saint walked out in a very bad humor to the river Ness, from the pebbles of which he selected one white stone, to be turned to an important use. Broichan, the Magus, had in his possession a female slave from Ireland. Columba, who seems to have held with him such intercourse as a missionary to the Choctaws might have with a great medicine-man, desired that the Magus should manumit the woman, for what reason we are not distinctly told; but it is easy to suppose strong grounds for intervention when a Christian missionary finds a woman, of his own country and creed, the slave of a heathen priest. Columba's request was refused. Losing patience, he had resort to threats; and at length, driven to his ultimatum, he denounced death to Broichan if the slave were not released before his own return to Ireland. Columba told his disciples to expect two messengers to come from the king to tell of the sudden and critical illness of Broichan. The messengers rushed in immediately after to claim the saint's intervention. Broichan had been suddenly stricken by an angel sent for the purpose; and as if he had been taking his dram in a modern gin-palace, we are told that the drinking-glass, or glass drinking-vessel, "vitrea bibera," which he was conveying to his lips, was smashed in pieces, and he himself seized with deadly sickness. Columba sends the consecrated pebble, with a prescription that the water in which it is dipped is to be drunk. If, before he drinks, Broichan releases his slave, he is to recover; if not, he dies. The Magus complies, and is saved. The consecrated stone, which had the quality of floating in water like a nut, was afterwards, as we are told, preserved in the treasury of the king of the Picts. It has been lost to the world, along with the saint's white robe and his consecrated banner, both of which performed miracles after his death. But the sanitary influence attributed to the water in which consecrated stones have been dipped, is a superstition scarcely yet uprooted in Scotland.

Sermons in Stones.

NE of the clubs has lately deviated from the printing of letterpress, which is the established function of clubs, into pictorial art. As it threatens to repeat the act on a larger scale, it is proposed to take a glance at the result already afforded, in order that it may be seen whether it is a failure, or a success opening up a new vein for club enterprise. In distributing a set of pictorial prints among its members, the club in question may be supposed to have invaded the art-unions; but its course is in another direction, since its pictures are entirely subservient to archæology. The innovator in question is the Spalding Club, which has already distributed among its adherents a collection of portraits of the sculptured stones in Scotland, and now proposes to do the same by the early architectural remains of the

North. In giving effect to such a design, it will produce something like Dugdale's Monasticon and the great English county histories.

If that which is to be done shall rival that which the club has achieved, it will be worthy of all honor. No one can open the book of the sculptured stones without being almost overwhelmed with astonishment at the reflection that they are not monuments excavated in Egypt, or Syria, or Mexico, but have stood before the light of day in village church-yards, or in market-places, or by waysides throughout our own country. As you pass on, the eye becomes almost tired with the endless succession of grim and ghastly human figures — of distorted limbs — of preternatural beasts, birds, and fishes — of dragons, centaurs, and intertwined snakes — of uncouth vehicles, and warlike instruments, and mystic-looking symbols — of chains of interlaced knots and complex zigzags, all so crowding on each other that the tired eye feels as if it had run through a procession of temptations of St. Anthony or Faust Sabbaths. When this field of investigation and speculation is surveyed in all its affluence, one is not surprised to find that it has been taken in hand by a race of bold guessers, who, by the skilful appliance of a jingling jargon of Asiatic, Celtic, and classical phraseology, make nonsense sound like learning too deep to be fathomed. So, while Rusticus will point out to you "the auld-fashioned standin' stane" — on which he tells you that there are plain to be seen a cocked hat, a pair of spectacles, a comb, a looking-glass, a sow with a long snout, and a man driving a gig, — Mr. Urban will describe to you "a hieroglyphed monolith" in the terms following: —

"The Buddhist triad is conspicuously symbolized by what the peasantry call a pair of spectacles. It consists of two circles, of which the one, having its radius 1¾ inch wider than the other, is evidently Buddha, the spiritual or divine intellectual essence of the world, or the efficient underived source of all; the other is Dharma, the material essence of the world — the plastic derivative cause. The ligamen connecting them together completes the sacred triad, with the Sangha derived from and composed of the two others. Here, therefore, is symbolized the collective energy of spirit and matter in the state of action, or the embryotic creation, the type and sum of all specific forms, spontaneously evolved from the union of Buddha and Dharma. The crescent, likened by the vulgar-minded peasantry to a cocked hat, is the embodiment of the all-pervading celestial influence; and the decorated sceptres or sacred wands of office, laid across it at the mystic angle of forty-five degrees, represent the comprehensive discipline and cosmopolite authority of the conquering Sarsaswete. The figure of the elephant — undoubted evidence of the Oriental origin of this monoglyph — represents the embryo of organized matter; while in the chariot of the sun the never-dying Inis na Bhfiodhlhadth threads the sacred labyrinth, waving a branch of the Mimosa serisha, which has been dipped in a sacred river, and dried beneath the influence of Osiris. The figures called a comb and a looking-glass are the lingal emblems of the sacred Phallic worship. The whole hierograph thus combines, in an extremely simple and instructive unity, the symbolization of Apis, Osiris, Uphon, and Isis, Phallos, Pater Æther, and Mater Terra, Lingam and Yoni, Vishnu, Brama, and Sarsaswete, with their Saktes, Yang and Yiri, Padwadevi, Viltzli Pultzli, Baal, Dhanandarah, Sulivahna and Mumbo Jumbo."

The honest transcripts in the club book clear away a great deal of that unknown which is so convertible into the magnificent. It was extremely perplexing to understand that the elephant was profusely represented upon memorials familiar to the eyes of the inhabitants of Scotland, at a period, if we might credit some theories, anterior to the time when Roman soldiers were appalled in the Punic war by the sudden apparition of unknown animals of monstrous size and preternatural strength. The whole flood of Oriental theory was let loose by this evidence of familiarity with the usages of Hindostan. But it is pretty evident, when we inspect him closely, that the animal, though a strange beast of some peculiar conventional type, is no elephant. That spiral winding up of his snout, which passed for a trunk, is a characteristic refuge of embryo art, repeated upon other parts of the animal. It is necessitated by the difficulty which a primitive artist feels in bringing out the form of an extremity, whatever it may be — snout, horn, or hoof. He finds that the easiest termination he can make is a whirl, and he makes it accordingly. Thus the noses, the tails, the feet of the characteristic monster of the sculptured stones all end in a whirl, as the final letter of an accomplished and dashing penman ends in a flourish. The same difficulty is met in repeated instances on these stones by another ingenious resource. Animals are united or twined together by noses or tails, to enable the artist to escape the difficulty of executing the extremities of each separately.

There is a propensity to believe that whatever is old must have something holy and mysterious about it. It is difficult to suppose that, in making an ornament, men who would be so venerable, were they alive now, as our ancestors, can have been in the slightest degree affected by the pomps and vanities of this wicked world. Hence there is never a quaint Gothic decoration, floral or animal, but it must be symbolic of some great mystery. So the reticulated and geometrical tracery on the sculptured stones has been invested with mythic attributes, under such names as "the Runic Knot." It has been counted symbolical of a mysterious worship or creed, and has been associated with Druids and other respectable, but not very palpable, personages.[1]

[1] It would not be difficult to trace a resemblance between some of the exceedingly elaborate sculpture of the New Zealanders and that of the sculptured stones, especially in the instance of the very handsome country-house of the chief Rangi-

Good theories are such a rarity in the antiquarian world, that it is a luxury to find one which, in reference to this sort of decoration, merits that praise. The buildings, both ecclesiastical and civil, of the early Christians of the North were, as we have seen, made of wattles or wicker-ware. The skill, therefore, of the architectural decorator took the direction of the variations in basket-work. We know that in the Gothic age those forms which were found the most endurable and graceful in which stone could be placed upon stone, became also the ruling forms which guided the carver and the painter; so that all wood-work, metal-work, seal-cutting, illumination of books, and the like, repeated the ornaments of Gothic architecture. It would only, then, be a prototype of an established phenomenon were it to be found that the sculptor of an earlier age adopted the decorations developed by the skilful platting of withes or wattles; and accordingly, this is just the character of the platted ornaments so prevalent on the sculptured stones.[1] But, however these may have been suggested, they show the

haetita, represented in Mr. Angas's New Zealanders Illustrated. Its name, by the way, in the native Maori, is Kai Tangata, or Eat-man House — so called, doubtless, in commemoration of the many jolly feasts held in it on missionaries, and others coming within Wordsworth's description of

"A being not too wise and good
For human nature's daily food."

[1] See "An Attempt to Explain the Origin and Meaning of the Early Interlaced Ornamentation found on the Ancient Sculptured Stones of Scotland, Ireland, and the Isle of Man, by Gilbert J. French of Bolton." Privately printed.

work of the undoubted artist, and furnish, as the advertisements say, "a varied assortment of the most elegant and attractive patterns."

Every one who in future attempts to unravel the mystery of these primitive sculptures must not only in gratitude but in common justice pay homage to the services of Mr. John Stuart, the secretary of the Antiquaries' Society of Scotland, to whose learning and zeal he owes the collective means of examining them. It will interest many to know that Mr. Stuart has been at work again, and has a second collection of transcripts, in some respects even more instructive than the first. These will show, for instance, the point of junction between the sculptures of the East and of the West, which, in their extreme special features, are widely unlike each other.

In the mean time, as the reader is perhaps tired of all this talk about books, and I would fain part with him in good humor, I venture to take him on an imaginary ramble in the wilds of Argyleshire, in search of specimens of ancient native sculpture, that he may have an opportunity of noticing how much has yet to be gleaned off this stony field. So we are off together, on a fresh summer morning, along the banks of the Crinan Canal, until we reach the road which turns southward to Loch Swin and Taivalich. After ascending so far, we strike off by a scarcely discernible track, and climb upwards among the curiously broken mountains of South Knapdale. When we are high enough up we look on the other side of the first ridge, and see the brown heather dappled with tiny lakes, looking like molten silver dropped into their hollows; while far below, one of the countless branches of Loch Swin winds through a narrow inlet, among rocks cushioned to the water's edge with deep green foliage. We are not to descend to the region of lake and woodland, betrayed by this glimpse, but to keep the wilder upland; and at last, in a secluded hollow near the small tarn called Lochcolissor, we reach a deserted village — a collection of roofless stone houses, looking, if one judged from mere externals, as if they might in their day have given shelter to Columba or Oran. In the centre of this group of domestic ruins is an affluent fountain of the clearest water. Standing over it is the object of our search — a tall, gray, deeply-lichened stone. At first it seems amorphous, as geologists say; but a closer view discloses on the one side a cross incised, on the other a network of floral decorations in relief. To trace these in their completeness, it would be necessary to accomplish the not easy task of removing the coating of lichen; and, by the way, if adepts in the cryptogamic department of botany shall succeed in finding a test of the precise age of those lichens, which they believe they have proved to be the growth of centuries, a key of the most valuable kind will be obtained for discovering the age of stone monuments.[1]

[1] Any one who desires to see the extent to which science can find employment in this arid-looking corner of organic life, may

Turn now in another direction. At the head of Loch Fyne, near Dunderar, the grim tower of the Macnaughtons — which, from some decorations on it, looks hugely like as if it had been built in the seventeenth century with the stones of an old church — we find a tuft of trees with a dike round it, called Kilmorich. It is a graveyard evidently, though it may not have been recently opened; the surface is uneven, and several rough stones, which may have been placed there at any time, stick through the earth. These, after a deliberate inspection, are found to have nothing of a sculptural character. But a small piece of rounded stone appears above the grass, and a little grubbing discloses a font, faintly decorated with some primitive fluting, on which a stone-mason would look with much scorn; and a scratching of a galley, the symbol of the Argyll family, or some other of the races descended from ancient sea-kings. This gives encouragement, and a sharper glance around betrays a singular-looking rounded headstone, with two crescent-shaped holes. There are corresponding holes on the portion under the sod, which thus completes the rounded head of an ancient Scoto-Irish cross. The next point is to find the shaft — it lies not far off, deep in the turf. And when we take the grass and moss from its face, it discloses some extremely

look at a "Memoir on the Spermogones and Pycnides of Filamentous, Fruticulose, and Foliaceous Lichens," by Dr. William Lauder Lyndsay, in the 22d volume of the Transactions of the Royal Society of Edinburgh.

curious quadrilateral decorations, quite peculiar, and not in conformity with any type of form which would enable its date to be guessed at within a century or two of the reality.

Passing through the rich woods of Ardkinglas, in a few miles we reach the burying-ground, called of old Kilmaglas, but now the well-kept churchyard, in which stands the modern church of Strachur. There are many who will remember the white house glimmering through the trees, and lament that memory is now all that it contains for them. Here are several fine specimens of sculpture. Some stones, not of the oldest type, have the crossed sword, symbolical alike of the warrior character of the dead and the religion of peace in which he rests. There is one with a figure in full chain-armor; and others, again, of an older date, ornamented with the geometric reticulations already discussed. Descending a few miles farther, in the small fertile delta of the Lachlan, and overshadowed almost by the old square castle of the M'Lachlans, there is a bushy inclosure which may be identified as the old burial-place of Kilmory. A large block of hewn stone, with a square hole in it, sets one in search of the cross of which it was the socket. This is found in the grass, sadly mutilated, but can be recognized by the stumps of the branches which once exfoliated into its circular head. Beside it lies a flat stone, on which a sword is surrounded by graceful floral sculpture.

Let us cross over again to the valley perforated

by Loch Crinan. Northward of the canal there is a remarkable alluvial district, through which, although it seems crowded with steep mountain summits, we can travel over many a mile of flat turf. From this soil the hills and rocks rise with extreme abruptness, in ridges at the border of the plain, and in isolated peaks here and there throughout its flat alluvial surface. Conspicuous, in a minor degree, is a great barrow like a pyramid, with a chamber roofed with long stones in its centre. Near it is one of those circles of rough stones called Druidical, and farther on there is another, and then another; some of them tall pillars, others merely peeping above ground. They literally people the plain. This must have been a busy neighborhood, whatever sort of work it may have been that went on around these untooled fragments of the living rock, which have so distracted our antiquaries in later centuries. If they were the means or the object of any kind of heathen worship, then the existence close beside them of the vestiges of early Christianity may be set down as an illustration of the well-known historical opinion, that the first Christian missionaries, instead of breaking the idols and reviling the superstitions of those whom they went to convert, professed to bring a new sanctity to their sacred places, and endeavored to turn their impure faith, with the least possible violence, into the path of purity.

Our next trial is at Kilmichael, about three miles from Loch Gilp. The churchyard is extremely fruitful in sculptured stones of various kinds — some floral, others geometrical, with wild beasts, monsters, and human figures. One of them was pointed out as the tomb of a member of the house of Campbell, who bore the name of Thomas, and was a great bard, and lived in London and other great cities — Thomas Campbell, in short. It seems to be true that his fathers were buried in Kilmichael churchyard, but my informant seemed to struggle with an idea that the stone covered with the sculpture of a far past century had been really raised to his honor. The next generation will probably assert this as a fact. The genesis of such traditions is curious. The stone called Rob Roy's tomb, which lies beside an ancient font in the churchyard of Balquhidder, is a sculptured stone raised for some one who had probably died in wealth and honor hundreds of years before Rob stole cattle.

By a slight ascent westward of the alluvial plain we reach Kilmartin, a village with a large modern church. Its graveyard is graced with many sculptured stones — twenty-five may be counted, conspicuous for their rich carving and excellent preservation. On one or two of the latest in date, there are knightly figures clad in chain-mail. A local antiquary could probably trace these home to some worshipful families in the neighborhood, but there are others beyond the infancy of the oldest authentic pedigrees. While the stones in the eastern counties are all of extremely remote antiquity, offering no link of connection with later times, these Highland specimens seem to carry their peculiarities with modified variations through several centuries into times comparatively late. There are among them stones bearing some types of extreme antiquity, and others which undoubtedly proclaim themselves as no older than the fifteenth or sixteenth centuries. It is sometimes a difficult task, in judging of antiquities, to make a sufficient allowance for the spirit of imitation. There is nothing certainly more natural than that a new tombstone should be made after the fashion of time-honored monuments, the pride of the graveyard in which it is to be placed. In Kilmartin there are two decided imitations of the more ancient class of the western sculptured stones. Though the symbols and decorations which they bear are of ancient outline, the heavy, and at the same time accurate and workmanlike, way in which they are cut, would mark them indubitably as modern, even if the one did not bear the date of 1707, and the other of 1711.

But the sun is dropping behind Ben Cruachan and the Jura hills. The time of holiday reading and holiday rambling has come to its end; and a voice calls the wanderer back to more sedate and methodical pursuits.

INDEX.

www.ingramcontent.com/pod-product-compliance
Lightning Source LLC
LaVergne TN
LVHW011149110826
845150LV00006B/1196